Early-Stage Technologies

INTELLECTUAL PROPERTY SERIES

Early-Stage Technologies: Valuation and Pricing by Richard Razgaitis

How to License Technology by Robert C. Megantz

Intellectual Property Infringement Damages: A Litigation Support Handbook, Second Edition by Russell L. Parr

Intellectual Property: Licensing and Joint Venture Profit Strategies, Second Edition by Gordon V. Smith and Russell L. Parr

Licensing Intellectual Property: Legal, Business, and Market Dynamics by John W. Schlicher

Intellectual Property in the Global Marketplace: Commercial Exploitation and Country-by-Country Profiles, Second Edition by Melvin Simensky, Lanning G. Bryer, and Neil Wilkof

Profiting from Intellectual Capital: Extracting Value from Innovation by Patrick H. Sullivan

Technology Licensing: Corporate Strategies for Maximizing Value by Russell L. Parr and Patrick H. Sullivan

Trademark Valuation by Gordon V. Smith

Valuation of Intellectual Property and Intangible Assets, Second Edition by Gordon V. Smith and Russell L. Parr

Value-Driven Intellectual Capital: How to Convert Intangible Corporate Assets into Market Value by Patrick H. Sullivan

Early-Stage Technologies

Valuation and Pricing

Richard Razgaitis

John Wiley & Sons, Inc.
New York • Chichester • Weinheim • Brisbane • Singapore • Toronto

This publication is designed to provide accurate and authoritative information in regard to the subject matter covered. It is sold with the understanding that the publisher is not engaged in rendering legal, accounting, or other professional services. If legal advice or other expert assistance is required, the services of a competent professional person should be sought.

Designations used by companies to distinguish their products are often claimed as trademarks. In all instances where John Wiley & Sons, Inc. is aware of a claim, the product names appear in initial capital or all capital letters. Readers, however, should contact the appropriate companies for more complete information regarding trademarks and registration.

Library of Congress Cataloging-in-Publication Data:
  Razgaitis, Richard
    Early-stage technologies: valuation and pricing
/ by Richard Razgaitis.
      p. cm.—(Intellectual property series)
    Includes bibliographical references and index.
    ISBN 0-471-32856-1 (cloth : alk. paper)
    1. License agreements—United States. 2. Technology transfer—Law
and legislation—United States. I. Title. II. Series:
Intellectual property series (John Wiley & Sons)
KF3145.R39 1999
346.7304'8—dc21   99-30149
                                       CIP

Printed in the United States of America
10 9 8 7 6 5 4 3 2 1

About the Author

Dr. **Richard Razgaitis** is a Senior Consultant at IPC Group, Inc. He has over 25 years of experience working with the development, commercialization, and strategic management of technology, 15 of which have been spent specializing in the commercialization of Intellectual Property. He has participated in the licensing-in and licensing-out of numerous technologies, including advanced materials, manufacturing systems, software and communications products. In addition, Dr. Razgaitis has been involved with commercialization efforts of technologies originating from federal laboratories, and he has negotiated commercialization agreements with clients in the U.S., Europe and the Far East ranging from Fortune 500 to small start-up companies.

Early in his career, he was a rocket scientist who worked at Cape Kennedy on the Apollo program from Apollo 8 through the famous Apollo 13.

Dr. Razgaitis is a Trustee of the Licensing Executives Society USA/Canada (LES). He speaks frequently on the commercialization of technology, specifically on valuation and pricing of technology, licensing strategy, and linking licensing and business strategies. He has taught segments of licensing courses sponsored both by LES and the Association of University Technology Managers (AUTM).

He has B.S., M.Sc., and Ph.D. degrees in engineering from the University of Illinois, Florida, and SMU, respectively, and an MBA from Ohio State University.

Dr. Razgaitis is a registered Professional Engineer in three states and the holder of four U.S. patents.

Bill Riley,
licensing mentor at Battelle and friend.

Acknowledgments

Much of my life has been spent in learning. Some would say I still have a long way to go (which is true, but details on that are more appropriate to a confessional). Here I want to offer heart-felt thanks to you many "teachers" of valuation and pricing.

For 14 years and 2 months, I had the privilege of working for Battelle in Columbus, Ohio. During the early years of this period I had the opportunity of working for Battelle Development Corporation (BDC), a wholly-owned subsidiary that had been responsible for commercializing Battelle and out-side-inventor technology since 1935. During those years at BDC, I hap-pened to be present during the retirement transition of an unusually talented group of individuals who took the time and had the patience to share with me over a period of years their insights from an incredible breadth of experience. Although the content of this book is mine, I would be remiss not to acknowledge the influences that this unique opportunity afforded me. Bill Riley, to whom this book is dedicated, hired me into BDC. Bill was an end-less source of experience-filled marketing and deal-making histories; many of those stories deserve a string instrument composition to elevate them to more-than-Irish ballads—really more like Homeric Epics. Bill's 29 years with Battelle, long-term participation in the Licensing Executives Society (including a term as LES President), and wise memory were, for me, like attending an academy of licensing learning.

Ken Shaweker was also a 30 year veteran of licensing experience, mostly at Battelle. He was BDC's IP Counsel. As our lead attorney, he was a model of reasoned judgment combined with sagacity in developing solutions to meet worthy business objectives and taught me lot about agreements and people. Steve Dickerson, another 30 year man and head

of BDC for many years, was tireless in his enthusiasm and pursuit of opportunities. In negotiations he was both gracious and quick-thinking, a
very potent combination. Dr. Charles Schwartz was, unbelievably, our
50-year man (I put this in the category of Hank Aaron's lifetime home
run record—amazing and not soon to be broken). His breadth and currency of technical insight was astounding; and as to kindness and patience, I have known only one other that deserves mention in the same
breath. Art Westerman ("just" a 40-year man) in addition to his business
development skills was a great writer and teacher of business writing
(sorry that I didn't learn better than I did).

There were many others at Battelle who were not part of the retirement
transition but who were part of my licensing and valuation 'faculty':
Barry Bissell, Bob Zieg, Bill Huffman, Roland Adoutte, Don Williams,
Gene Eschbach, and many others. I owe a very special debt to four very
talented administrative assistants whose teachings often had to be by the
rescue method: Carol Cremeans, Shirley Russell, Shari Dean, and Mary
Ann Dillon.

My association with the Licensing Executive Society (LES) has been a
constant source of learning from many people who have also become
friends. If I start mentioning names, I would never know where to stop.
LES is simply an outstanding group of individuals who have universally
been both gracious and wise, an uncommon combination.

I am likewise indebted to my many teachers at Bellcore, now Telcor-
dia Technologies, part of SAIC, another very special organization. In
the midst of revolutions in communications technologies, and the networking marketplace, and even in our corporate structure, there were
many who took the time to help and educate.

I would also like to thank my present colleagues at IPC Group and in
particular Dan McGavock, Jim Malackowski, and Mike Lasinski.

Perhaps I owe my greatest learning debt to those many individuals
with whom I negotiated, or attempted to negotiate, licensing agreements.
Your reasoned and articulate explanations of how you viewed the subject
opportunities have swirled through my memories many times and continue to do so even many years later. It is an axiom of negotiation that
deal-making is a mutual-learning experience. I don't know how mutual it
has been, but for me it has been the learning laboratory and my thanks
goes out to all of you.

This is not the kind of personal book that causes me to focus on the
contributions of my family. But it has been their encouragement and
patience and source of earthly purpose that has kept me going: so to
you, Carol (my loyal wife of 32 years) and children of whom I am so
proud—Rich, Rennie, Christy, Jodi, and Leslee—I say "thanks." These
six have all at one time or another asked "What exactly is it that you

do?" This book provides a good bit of the answer (hey, guys—I know it's hard to believe anybody actually gets paid for this, but this is what I do).

Lastly, my thanks go to Martha Cooley and her associates at Wiley publishing. Thanks for encouraging my writing when things were sometimes going slowly.

Contents

Preface

This book is about the valuation and pricing of technology. By "technology" or "early stage technology" is meant potential new business opportunities that are at an early or mature state of Research & Development (R&D) and not yet to the point of having been *productized* and introduced commercially. Valuation is about determining what something is worth intrinsically. It is something that both the seller and buyer need to do for many purposes, not the least of which is to determine whether there is a basis for an agreement. Pricing is about negotiating and communicating. It is something that is done by both seller and buyer once a valuation is done. Generally speaking, valuation is something intrinsic, whereas pricing is external; valuation is an idea, pricing is an agreement.

TR R A DE™

As a framework for this book, and linking the idea of licensing value creation to the traditional meaning of *trade* as a value-creation event, we will use the acronym *TR R A DE*™. This term summarizes what this book is about: Technology Rights (TR) becoming the economic basis of a deal (Deal Economics, DE) as determined by Risk characterization (R) and the Art (A) of creating deal-making opportunities.

JUDGMENT

Technology licensing in particular exhibits an apparent paradox: the licensed subject matter to be valued is subject to highly structured and rock solid scientific laws and principles, but the deal-making, including valuation, can appear to be subject only to whimsy. The paradox is only apparent. The world of certainty is a limited one. Where life is lived is inherently where generalizations apply and a certain fuzziness is inevitable. We live in a place that constantly requires us to make estimates and predictions, knowing that ideas submerged in words like *truth* and *certainty* and even *knowledge* do not really fit. Estimates and predictions can be faithful to underlying assumptions and beliefs, so that they are valid and self-consistent, but they cannot be *true* in the sense that knowledge of a historical occurrence or a scientific fact can be. This condition is not really a limitation; it is the nature of practical everyday life.

For some, the lack of certifiable, demonstrable, knowable outcomes leads to the following question: is valuation a pointless exercise? Although it can be, in general (another generalization) it is not. There is substantial value in performing a valuation. As we shall see in this book, there exist methodologies, underlying principles, and ideas that can be of great benefit in the determination of fair value creating agreements. As no one can know whether one's future includes an automobile accident, such lack of certitude does not induce reasoned individuals to drive without learning how, or following the rules of the road, or exercising caution, or staying sober. So here in the domain of valuation, the impossibility of certainty should not lead one to assume that there is no method or tool of value, or that rules of experience cannot be of help, or that the counsel of the wise cannot guide, or that sober, reasoned judgment is not of real practical benefit.

This form of thinking, often termed "wisdom" or "reasoned judgment," is as old as the Bible and, in another domain, Aristotle. This book is about applying such reasoned judgment in the arena of technology valuation. It is an Aristotelian principle that one should not expect more precision from any subject than that subject matter is capable of providing. So in providing such reasoned judgment in matters of valuation, especially in the context of early stage technologies, it should not be expected that comparable levels of knowledge or certainty are possible as that of the scientific underpinnings of the technology being licensed. Fortunately, comparable levels of knowledge are not needed to be of benefit to the user.

The purpose of this book is to aid the practice of technology licensing. The target reader is the licensing practitioner. In the case of the experienced practitioner, it is hoped that the experience of reviewing a codification of valuation methods and principles can be useful in integrating what such an individual may have learned through one-by-one experiences. Further, this book addresses some methods, such as Monte Carlo, that may not be familiar to even experienced licensing professionals. In the case of those new to licensing, this book may function

well as a textbook suitable for one-semester self-study. For those between the stages of beginners and old timers, this book may be a useful
reference and introduce some ideas and insights usable in everyday business practice. It is also hoped that this book could serve as a text for specialized classes in valuation.

DISCLAIMER

It many not be necessary, but it is probably prudent, to point out what
should be obvious: this is not intended as a proof text in support of a litigation. The context of the valuation methods considered here and my associated observations and suggestions is in support of opportunity
licensing, not enforcement. Further, each licensing and valuation opportunity is specific to the given fact situation; so it is unwise and can even
be misleading to take a passage of static words and assume that it can be
applied without consideration of the specific circumstances by the exercise of reasoned judgment.

Early-Stage Technologies

1

What Is Technology Licensing?

INTRODUCTION

This book describes how to develop a value for technology rights being offered or bought. There are many books that treat the subject of valuation in various business contexts; this one focuses on valuation of technology licenses and assignments.

DISTINGUISHING TECHNOLOGY LICENSING
FROM BUSINESS AND PRODUCT LICENSING

One can think of three discrete species of licensed rights: businesses, products, and technologies. Business transactions, which are usually outright sales or assignments, are those situations where a going concern with manufacturing, sales and marketing, established customers and channels with a revenue and profit history, and all the other elements necessary to operate as a stand-alone entity are being transferred. "Products" licensing relates to those license transactions that enable the buyer to duplicate the making of some device, system, or service that has already been completed and proven by the seller. In this situation, the buyer will need to provide the necessary surrounding business assets to realize a profit from the license. The term "technology agreements," on the other hand, commonly is used to designate transactions for pre-commercial designs and data, normally without the evidence of large-scale manufacturability or even a single legitimate customer. In some cases, the final or best formulation has not yet been established. Another way of thinking of "technology" is as a work product of research and development (R&D). Put yet another way, R&D is a business operation which has as its successful result "technology." Such a R&D work product can range all the way from a raw concept, at one extreme, to the results of

1

many years and many millions of dollars' worth of investigation with comprehensive data books, samples, test results, financial projections, and business plans, as well as outside verification by certification agents and potential customer feedback from trials.

The key ingredient missing from technology licensing that is present in both business and product licensing is a commercial track record. Without such ingredient, the customary approaches to product and business valuations do not work because the underlying data relied on do not exist. To make this more concrete, consider an automotive example. In early 1999, Ford Motor Company made an offer to buy and ultimately bought Volvo's automotive business. In developing the valuation of this transaction Ford, as the buyer, was able to study many years of financial and operational data as well as forecasted performance based on such data. This is the nature of sale of "business" transactions. Alternatively, Ford could have licensed from Volvo the right to make and sell Volvo cars in the United States in Ford plants based on Volvo proprietary information and patents. Again, in such a situation, Ford would have been able to study an extensive historical basis of the costs and revenues of making a Volvo car, and use such information to develop projections of profitability. This would have been a "product" transaction, because Ford would have had to use its business assets to make and sell the cars. An example of a "technology" transaction would be Ford's acquisition of the rights to an untested Volvo invention that Ford could then develop and use in their manufacture of Ford cars, or for some other business purpose. With such technology transaction species, there is no product or business history because what is being licensed is newly developed and has not yet reached the stage of a "product." Although the tools and methods discussed in this book can be of use in business and product transactions, the main objective here is in support of technology licensing.

Technology licensing is becoming an increasingly important transaction category but does not have the abundance of tools and experience available to business and product transactions. This book is intended to contribute to the field of technology valuation.

SELLERS AND BUYERS IN TECHNOLOGY LICENSING TRANSACTIONS *(TR R A DE™)*

The vehicle of technology transactions is a contract between a seller and buyer, normally a license. Such license conveys technology rights from the licensor, or seller, to the licensee, or buyer. For simplicity, hereafter the licensor will be referred to as the seller, and the licensee as the buyer.

The transaction between buyer and seller is a trade. Sometimes the trade is as simple as money from the buyer in exchange for assignment of a patent by the seller. In most cases, the trade is much more complex. But it is always a trade. Building on this fundamental idea we have devised the acronym *TR R A DE*™ to structure our discussion. Within the scope of the book, all transactions are founded on the *TR R A DE*™ framework:"*TR*" is used to designate *Technology Rights* conveyed in the licensing transaction. "*R*" is the risk involved in any transaction, "*A*" represents the art of deal-making, and "*DE*" is deal economics. Each of these elements of a transaction will be further discussed throughout this book.

Depending on the complexity of the transaction, there can be numerous other agreements accompanying the license. For the transfer of physical assets, such as lab equipment or technology prototypes, there may be a separate purchase agreement. For circumstances where key employees are to leave the seller and join the buyer, normally there will be employment agreements. If the seller agrees to provide subsequent technical assistance to the buyer, there will be a separate services or consulting agreement. If the buyer is going to provide a licensed product to the seller for the seller's use in some other product, there will be a supply agreement. Sometimes, the parties choose to create a separate non-disclosure agreement so that it stands independently of the license. In the case of equity transactions, there are numerous other agreements that are needed related to stock purchase, incorporation, and shareholder issues. The legal details of all such licenses and related agreements are outside the scope of this book. Here we will focus on valuation and pricing and refer to the bundle of contracts as a singular license agreement, or "deal."

The process of valuation and pricing determines the transaction *deal economics*, (the "*DE*" in our acronym). So, in shorthand form, this book is about *TR* for *DE*.

TECHNOLOGY AND INTELLECTUAL PROPERTY

Technology Rights are usually expressed in three forms of intellectual property (IP): patents, trade secrets (also known as: "know how," or proprietary technical information), and copyrights. Such IP can be considered as the form by which the technology rights are documented, protected, and conveyed.

It will be assumed that IP protection exists when considering the valuation of technology. There is always some uncertainty about the breadth and strength of such protection, and this uncertainty factors into the value determination. If there are issued patents, there can be some uncertainty surrounding interpretation of claim language or even the validity of the patent itself. If the patents are still pending, then there will be uncertainty about what will be allowed by patent offices in various countries of the world. There can also be uncertainties about trade secrets. It may not be

well understood how "secret" the trade secret really is; it could be that
many other labs and companies have independently arrived at the same
information or soon will do so. Also there is always some risk of inadver-
tent disclosure of the trade secret by the seller or buyer or by some third
party that would damage the value of the underlying technology asset.

The extent and strength of IP protection are dimensions of a valuation.
An extreme example of such effect is the absence of value if the invent-
ing organization publicized all the details of its invention in such a way
as to preclude obtaining a patent or any other form of IP protection. So
the absence of protection can and normally does preclude value. However, the converse is not true: it is possible to have very strong patent and
trade secret protection and still not have much or any value because, for
example, of the absence of a market for the product made by the underlying technology. Thus, IP protection is a necessary but not a sufficient condition for value to exist.

Considerations about which forms of IP should be used in which contexts, and analysis of the strengths and weaknesses of each, are outside
the scope of this book. In the valuation examples considered it will be assumed that the *TR* are protected in some way or combination of ways.
When risk issues are considered, or when comparisons are made to reference agreements, then strength and extent of IP protection will be identified as a factor to be considered when performing a valuation.

SOURCES OF EARLY-STAGE TECHNOLOGY LICENSING

In the opening discussion of this chapter, we recognized that technology
licensing is just one of three broad categories. The natural question
arises, is technology licensing important in the business world? The answer is yes, and it is becoming increasingly more important.

In the United States alone, annual R&D expenditures are estimated to
be $236 billion in 1999 according to the annual Battelle-*R&D Magazine*
forecast.[1] Assuming as a rule-of-thumb that the United States represents
approximately 33 to 40 percent of technology markets, this suggests
worldwide R&D spending to exceed $600 billion per year.[2] The perpon-
derance of such investment is in thought and its physical manifestation,
the time and mental energies of the most creative engineering and science
people alive.

One important category of technology licensing arises as a result of
the R&D being funded in organizations that do not also house commercial operations. In 1999, the Federal Government will fund $68 billion in
R&D primarily performed at government R&D labs, universities, and institutes in addition to the $10 billion that will be spent by universities and
other nonprofits.[3]

According to 1997 survey results from 175 responding U.S. and Canadian universities, teaching hospitals, and patent commercialization companies, their total sponsored R&D expenditures in fiscal year 1997 was $22.7 billion.[4] During FY 1997, this group totalled 11,303 invention disclsoures, 4,267 new patent applications, and 2,645 new U.S. patents. When such R&D results in an apparently useful new anti-cancer drug, or a more potent laser, or a new diagnostic instrument, a technology license is the tool used to transfer the rights to an organization that will complete the commercial development and enter commerce. When R&D projects are technically successful, some form of technology license is the means by which the fruits of the work can be transferred to a commercial entity and realized to benefit the technology buyer and seller. Because such institutions, with very few exceptions, do not convert the fruit of their technology into products and businesses, commercially successful R&D is licensed to entities who do; in FY 1997, this group of 175 institutions reported 3,328 new licenses and options to licenses.

In addition to the significant government funding for R&D, companies also spend huge sums on R&D in their own labs. In 1999, it is estimated that U.S. companies will spend $157 billion on R&D, mostly in their own labs.[5] The preponderance of such industry R&D funding is designed to create technologies that the company itself will commercialize. However, it is a common outcome that companies create more technology than they can exploit in the businesses they operate and the markets they serve. Even with the prevailng trend of running much more focused R&D operations, companies inevitably create technology that does not find a "home" in a business unit. Sometimes this is because of a change in direction since the time that a specific R&D project was launched. In other cases, it just happens that creative people in the labs come up with "Aha's!" that are outside the business scope of their company. In still other cases the technology is needed and used in a company's product, but it can also be used in other fields; licensing is a way to extract hidden, additional value from such technology. Regardless of the reason, a company finding itself with "orphan" technology should consider how technology licensing can be used to extract value from the asset and benefit its shareholders.

An important segment of the venture capital industry invests in technology startup situations. Although more weight is put on the management team and the associated business plan, when the startup is based on a technology, then valuing the technology should be part of the overall valuation of the startup. As patents are being increasingly used by established companies to fend off unlicensed upstarts and new entrants, assessing the value of the technological intellectual property should play an increasingly important part of venture capital valuations.

Another context for technology valuation arises when a company transfers technology from its R&D lab in one country to a business unit in another country. There are tax issues associated with making sure that an appropriate imputed payment (royalty) is made intra-company.

A final example, but by no means a final category, occurs with in process R&D. Although beyond the scope of this book, this situation arises when two companies are merging. At the time of the merger the companies may seek to write off some of that intangible value in an acquired company that would otherwise have to appear as goodwill and would thereby be amortized, adversely affecting company-reported earnings. The accounting environment relating to such matters is rapidly changing.

ISSUES IN EARLY-STAGE TECHNOLOGY LICENSING

Valuation in business is about forecasting the future value of operating profits and cash flows. The buyer is paying to enjoy a stream of future positive cash inflows that it could not otherwise experience. When there is a history of sales, costs, and profitability there is generally a stronger belief that the future can be predicted. This is based on an innate belief that the past is a harbinger of the future. Due diligence in such cases focuses on two issues: confirming the historic data, and testing various hypotheses as to why the future should be worse, the same, or better than the past.

With technology licensing there is no "past" in the above commercial sense—or as is sometimes expressed tongue-in-cheek, "your track record is all in front you." So, the issue of forecasting is the same, but all the data needs to be developed from scratch. It should be recognized that when a new technology is to be deployed in making an existing product there are "data" on which to develop a history. Although this is certainly not an optimal situation, it does have advantages. With product and business licensing, it is easy to become so anchored in the past and its extrapolation that one can miss flaws in the data and hazards, or opportunities, in the future. In a sense, when developing a forecast for technology licensing, it is easier to consider everything because one starts from a blank or near-blank piece of financial paper. Absence of data also helps prevent the rigid mindset that the future can be determined by the past. In general, there exists an "inertia effect" that keeps business circumstances from changing overnight, which supports the notion of relying on historic data. However, in the 1990s we have seen such numerous revolutions in business models—internet information, electronic commerce, and telecommunications, for example—that one should be ready to scrutinize any forecasts regardless of the extensivess of a historical record.

Overall, the uncertainty in technology licensing is higher than product or business licensing. This difference can be narrowed by skillful due diligence and analysis, but the fact remains that converting the results of

R&D in a manufactured and sold product involves additional hurdles and possible opportunities for failure.

PRICING VERSUS VALUATION

Valuation and pricing are two terms used for closely related ideas. As used in this book, the term "valuation" means the direct output of the valuation tools and methods developed in Chapters 4 through 10 without consideration for how such value should be presented or packaged to make it attractive or acceptable to the other party.

"Pricing" is about using the valuation findings to reach an agreement. Pricing is the internal and external communication of perceived value. Pricing is also the concrete answer to valuation, the specification in monetary or equivalent terms of what is offered for sale. Valuation, as we shall see, tends to produce a range of numbers, either as a result of different methods used or as an expression of uncertainty in value; pricing is the proposed number. Yet another way of expressing the difference is this: Valuation is an opinion; pricing is a commitment.

Finally, pricing is the customary way in which parties say "yes" or "no" to a deal; in most cases, once a potential buyer has passed through an initial screening process for strategic fit, there is a price at which the buyer will buy and a price above it for which the buyer walk away.

Pricing also relates to transaction time. Although technology licensing is not normally amenable to "blue light specials" (àla K-Mart), a seller may establish a lower price for a quicker deal and this would be a legitimate strategy. If the time period is so short as to preclude a reasonable period for due diligence, then the buyer will only consider a "fire sale" offer—a price so low that, within a very wide range of conceivable outcomes, the buyer is confident that the deal is worth doing. If the due diligence time period is reasonable but short, and the seller is offering a price that can be derived by a reasonable valuation, then this approach can create a higher priority due diligence effort by one or more buyers. Conversely, a seller may adopt a high price strategy and be willing to conduct a more expensive and lengthy marketing campaign. Because technology tends to age more like apples than fine wine, one runs the risk of being passed by by playing too hard to get.

Pricing issues, then, relate to negotiation tactics and, in some cases, company strategy. Valuation is focused on the underlying asset's intrinsic worth. Both issues will be addressed, although the focus will be on the latter.

A highly recommended book is one of the less-famous Arthur Miller plays, (appropriately titled) *The Price*. Like other great works, this play has multiple levels of interpretation. The presented level is the price of some used furniture.[6] The seller, one of two brothers in the play, has invited a used furniture dealer, an 89-year-old Russian, to bid on the family furniture of his father's estate. There is wonderful interplay between the brother and the savvy buyer. The brother keeps wanting to hear "the price." The buyer keeps providing him insights about the furniture, business, and life in general because in broken English "the price of used furniture is nothing but a viewpoint and if you wouldn't understand the viewpoint is impossible to understand the price (sic)."[7] This apt comment about a viewpoint determining the price summarizes much of what will be later developed in this book.

CONCLUSION: OVERVIEW OF THE REST OF THIS BOOK

In Chapter 2, we will consider possible components involved in a licensing transaction, rights and other things conveyed by the seller and money and other things paid by the buyer, and risks embodied in the future projections. *Risk* is so important a factor that it is used to represent the second *R* in *TR R A DE*™.

Chapter 3 provides an introduction to the six valuation methods presented in Chapters 4 through 9 (one method per chapter). Risk is dealt with in quantitative terms in Chapter 7 through the use of a Risk Adjusted Hurdle Rate, RAHR (represented by the symbol "k").

Chapter 10 deals with some special issues when equity is a component of the transaction, especially with startup situations.

Finally in Chapters 11 and 12 we consider how the value of license agreements can be structured and negotiation principles. Such structuring and negotiation are what make technology rights deal-making an *Art*, the letter *A* in our acronym *TR R A DE*™.

To recap, this book will deal with *Technology Rights (TR), Risk (R), Art (A)*, and *Deal Economics (DE)*.

> Troilus: What's aught but as 'tis valu'd?
> Hector: But value dwells not in particular will.
>   It holds his estimate and dignity
>   As well wherein 'tis precious of itself
>   As in the prizer.
>   Troilus and Cressida II[8]

NOTES

1. R&D Forecast, *R&D Magazine*, January 1999.

2. Strictly speaking, only a portion of this total "R & D" investment belongs in the category of early-

stage technology. What is called "R & D" in companies is more appropriately termed new product development. Such investments are tied closely to the company's direct and immediate lines of business and, therefore, if licensed would be more like product or business licensing.

3. Ibid.

4. AUTM Licensing Survey, Published by Association of University Technology Managers (AUTM), 49 East Norwalk, CT 06851-3919.

5. R&D Forecast, *R&D Magazine*, January 1999.

6. The hidden levels have to do with the price of life paid by two brothers, their wives, and the brothers's parents. The play focuses on the price of the furniture, but the other "prices" keep reappearing. It is a wonderful story.

7. Arthur Miller, *The Price* (Penguin Books, 1968), Act I, p. 38.

8. *The Yale Shakespeare, The Complete Works*, Barnes and Noble, 1993, p. 336, line 54ff. Thanks to Edward J. Bander who identified this excerpt in the context of valuation in *The Breath of an Unfee'd Lawyer: Shakespeare on Lawyers and the Law*, Catbird Press, 1996.

2

Rights, Risks, and Psychology of Valuation and Pricing

INTRODUCTION

This chapter deals with three issues that underlie the rest of this book: the identification of the technology rights transferred in the license, the perceptions and characterizations of commercial risks, and the psychology of valuation (and pricing) in the context of making projections with a high degree of uncertainty.

Licensing is really about trade, hence the acronym *TR R A DE*™ introduced in Chapter 1. Trade means an exchange in which two parties transfer to one another different things, but *both* perceive they received more in value returned or a more useful form of value than what was given up. If both parties did not view the trade in this way, it simply would not take place. Further, both parties necessarily prefer to possess that which was acquired in lieu of that which was given up. Thus, trade is a value-creating event for both parties.

In common forms of trade the exchange is easy to value and rapid to execute, whether it is trading $1 for two bananas, or one party providing piano lessons in exchange for the other party mowing the piano teacher's lawn. With technology licensing, there is a wide range of elements that can be offered by the seller and by the buyer. The specification and valuation of these elements is the subject of this book. In this chapter we will consider further the *"TR,"* or *Technology Rights* issue introduced in Chapter 1, and the *"R,"* or *Risk*, the second R in *TR R A DE*™.

IDENTIFICATION OF TECHNOLOGY RIGHTS TRANSFERRED

Both the buyer and seller have beliefs as to what should be on the list of rights transferred. It is not uncommon to find that even well into a negotiation one or both parties are surprised to learn that something they had assumed was part of the deal is not in fact being offered. This discovery leads to setbacks in the negotiation process and, in some cases, a complete breakdown in the relationship. In all cases such a misunderstanding will lead to an error in valuation because valuing a technology needs to be done in the context of all the assets, which includes a specification of the rights being transferred. Consider three kinds of licenses: (1) outright sale, (2) non-assert, and (3) limited license.

Outright Sale Agreements

In the case of an outright sale, what is being offered is the ownership of the patents and related IP rights, such as trade secrets (know how). This would appear to be simple: "Here it is, you buy it." However, the buyer and seller can have different perspectives on what "here" and "it" means. The buyer may expect and reasonably need some hands-on learning, often termed "tech transfer" assistance in order to be able to make use of the technology; this could involve months of access to the seller's experts. In special cases, the buyer may even require that certain key employees of the seller become employees of the buyer, because the need for such expertise is perceived to be ongoing and critical to the commercial success of the project. The buyer may also expect to receive ownership of equipment and fixtures that were used in the R&D process. The buyer may also want representations and warranties concerning the seller's rights to the patents and other forms of intellectual property, guarantees that the patents are valid, assurances that the use of the technology as described by the seller does not infringe a third party's patents, and so on. The buyer may also want a representation that it will not require the use of any other patent owned or controlled by the seller even if such patent is not directly related to the technology.[1] Likewise, even with this simple agreement, the seller may expect more from the buyer than just money. For example, the seller may want the retained right to practice the patents or at least to be free from the threat of being sued by the buyer for infringement of the transferred patents' claims (a so-called "non-assert" provision). If the valuation includes royalty or other forms of future conditional payments, the seller may insist on minimums, guarantees, and reversion rights, depending upon future outcomes.

Non-Assert Agreements

In a "non-assert" license, the buyer is essentially acquiring freedom from a future lawsuit by the seller; it represents the opposite extreme from the initial example of outright ownership. On the surface, this also appears to be a simple agreement—basically, the buyer is paying for something *not* to happen. (In reality, the buyer does "get" something: assurance that it has the freedom to practice within the scope of the seller's patents included in the agreement.) Yet despite the apparent simplicity of this type of license, there are numerous elements of the deal requiring clarification as being included or excluded. For example, what about future patents that the seller may invent or obtain? Are such unspecified and even presently unknowable patents included within the scope of the non-assert? Will the non-assert right apply to all countries in which corresponding patents have been obtained? Does the seller have to represent that it will require any competitor of the buyer to pay the seller at least as much to acquire such a non-assert (the so-called "most favored nations" clause)? In turn, the seller may want some form of reciprocal non-assert for the same, related, or completely unrelated technology.

License Agreements

With a limited license or simply a "license," the grant to the buyer is more extensive than the non-assert but less than an outright sale and considers many dimensions of business practice. Will the buyer be able to make anything it wants under the license or only certain products or categories of products? Will it be able to make, use, and sell, or just one or two of these rights? In which countries will such rights be enabled? How long will the license last? Will the buyer have the right to license third parties (the so-called "sublicensing" right)? Will the buyer be able to sell its right to a third party (assignability)? What will the seller be obligated to provide? Commercial data? Customer lists? Equipment and facilities? Tech transfer support? Improvement inventions? Defense of the patents? Who pays to maintain the patents in all their various jurisdictions? What happens if the patents are later found to be invalid? Can either party terminate the license without cause and cost? If not, under what conditions could termination be effected? Will agreements to supply raw materials or buy or provide finished products be part of the trade? Obviously all these questions require interaction amongst the technical, business, and legal people on each side and should be factored into making a valuation.

The answer to each one of these and many other questions affects the value of the transaction, some more so than others. Accordingly, the specification of the *"TR,"* the *Technology Rights* which is used here to encompass all such terms, is essential to performing a valuation.

It should also be said that this is not a legal textbook. Therefore the reader is encouraged to refer to many such texts on legal issues to obtain a fuller and authoritative treatment of such agreements.[2]

Technology Rights^{TR}

Common Examples of TR That Could Be Offered by a Seller

- Rights to specified patents, in identified countries
- Rights to patents pending, in identified countries
- Rights to patent disclosures not yet filed
- Rights to specified technology trade secrets (know how)
- Use of other forms of proprietary information such as customer lists
- Prototype equipment, fixtures, specific facilities
- Access to experts for a specified amount of time in a specified period
- Rights to solicit for employment specified inventors or other key employees
- Inclusion of improvement inventions within a specified scope and time period
- Rights of the buyer to sublicense the technology
- Rights of the buyer to assign its rights
- Defense of the buyer in the event of a patent lawsuit by a third party
- Enforcement of the patents against third party infringers
- Indemnification against loss as a result of harm to third parties
- Resources (people, equipment, activities) that the buyer can use to do further development or trials.

Payment Forms

Common Examples of Payment Forms That Could Be Offered by a Buyer

- "Cash" on signing (usually as a wire transfer—if it were literally cash, it could not be expected to be very much money)
- Fixed payments due at future specified dates
- Fixed payments due at specified events, such as FDA approval, or commitment to build a commercial-scale plant, or first commercial sale
- Obligation to fund additional R&D at the seller to develop the technology further or to fund other areas of R&D, with or without rights to such other R&D
- Obligation to provide consulting agreement funding to named employees of the seller
- Requirement to supply the seller with licensed product at no cost or

at less cost than offered to third parties or at parity cost but on some other preferred basis such as a specified quantity or delivery in priority to all other sales
- Grant back of buyer's improvement inventions to enable the seller to use or license to third parties such additional technology
- The ability of the seller to also sell into a market created and established by the buyer
- Earned royalties (royalties paid as a percentage of sales or some other measure of usage)
- Minimum royalties (specified period payments to maintain the license)
- Guaranteed royalties (mimimums due even if the license is terminated by the buyer)
- Obligation to maintain the patents
- Obligation to enforce the patents against third party infringers
- Decommissioning and cleanup of the seller's facilities related to the licensed technology

Special Circumstances with "Cashless" Buyers

In some transaction situations the buyer is unwilling or unable to pay in cash, either on closing or in the near future. Startup companies are one notable category; even successfully backed startups are notorious for creativity in the avoidance of writing checks. Another category of cashless buyer is an economically distressed buyer who may have a very solid plan for profitability but is in a cash-poor position at closing. A third example is third world and even second world companies; once one leaves North America, Western Europe, and Japan, it is common to encounter negotiating situations where the buyer is unable or unwilling to pay in hard currency, especially upfront.[3]

In the case of startup companies, we will consider special issues of equity in exchange for *TR* in Chapter 10. For distressed companies, there are usually two avenues available to make the deal economics (DE) work. One way is by delaying or reducing payments otherwise due until the commercialized technology is anticipated to yield positive net cash flow and compensated by increased later payments because the seller in fact has become a risk capital lender as well as a technology provider. A second way is by creative investigation into non-cash ways that the buyer can remunerate the seller, such as supply agreements under highly favorable terms either of the licensed technology or some other product made by the buyer.

In the case of third world companies, in addition to the two ways used with cash-poor companies there has arisen a third and ancient way:

barter. The way barter works in a licensing context is generally as follows. The buyer agrees to pay a third party in the buyer country using the buyer's country's currency for a determined quantity of an exportable commodity with a quantifiable value. The third party then ships pre-paid the exportable commodity to a fourth party in a first world country. The fourth party then pays for the shipment by paying the technology seller in a bankable currency. There are numerous variants possible. For example, there could be multiple intermediaries buying and re-selling the exportable commodity until it becomes a bankable currency to the technology seller. Another variant is that the third world company "pays" some third party not in the third world currency but with some other commodity that it makes or resells. Clearly the use of bartering is much more complex, not to mention risky, than being paid in a first world currency. However there may be licensing opportunities where a third world company is the best route to the marketplace. In such a situation entering into a barter transaction may be warranted.[4]

Special Circumstances with "R&D" Sellers

There are numerous examples of technology sellers who perform R&D as their core "business." Included in this category would be universities, government labs, and private R&D entities such as SAIC, Battelle, AD Little, and SRI.

One element of value to such R&D sellers is to have funding to sustain active programs within the field of the licensed subject matter or in other fields. This can lead to circumstances where the license fee(s) can be committed in a way that benefits both the seller and the buyer. For example, a portion (or all) of the upfront license fee could be committed by the seller to further a not yet investigated area related to the licensed technology and which, if successful, could become the basis for a second generation product line. By earmarking such expenditure, with terms and conditions regarding rights to new inventions, the buyer can get more for its payment than just the subject license and, thereby, justify paying more than sought by the seller just for the offered *TR*. From the perspective of the R&D seller, valuation in these situations brings in other factors and rules of thumb, such as the "man year rule" or the "invention factory rule"[5] which are outside the scope of this book.

Defining the Technology Rights (*TR*) of the *TR R A DE*™

Ordinarily one expects the seller to be primarily responsible for defining and pricing the opportunity being offered. However this generalization has limitations. In many cases the licensing opportunity derives from need discussions originated by the buyer. In other cases the opportunity is created by both parties by mutual recognition of the possibility that a licensing deal can create value for both parties.

Regardless of the context, it is important that early in the discussions both parties agree on what is in and out of a possible deal. Ultimately such detail becomes an essential component of the executed agreements, often in the form of attachments of formal specifications. At the negotiation stage, the contents of the offer can be expressed as informally as bulleted points on a vugraph or transparency all the way to an offering book for more complex situations, although one should always obtain legal advice on such matters. Such summaries are included in documents known as "heads of agreement" or a "term sheet;" normally these documents have laid out, in addition to the *TR* specification, other key business terms including some of the key financial terms (*DE*).

If the negotiations are to be in the context of an auction, (covered as Method 6 in Chapter 9), then the deal definition comes from the seller and is formal and fixed. More frequently, the deal definition (*TR*) is itself a subject of negotiation between the parties. It is said that no two deals can ever look alike because the buyers and sellers are unique and want and value different things.

Another virtue of early definition of the *TR* is that deal-breaking issues can be identified. Examples of buyers' expectations that might become deal-breakers include the following:

- Representations and warranties that the patents offered are valid, or that the technology "works." Essentially, asking the seller to take the risk without the responsibility or control of getting the technology from the R&D stage to successful operation at a commercial scale.
- Commitment to enforce the patents against any and all infringers irrespective of the economic significance of such infringement.
- Inclusion of other patents or technologies which may not directly relate to the scope of the license.

Such issues can arise for many reasons. In some cases buyers are mistaking a technology license for a product or business license: by definition, a technology license requires a buyer to take responsibility for getting it from "here" (R&D work product) to "there" (commercial fruition). In other cases, buyers have low tolerance for risk, either because they see the overall risk of the project as being extraordinarily high, or they just have low tolerance for risk. In still other cases, buyers will keep asking for more *TR* until they hear a firm "no" simply as a negotiating strategy: How do we know we got all we can until they are ready to throw us out? (This is sometimes known as the "Brooklyn Negotiating

Strategy.") Regardless of the circumstances, it serves both parties well to reach this understanding early, and record such understanding in writing even if in the form of a summary table. Such record keeping can be particularly useful when other parties within the buyer's organization join the negotiations at a later stage and presume or feign to presume certain things are included in the deal that have been excluded. Also, at the stage of documenting the *TR* table it is essential that the parties representing the seller gain organizational unanimity of the scope of what is being offered to avoid creating "take away" situations late in negotiations; such situations are always harmful to the negotiation process and can lead to the breakdown of a pending agreement.

Just as there are deal-breaking requests made by buyers there can be seller *TR* offers or structures that can be deal-breaking to a buyer. Examples include:

- Guaranteed commercial outcomes which, if not met cause the buyer to face substantial punitive consequences
- Requiring the buyer to grant back its improvements so that the seller can then license or disclose such improvements to third parties to compete with the buyer
- Requiring broad cross-license rights from the buyer's extensive patent portfolio in areas unrelated to the subject matter of the license.

Again, to avoid facing a broken deal after substantial effort, it is in the interest of both parties to work out the deal content issues early in the due diligence process. Another crucial reason for such *TR* definition is its necessity in order to assess *Risk* (*R*) and determine the appropriate *Deal Economics* (*DE*).

What about the feasibility of creating a pricing table for each possible (non deal-breaking) element of a transaction that can be used with any potential buyer or what is known as "ála carte pricing?" Unfortunately, such pricing works in restaurants and even when buying automobiles but it generally isn't feasible in technology licensing. In general, there are too many elements that can be negotiated that simply cannot be quantitified on a one-by-one basis in a pricing book. Some exceptions exist. One such exception occurs when the technology can be used to make two different products (say, A and B) and in three different territories (say, 1, 2, and 3); in such cases it is possible that a limited pricing table can be created along the following lines:

- The *TR* for "A" and "B" are priced separately for use in all territories (1, 2, and 3) making a two-element pricing structure, or

• The *TR* for all products (A and B and any other) are priced separately for each of three territories (1, 2, or 3) making a three-element pricing structure.

The former situation makes sense when the buyer is a large international company that is likely to want to pursue worldwide exploitation of one, but not both, products. The latter situation makes more sense when the buyer is a smaller company whose marketing interests are focused in one territory but wants to put the underlying technology to as many uses as possible.

In this example, it is possible (in theory) to conceive of creating a matrix of rights: two products in two rows and three territories in three columns and pricing each of the six resulting cells. It has been reported that term sheets have been offered that have nine products matrixed against nine territories creating 81 cells all for one underlying technology. Such an approach may be workable for special situations such as licensing soft drink franchises in various countries, and it is conceivable for special technology licensing situations such as nonexclusive rights to a medical diagnostic tool protected by worldwide patents. In general, however, segmenting license prices into more than two or three components is rare. And rarer still (in fact, unheard of) would be a *TR* term sheet that shows the added cost of each of a dozen elements possible in an agreement.

RISK

A dictionary definition of "risk" when used as a noun conveys an idea of possible loss or injury. When used in a license valuation context, "risk" means that the seller and buyer understand that things could turn out adversely in the context of the projected "most likely" situation assumed when performing a valuation. Risk can be thought of as the likelihood and impact of an outcome less favorable than the "most-likely" one.

In this sense risk is tied to the optimism (or pessimism) used to create the valuation. By itself, risk does not have meaning. Like the old vaudeville joke—"How are you doing?" ("*Compared to what?*")—risk needs a point of comparison. For example, if a buyer were knowingly to make very optimistic projections of how soon the technology could be brought to market, and of the top line growth in sales and the bottom line profit margins, then there would be a very high likelihood that such a project will not meet such projections. Put another way, this would be a high-risk deal for the buyer.

However, if the buyer were instead to make very pessimistic assumptions on time to market entry, sales, and margins, then the risk becomes lower, though it is never zero, because there is always the risk that the entire project could fail prior to the first sale.

Does this variability of risk mean that no rational basis exists for creating valuations and assessing risk? The answer must be "no," or this would be a very short book. There is another dimension to risk not considered in the previous examples, namely, the "upside" potential. Generally sellers and buyers are equally interested in upsides as well as downsides. In the optimistic projections the "downside" (i.e., risk) is large and likely, and the "upside" small and unlikely. In the pessimistic projection, the situation is reversed. Generally both the seller and buyer are interested in grasping and characterizing such upside potential in their projections and valuations; examples of this will be presented in the Monte Carlo Method in Chapter 8.

Consider a simple example. Suppose the seller offers a buyer the right to flip a coin and to be paid by some third party based on the number of successive "heads" that turn up. Specifically, the deal for the buyer is this: if the first flip is "heads," the buyer gets $1 million, if the second flip is also "heads," the buyer gets $10 million (total), and if the third flip is also "heads," the buyer receives a total of $100 million; however, at the first "tails" the game is over. There are the following four pay-off possibilities for the buyer who acquires this seller's "technology" (where H stands for heads, and T for tails):

  H-H-H = $100 million
  H-H-T = $10 million
  H-T = $1 million
  T = $0

How would a rational buyer characterize the risk and value such an opportunity? The mega-optimist[6] would say this is a $100 million opportunity with high risk while the mega-pessimist would say there is a 50:50 chance it is worth nothing. The statistical value of the coin flip possibilities is shown on the opposite page using a decision tree format. The value of each mode is simply the average of the two subsequent outcomes as each possiblity is equally probable.

So, statistically the value of this opportunity is $14 million.

This means that statistically, if a buyer could acquire many such technologies, say 20 or more, it would very likely experience an *average* benefit of $14 million over the 20 or more "licenses" even though no one license yielded or even could have yielded exactly $14 million because the only possibilities are $0, $1, $10, and $100 million. From this long-term/many-deal perspective, the buyer should be willing to pay a seller of such rights almost up to $14 million to secure the right to "play" (assuming it does not have to make any other investments or deploy other buyer assets).

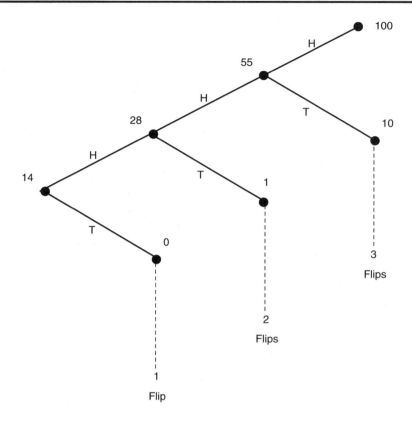

Say the parties agree that the buyer will pay $11 million for this opportunity. The most *frequent* outcome would be that the buyer would lose money on the deal, because half the time the buyer would get zero (tails first), and of the other half of the time the outcome would be evenly divided between $1 million and either $10 million or $100 million. Yet, if the buyer can play enough times, then the $100 million prize will occur with sufficient regularity that even paying the seller $11 million would be profitable to the buyer. For the 20-deal example, the buyer would average a profit of $3 million per "license" and, could thereby expect a total profit of $60 million.

Practically speaking, technology licenses require many years before great successes can be realized (failures can come early). Buyers and sellers recognize that in their business lifetimes they will generally not have a statistically significant number of deals that they can be so confident in such statistical methods, though for large corporations doing many deals such analysis is reasonable and appropriate.[7] Accordingly, it appears that buyers generally discount very high but rare upsides in their valuation analysis. Sellers, of course, normally take pains to point out to prospective buyers the existence of the upside potential.

Venture capitalists in particular receive offers that sound like the above coin toss payoff example. Here is an actual letter:

"What we are asking for is Forty Million Dollars ($40,000,000), which will provide the capital needed.... As planned, at the end of the two-year period we will have ramped up to 100 percent with an expected pre-tax profit of $211,832,258."[8]

Although one appreciates the precision of the projected returns, any reasonable buyer recognizes that what is being pitched here is a very high risk opportunity, or worse. It is useful to consider the kinds of risks that a buying opportunity may entail.

What kinds of risks exist? Fully enumerated, there are at least 36, as Dilbert contends in Figure 2.1. However, for our purposes the risks can be grouped into four categories.

R&D Risks

Although there is no bright line of demarcation at the end of R&D and the beginning of design for manufacturing, usually what is meant by "R&D" is the demonstration of a practical means of doing something. In this context, "practical," means that the quality control, the speed, and the cost of making the product appear to be sufficient and the product can be made and sold at a profit.

The nature of R&D is to attempt to anticipate all the issues that require resolution prior to design for manufacturing. The problem is that one can never anticipate the things one does not think of and one can never be sure that everything that should have been considered was considered. There are many famous catastrophes,[9] and lesser ones, that show the danger of R&D hubris.

In some technology licenses the seller purports to provide *TR* that is

Figure 2.1
DILBERT © distributed by United Feature Syndicate. Reprinted with permission.

complete with respect to its R&D. In other cases, the seller notes known unfinished R&D. In all cases, the buyer in its due diligence needs to consider not only the investment in time and money to complete all the R&D, seller's perceptions excepted, but also to characterize the risk associated with successful completion.

The real risk of failure at the R&D stage is not normally that the technology cannot be made to work but that it is too difficult and costly to be made to work. With rare exceptions, to be commercial it is necessary that the technology is extensively used and, so costs are important.

Manufacturability Risks

Manufacturability risks refer to all the perils that one faces in creating a production environment that will repeatably and cost-effectively produce the product designed by the R&D process. These risks are associated with converting a technology that has been demonstrated in a limited number of examples at lab scale into something that can be replicated many times at a commercial scale. Also involved in such conversion is the idea that less skilled people will be deployed in the manufacturing process in order to keep costs low.

There are many ways technology can fail at this stage. In chemical processes, R&D is frequently done in a batch mode whereas in many commercial high-volume operations, it needs to be done in a continuous mode to be profitable. This can be a difficult transition.

In commercial operations one needs to be concerned with waste product disposal issues. In the R&D process, certain internal recycling operations may have been assumed that in a commercial context turn out to be difficult to accomplish.

In the case of semiconductors, the ratio of good parts to total parts made, or the yield, is the critical factor in the process economics. Although there may be extensive data at the R&D scale on yield, it is possible that when a large-scale production facility operates, the yields will not be as high as needed, or that significant additional development will be required to achieve necessary yields.

Marketing Risks

Even with a product that performs as designed and can be sold at low cost because of efficient manufacture, it is not certain that a sufficient number of customers will purchase the product to warrant its existence.

It is surprisingly difficult to predict what customers will do with respect to a specific offer-for-sale opportunity. This is compounded in technology licensing because at the time of the license the exact nature of the product features and cost may be unknown. Also, the "market" changes its opinion with time. If you asked people in 1990, if they wanted an "internet," what would they have said? If you asked people in 1985, if they wanted a "fax machine," what would they have said? A "PC" in 1980? A "microwave" in 1970?

It is important to recall such examples as the PC Junior (IBM), Corfam (Dupont), supersonic airlines (Boeing), Betamax (Sony), Video On Demand (Time Warner) and many others to realize that even very good companies with smart people spending large sums on market research have been humbled, regularly.

Competitive Risks

When considering the risks associated with a *TR* buyer making products and selling to its customers, it is easy to lose sight of the fact that this is more than a two-party process. When a technology and its derived products are being evaluated at the licensing stage, assumptions are made about what competitive products will exist when the subject one is introduced and how competitors will respond. All companies are searching to meet customer needs. While a technology buyer thinks it can disadvantage such competitors in the competition for customers, there are known competitors and unknown who are thinking and planning the same thing. This unending stream of suitors for customers is a wonderful situation for the marketplace, but it creates a risky environment for companies making new product plans.

If a technology is going to yield products that will displace currently sold products, one can be sure that the competitors making such products will not stand by and say, "sure, you go ahead and take my customers because I'll just do something else" (such as go out of business). Competitors have shareholders who expect profits and management who is accountable for same, and salespeople with quotas, and product managers who are hired and fired based on their ability to create and maintain a competitive edge. All these people and companies are not going to give up without a fight.

Even if a technology is intended to create new products and services for new markets, the competitive response is still there. All companies are looking for opportunities for new revenues and higher margins. If a new product is introduced in a new market, it will spawn a competitive response provided the business looks attractive. When a football coach is watching his first string team beat up his third string team on a Wednesday, he should not assume that Saturday's game is in the bag; his opponent's first string is also beating up its third string that same day.

Legal Risks

One simple example of a legal risk is Prohibition. Early in the twentieth century the government outlawed the making and selling of alcoholic beverages. More recently, the government has put such hurdles in the use of nuclear power as to effectively extinguish that industry in terms of new plants. Designers of new encryption techniques face serious scrutiny for use and export. The cost and therefore, utility, of many chemical products is significantly affected by environmental regulations. In recent years there have been cost penalties and outright prohibitions associated with the use of certain chemicals in packaging (polystyrene cups for example).

Another form of legal risk is contained with the very nature of patents. In the United States, approximately 2,000 patents are issued every Tuesday that, for approximately 17 years, bar the making, using, and selling of a defined and claimed process or product.[10] Because U.S. patent applications are secret until they are issued, and there are literally several hundred thousand such pending applications, it is conceivable that one of those pending applications could mature into a valid, enforceable patent that would prevent one's practice of a licensed technology.[11]

With software technology such patent-blocking risks have increased significantly. Although software patentability has been established for some years now, it has not been a significant business issue. It appears that with the increasing proliferation of software tools and processes coupled with the enormous market value of software companies (Amazon is presently more valuable than Sears), in the future the blocking effect of software patents will increase the risk of deploying new technologies.

Overall Characterization of Risk

There is no formula that can be used to derive the risk of a technology licensing project. There has been significant study in two related aspects: success rates for new product development and for pharmaceuticals in particular. A recent study published in *Research Technology Management* summarizes 16 prior studies on the commercial success rates of new product launches; these studies claimed success rates from a low of 40 percent to a high of 67 percent.[12] Further, this study examines data looking at seven stages in the new product development process, starting with "raw ideas" and ending with "economically profitable." The study concludes that the ratio from Stage 1 (raw idea) to Stage 7 (economically profitable) is 3000 to 1: that is, it takes 3,000 starting raw ideas to make one profitable success. Most of the mortality, according to the study, occurs in the R&D process (although that is conditional upon certain definitional issues) Depending on one's interpretation of "completion of R&D," the data suggests that from 4 to 100 projects are required for one commercial success. This leads to the conclusion that both of the following statements are true: (1) 60 percent of new product projects succeed (from Stage 6 to Launch/Stage 7) *and* (2) 99.7 percent of ideas submitted fail (from Stage 2 to Stage 7).[13]

An interesting question and relevant issue to technology licensing is this: do technology licenses have a higher success rate? The argument can be made that the answer is yes for two reasons: (1) there exists a willing buyer who, at arms length and without compulsion, elects to pursue the subject opportunity, and (2) by separating the inventing/R&D performing organization from the manufacturing/selling organization, it is possible that a better result will occur, despite "hand off" (tech transfer) issues, because each could be the best at what they do.

Another area in which considerable study has occurred is the development of pharmaceuticals. One widely cited figure is that it takes 10,000 active molecules identified to create (on average) one pharmaceutical sold in the marketplace; this would suggest that the mortality, if that's the right word, in the pharmaceutical development business is approximately three times the 3,000:1 findings for typical industrial products. A study attributed to Shearson Lehman Hutton suggested the following ratios at various stages: 20:1 at IND (the filing of Investigation of New Drug), 10:1 at Phase I Clinicals, 4:1 at Phase II, 1.8:1 at Phase III, and 1.2:1 at New Drug Application (NDA).[14]

As will be discussed in detail in Chapter 7, the overall commercial risk is normally characterized by one numeric factor designated by the symbol "k." Such "k" is known by a variety of terms: risk factor, hurdle rate, Risk-Adjusted Hurdle Rate (RAHR), and return-on-investment required (or expected); we will generally use RAHR. It is the one value by which all the previously mentioned risks are expressed, and it is used to assess the present value of a prospective future benefit.

Chapter 8 will deal with the Monte Carlo Method, a powerful and more recently developed tool for characterizing risk. With this approach we will see risk expressed as a probability distribution of financial outcomes somewhat like the heads and tails example used earlier.

Just as with the "price of used furniture,"[15] risk is a *perspective*. Inventors tend to see risk as primarily embodied in the creation of the original concept; from their perspective, the risk post-invention is, in comparison, small. R&D managers, having a broader perspective, see the successful R&D project as having wrung out most of the risk. Design-for-manufacturing people see the primary risk in creating the cost efficient, reliable "factory" that actually makes things. Marketing people see the identification of customer segments and the cost-benefit equation and competitive response as being the real risk. Salespeople see the risk as being what it takes to get a customer to lift his or her pen and sign a purchase order. Lawyers see risk everywhere; it's their calling. And, shareholders don't want to hear about risk; they just expect to see 20+ percent growth in share price (or else).

PSYCHOLOGY OF NEGOTIATIONS AND BUYING

The personalities and processes of the seller and buyer significantly affect the perceived value and associated risk of a deal, and the (speed or lack of it) of reaching an agreement. Generally in license negotiations, sellers play the official role of optimists, providing reasoning that leads to higher estimates of future successes, while buyers are the pessimists dedicated to thinking of things that can go wrong. Clearly the respective motivations drive such perspectives: the seller wants to receive a high price, whereas the buyer not only wants to acheive the highest profit possible, but also wants to avoid a situation where the company has paid more than can ever be realized by its commercial efforts.

If both parties conform to their natural inclinations, deals would be rare events—they would occur only in those cases where a pessimist perceives the opportunity more valuable than an optimist! This is similar to the joke about the optimist being one who believes we live in the best of all possible worlds and the pessimist fearing that this just might be true. So, in order for deals to occur, sellers will need to gain a comprehension of the downside that any buyer faces in converting a technology to a business, and buyers will need to grasp that really good things can happen and maybe the overall risks are not as great as they may seem.

From this perspective, negotiation is a teaching process whereby buyers persuade sellers to think less of their technology and sellers persuade buyers to think more of the opportunity.

Buyer Perception and How It Can Affect Value

There are many factors that can affect this mutual teaching and persuasion process. For starters, seller professionalism and credibility is important. There is no practical way that a buyer can completely replicate every assertion of a seller without redoing the entire R&D program. If the buyer perceives the seller to be the "Joe Isuzu" of technology licensing it will either lose interest in the negotiation or so low-ball its offers that a deal becomes unlikely.[16]

Exhibit 2.1 shows the results from a study run with two groups, a test

Exhibit 2.1   Subjective Factors Affecting Buyers

"Consumer Products Book"	Mean in Setting A	Mean in Setting B	(B-A/A)
Dress 1	$27.77	$41.50	49%
Dress 2	$21.09	$33.91	61%
Tent	$69.95	$77.73	11%
Men's Sweater	$13.91	$20.64	48%
Lamp	$28.36	$40.41	42%
Electric Typewriter	$131.45	$165.36	26%
Chess Set	$35.29	$43.15	22%

Source: Feinberg, R. A., APA Proceedings, Division of Consumer Psychology, 1982, p.28

group, and a control group.[17] The results for the control group are shown in the first column under "Setting A." A statistically significant number of individuals were asked, one at a time, to review a notebook describing the seven items shown at the left. Based on such descriptions each individual was asked to say how much they would pay for the item with the understanding that no transaction was to take place. The entire process was repeated for "Setting B," with the results showing that in every case the mean value of willingness to pay was higher than Setting A ranging from a low of 11 percent higher to more than 60 percent higher.

What was different in Setting B? The experimenters placed a "Master-charge" logo (the experiment was conducted prior to the name change to Mastercard®) on a desk near the notebook. Even though it was clear that no actual purchase was to take place, the interpretation was that the mere presence of a credit card as a means of payment unconsciously influenced the evaluation of the willingness to pay. It is this belief that makes retail stores go to great lengths to display every credit imaginable on their entrance doors and at their counters; they know, or believe, that people will pay more if they can pay with plastic.

How does all this relate to technology licensing? Consider the following two examples. In the first case the seller is an unknown university located well off the beaten path, requiring a planes/trains/and automobiles experience to get there. The principal investigator on the project believes that duct tape and alligator clips are the primary tools of good R&D labs. Moving aside some coffee-stained old newspapers, the buyer examines some of the data recorded in pencil on looseleaf paper. For lunch, the prospective buyer is treated to fast food. As the buyer leaves, the principal investigator commends the prospective buyer for having been the first person to have ever bothered to look at the project.

Suppose the exact same technology was instead found in the following setting: Harvard University. The buyer has difficulty arranging a visit because, apparently, many other prospects have been previously scheduled. When greeted at the lab, the principal investigator looks as the lab does, impeccable. The latest in data acquisition tools are everywhere. There is a hum of efficiency and excitement among the technicians and grad students. The data is available in electronic form as well as copious and artistic notes in a shelf of lab notebooks. Lunch is at the Harvard Faculty Club and Henry Kissinger stops by to congratulate the principal investigator on receipt of his or her second Nobel Prize and asks how the new breakthrough invention (being discussed) is going.

Would a prospective buyer come away from the second experience thinking more highly of the opportunity than from the first? Would it make a difference in perception if at the buyer's organization it becomes known that a license is being considered from a prestigious university and a "name" professor?

The lesson here is that sellers should do all they can to present themselves and the opportunity in the best light possible. This is not to say that one should become Joe Isuzu, because that actually would be counterproductive. Rather, the seller should make every effort to present as thorough and well-considered a presentation as possible. Optimism can be expressed by using scenario-projections such as "conservative," "most likely," and "optimistic."

The same lesson also applies to the buyer. Typical licenses provide conditional payments to sellers in the form of royalties or equity based upon the ultimate outcome once the technology is in the hands of the buyer. Sellers want to have their technology in the best, most-professional (and enthusiastic) hands. So, buyers need to temper their skepticism lest they appear so negative that the seller wonder's why they are even interested. However, the same caution against becoming a Joe Isuzu buyer applies.[18]

CONCLUSION: TWO FINAL POINTS
ON BUYING AND SELLING

Returning to the Arthur Miller play, *The Price*, we are reminded that valuation is a function of perspective and, is therefore individual. Two different prospective buyers each following legitimate valuation approaches can come to two significantly different valuations because of widely differing perspectives on what is "most likely" as an outcome and the attendant "risk." For the seller, the challenge is to find that prospective buyer who, because of some combination of experience, general optimism about the future, relevant assets, and especially with significant needs for new products, will grasp some of the seller's upside enthusiasm. "Hungry" buyers tend to see more opportunity.

> He who is full loathes honey,
> but to the hungry even what is bitter tastes sweet.
> Proverbs 27:7

And, finally, pricing is the leverage point of all negotiations. No buyer will ever say to a seller, "This is a great deal, are you sure we would be paying you enough?" That is about as likely as a hockey player apologizing for causing a collision. So, regardless of the price, the seller will hear (even right up to the moment of contract signing) that the price and risk are too high.

> "It's no good, it's no good!" says the buyer;
> then off he goes and boasts about his purchase.
> Proverbs 20:14

NOTES

1 Such represenatation are generally not appropriate to technology licensing as by definition, the seller is not likely to know or be able to control how the technology is ultimately put into practice by the buyer.

2. John W. Schlicher, *Licensing Intellectual Property*, Wiley Intellectual Property Series, 1996; Harry R. Mayers and Brian G. Brunsvold, *Drafting Patent License Agreements*, Second Edition, Bureau of National Affairs, 1987.

3. These comments are not intended to apply to large multinational companies that may be headquartered in a country outside the geography of North America, Western Europe, and Japan. Such companies are capable of writing large checks in any currency.

4. "Bartering as a Means of Technology Transfer," presentation by Steven R. Maimon of the Hunter Group, Inc., given at the Licensing Executive Society Summer Meeting at Williamsburg, VA.

5. "Valuing/Dealing with Non-Cash Consideration," presentation given by Richard Razgaitis at the Licensing Executives Society Advanced Licensing Course, Charleston SC, March 13, 1997.

6. Defined as that person who believes he could douse hell with one bucket—while the pessimist fears that the optimist could be right.

7. A more practical measure is the number of deals in the career horizon of the buyer. Given the increased pressure on near-term returns, individuals may be far less prepared to consider statistical returns.

8.Michael S. Malone, *Upside*, September 1992.

9. Two examples come to mind. The first one is home movies of the gyrations and collapse of the Tacoma Narrows bridge that failed less than a week after being opened; there was an era where this was required viewing for every engineering freshman. The second example is of the numerous early aviators with their now-bizarre looking "aircraft" failing with sometimes comic and sometimes tragic outcomes.

10. The life of a U.S. patent is 20 years from filing. Assuming it takes three years to get from filing to issuance, the useful life on issuance would be 17 years.

11. Although it is possible that the holder of such blocking patent would be amenable to providing a

license, there is no assurance that this is the case and the economics of such a second license could significantly harm the overall economics of the original transaction.

12. Greg A. Stevens and James Burley, "3,000 Raw Ideas = 1 Commercial Success!" *Research Technology Management*, published by IRI, May–June 1997, p. 16-27.

13. Ibid.

14. "Commercializing Biomedical Technology," in *Licensing Economics Review*, June 1991, p. 9, cited an Immulogic Pharmaceutical Corporation presentation at an international conference on Commercializing Biomedical Technologies, held at Harvard School of Public Health, April 1991.

15. *The Price.* Miller, Arthur, Penguin Books, 1968, Act I, p. 38.

16. In the late 1980s, the Isuzu automobile company ran a series of television advertisements that made fun of the car salesperson's character by having one Joe Isuzu say the most outrageously puff statements ever heard coupled with small on-screen footnotes providing the corrections.

17. Feinberg, R.A., APA Proceedings, Division of Consumer Psychology, 1982, p. 28.

18. Dear Isuzu Lawyers: I actually like Isuzu cars; I own two of them at the moment. So, the use of "Joe Isuzu" is not intended as an adverse reflection of the product of the Isuzu company or its employees, dealers, or shareholders.

3

Overview of Valuation Methods

In this chapter we will anticipate the six methods to be studied in Chapters 4 through 9. We will also consider how the use of royalties and equity greatly aid in dealing with high-uncertainty valuations. Finally, we will consider the appropriateness of using seller's cost as a valuation "method" or basis. This is an important issue because it so commonly, and generally inappropriately, arises in technology licensing discussions.

KNOWLEDGE VERSUS CERTAINTY: THE VALUE OF METHOD-BASED JUDGMENT

Beginning in Chapter 4, we will consider the first of six valuation methods. The purpose of this chapter is to provide an overview of these methods and the context of their intended use. Also, we will address the issue of seller's incurred cost as a measure of value.

There are two polar perspectives that could be applied to the subject of technology valuation: (1) that there exists a rigid, certain method that yields one and only one answer independently of the evaluator, or, at the other extreme, (2) there cannot exist any real "method" for dealing with high-uncertainty situations such as technology licensing, so any proposed "method" is simply disguised guesswork. The first perspective directs one to slavishly follow the result while the second perspective says not to bother creating a result in the first place.

The six valuation methods embodied in Chapters 4 through 9 reject both of these polar views. There exist tools and approaches that *are* worth applying because they provide practical guidance and rescue one from pure guesswork. On the other hand, the very nature of the problem being addressed does not admit to the kind of certainty that a purely analytical perspective would expect.

This position of extolling a position of intermediacy between certainty and ignorance has a long history. Aristotle argued that it is a sign of an educated mind *not* to expect more certainty from a subject than it can possibly provide. If we deal with geometry or algebra, we anticipate and require certainty; it just cannot be possible that adding a column of numbers can produce a result that depends upon the opinion of the adder, or the circumstances of the moment, or that the Pythagorean Theorem is just one man's opinion. However, when we deal with artistic interpretation, we understand that the observer is a participant in the art in the sense of its interpretation; so it is that art can "mean" different things.

In ancient Greek thought there was an important word for this position of intermediacy: phronēsis, (fro-KNEE-sis), usually translated as "judgment." The use of the valuation methods discussed in Chapters 4 though 9 is an example of that kind of judgment. Because we are dealing with unique technologies and specific profiles of sellers and buyers, and particularly with the issue of forecasting future events, it cannot be that a certain, unarguable result can be produced. Yet there are tools that can, with skill, experience, and judgment, provide very valuable guidance to an important business question: How much is this deal worth?

Drawing on another parallel, in the early days of computers a term was coined to explain bad outputs—GIGO, or garbage in...garbage out. The computer cannot improve bad or false data or improperly crafted algorithms (at least not yet). Similarly, the methods discussed in Chapters 4 through 9 rely on information and application that is as close to mirroring reality as is possible; otherwise, it can be GIGO here too.

AN OVERVIEW OF THE SIX METHODS

The first method considered, in Chapter 4, is the use of Industry Standards. This is based on the idea of working to find as many relevant agreements as possible that bear some resemblance to the technology and deal in question. For reasons that will be discussed, it is rare that a "right on" comparable agreement is found that can be directly used to infer a value. Rather, an interpretive process works on families of agreements to characterize the nature of the terms agreed to in other agreements so as to give guidance to the subject valuation.

In Chapter 5 we consider the Rating/Ranking Method. This method provides a more formal way of characterizing how one technology and/or one agreement differs from another. It requires a reference agreement or standard in order to base a valuation. For this reason it is normally used in conjunction with the Industry Standards Method.

The use of Rules of Thumb is considered in Chapter 6 as the third method. Such rules, guidelines really, are generalizations derived from observing how parties reached previous agreements. The most common form is the so-called 25 Percent Rule. It establishes a principle for apportioning a percentage of the revenues received by the buyer based on the anticipated profitability.

Chapter 7 presents the Discounted Cash Flow Method. This method introduces the Risk Adjusted Hurdle Rate (RAHR, designated by "k") as a means for characterizing the overall commercial risk. Using such a risk factor, the magnitude and timing of future cash flow benefits can be analyzed and apportioned between the seller and buyer.

Advanced methods are considered in Chapter 8, principally the Monte Carlo Method. This method is similar to the Discounted Cash Flow Method except that it relies on probability analysis of estimated ranges to produce a statistical prediction of the expected value. In addition, we will consider in this chapter some other non-traditional perspectives on valuation that deal with high-uncertainty and/or long-term payoff situations.

Finally, the Auction Method is presented in Chapter 9. In a sense, Chapter 9 brings us full circle back to a market-based approach that is the basis of Chapter 4. However in the case of auctions, the seller creates a market for the specific opportunity being offered for license.

In Chapter 10 some special valuation issues relating to the seller taking an equity position in the buyer (usually as a startup) are reviewed. In general, these issues rely upon the six basic methods developed throughout the book.

Finally, in Chapter 11 we consider how valuations determined can be expressed in various forms of payment. And in the closing chapter, Chapter 12, some principles of negotiation are discussed.

THE POWER OF SCALED PAYMENTS: ROYALTIES AND EQUITY

The most difficult situation in high-uncertainty valuations, such as technology licensing, occurs when the result has to be a single number payable at closing. Here all the future uncertainty has to be shrunk to the most certain of all entities, that of a single, fixed number now. Although the methods to be presented in this book, working in concert with good judgment, are capable of performing such a feat, there is no escaping the fact that when dealing with high-uncertainty futures there is an acute tension in creating an absolutely certain present.

The establishment of royalties, however it originated in the antiquarian past, is a powerfully enabling tool for dealing with uncertainty. Because the amount of payment is tied to a rate multiplied by a to-be-determined number, usually sales, there is a built-in way of causing large payments for large outcomes (at least in terms of sales), and vice versa. Accordingly, using royalties makes the valuation task easier because all the future uncertainty has to be reduced to a single *rate*, not a single number (dollar amount). This is by no means easy, because there is a wide variation in what an appropriate rate should be. However, it is important to note and credit the great utility of "royalties" as a tool that can be used in conjunction with all six valuation methods.

Likewise, equity is a powerful way to make a valuation correspond to outcomes. Equity, even more than royalty, is more closely tied to value because of its connection to profitability which, over time, determines the market value of a company, present internet valuations excepted. As we shall see in Chapter 10, there are some limitations on the use of equity. Nonetheless, when equity can be used it is a tool, like royalties, applicable to all six valuation methods.

VALUATION METHODS/TOOLS USED IN COMBINATION

There are two senses in which the valuation methods are used in combination. One way is that a technology is commonly valued using two (or more) different methods so as to compare the results. When different methods lead to similar ranges, it increases one's confidence in the utility of the result. When the methods do not lead to similar results, then it is time to reexamine the assumptions and retry the methods.

Another sense in which methods are used in combination is that each of the methods can be thought of as a tool to support other methods. For instance, the Discounted Cash Flow Method helps create equivalencies in cash value for different times and conditions that can be used to help better identify and interpret a comparable license (Method 1 in Chapter 4). Rating/Ranking (Method 2 in Chapter 5) is often used with Industry Standards and with Rules of Thumb. Monte Carlo (Method 5 in Chapter 8) is built upon Discounted Cash Flow (Method 4 in Chapter 7). Auctions (Method 6 in Chapter 9) are normally evaluated using other methods such as Industry Standards and Rules of Thumb. Rules of Thumb are frequently used with Discounted Cash Flow to apportion profitability between seller and buyer.

Accordingly, it would be a mistake to latch on to one method as the one and only way of conducting valuations. It would be like choosing to have only one tool in your tool box.

WHAT ABOUT COST AS A METHOD?

You may note from the previous outline that the seller's cost is not considered as a valuation method. Some, might consider this as missing the most obvious method. However, with few exceptions (as we shall presently discuss), seller's costs are irrelevant. As the following illustration shows, the seller's cost could be a benchmark as to the buyer's costs to design around the offered license.

Seller's Cost Perceptions and How They Can Affect the Deal-Making Process

One common issue affecting a seller's perception of value and price of an opportunity is its costs incurred. There is a logic to this perception because, after all, the cost is what the seller paid for the technology, so why shouldn't the buyer be willing to pay at least the same amount? However, the logic is false in the following sense. What the seller bought was an option to a business opportunity that would result from an R&D success. If the R&D project is a success, then the seller would be foolish to consider its costs as the value. If the R&D project fails or underperforms, then the seller needs to be reminded that it bought an option, and options can go up and go down; in this case, it went down, perhaps even to zero.

Although it is an extreme example, consider buying a ticket in a lottery. If one pays $1 for the ticket, one has bought an option on, say $1 million, if all the little numbers on the ticket line up with all the little balls in the scrambling machine. If they do, the option price of $1 is irrelevant to the ticket's value because it is (in such case) exercisable for $1 million. If the balls do not replicate the ticket holder's string of little numbers, then the option price of $1 is also irrelevant to the ticket's value because it has an option on nothing. So regardless of what happens, the purchaser of a lottery ticket can be certain that his or her ticket will *never* again be worth $1, because costs are irrelevant. Consider a real-life technology example (one of many). Kendall Square was once a high flying computer company. In August 1993, the company was valued at $360 million and shares were selling for $25 apiece. In October 1994, Kendall Square was selling for less than 5 cents (cents!) a share. In between those dates, one poor soul had invested $65 million in real money.[1]

In the case of technology that turns out to be a disappointment, seller's sometimes still believe that its cost should invoke a combination of perceived significance and pity on a buyer. Here's another example. In 1990, the investors of Optical Data, Inc. threw in the towel on their $10 million investment made over a nine-year period. A business journal article summarized the decision as follows: "Though it was touted as breakthrough technology, the company was never able to create a market for its products."[2] The resulting patents were being offered at $1 million. Although the linkage between the stated value ($1 million) and the historic costs ($10 million) is not overtly stated, the implication is made that there is a bargain in the offing as the IP can be had for "only" 10 cents on the dollar.[3]

An Example Negotiation Driven by the Seller's Perception of Its Costs Determining Value

For projects that a seller believes will be successful, it tends to view value in a return-on-investment way. Although this is closer to being value-based thinking, this idea is flawed as well, as Exhibit 3.1 will illustrate. This example shows how sellers and buyers can misapprehend each other. In one case they miss a deal and in another they reach a deal but through a false rationale.

Shown in the left column is the seller's R&D cost with an added "justifiable" margin that the seller believes it should be entitled to based on its costs. Such a perspective is really based on a manufacturing model of R&D: that selling prices can be determined by some form of "cost plus" pricing, even though such an approach is increasingly rare even for commercial operations.

In the right-hand columns of Exhibit 3.1, the buyer's perceptions of value are shown. For "Case A" we see three components to such perceived value: (1) the cost if the buyer had to repeat the R&D, plus (2) the incremental cost to avoid the intellectual property barriers surrounding the seller's technology (i.e., patent claims), plus (3) the value of having the head start of picking up the seller's project without attempting to independently recreate the results. In Case A, the buyer's perceived total value is shown as being just below the seller's costs. And here is an illustration of a cost-based valuation which is valid. Therefore, the seller's

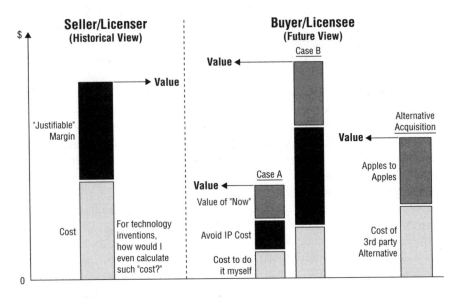

Exhibit 3.1   Seller and Buyer Perspectives on Cost and Value

initial reaction will be negative to a buyer's offer of such an amount because it would have the effect of acquiring the technology for less than the seller's own costs. Sellers naturally resist the idea that successful projects can be worth less than they cost. Unless the seller can be persuaded that the buyer's value is in fact an accurate representation of value, then no deal will be done.

In Case B, the same components of value have resulted in a buyer's valuation to be greater than the seller's perception. In this case a deal should be readily possible but only because it so happens that the seller's perception of "justifiable margin" matches the buyer's perceptions of the three components of value that it considered. So the deal is, in a real sense, an accident.

Shown to the far right in Exhibit 3.1 is yet another dimension of buyer valuation. Every investment that a buyer considers making should be compared to other uses of the investment resources. The decision to acquire the seller's technology should be made only if that decision happens to be the very best use of the incrementally available investment resources. This column shows that there is an alternative that can be acquired for much less than the seller is offering for the subject opportunity. Because no two opportunities are ever exactly alike, the buyer has to add or subtract an "apples to apples" comparison between the third party alternative and the seller's proposal. In this example, the buyer has concluded that the seller's technology does have an incremental value above the third party's alternative, but not enough to reach the seller's perceived value. If the seller perceives that the third party alternative is something that will affect only this one prospective buyer, then even a demonstration of the basis of such lower valuation will be unpersuasive to the seller. However, if the seller can be convinced that all potential buyers will have third party alternatives like or approximately like this one, then a seller might be convinced that its perception of "justifiable margin" is wrong. This suggestion sets the stage for the first valuation method, the use of industry standards, in Chapter 4.

What Do Sellers Sell?

What do seller's sell? Value. "Price is never the *cause* of value."[4] Price, or valuation, is the quantification of value. Buyer's buy value, never the seller's costs.

There can be negotiation utility in knowing the seller's costs, although such knowledge and use can be confusing. Let us imagine a technology created by the seller at a cost of $1 million that has, by some combination of valuation methods, a present value of $10 million, the inverse of the previous Optical Data Company example. The parties agree that they will divide up the $10 million payment into an upfront component and a royalty component. There might be good reason why the seller would like as a downpayment an amount equal to the costs incurred, namely $1 million if it is warranted by the value. This creates a comfortable logic that the seller got back its costs upfront and will achieve its return on investment from future royalties. In this case, it is likely that the buyer will find this acceptable. However, the logic and comfort of such math only works because the value determined independently of cost turned out to be 10 times the cost. If it is equal to the cost, or worse, then the math does not work.

Finally a suitable use of cost is for the seller to measure the value-generation performance of its R&D function. If over time the seller finds that the cumulative payment received (value) is less than a suitable return on investment (i.e., costs) then the seller should conclude that R&D is not a good business to be in, at least as it has been constituted.

CONCLUSION

The need to make assumptions and create models and scenarios to obtain a valuation can be troubling. What if the assumptions are wrong? What if the models are incomplete? What if the scenarios were too optimistic or too pessimistic?

The problem is that all these issues are present every day. When buying the stock of a publicly-traded company, one is forecasting the future in terms of the company's revenues and profits, the attitude of its customers and competitors, the skill and staying power of its management, and even the enthusiasm for other investors in bidding up or selling down the stock.

Valuation of business and product licensing transactions is similarly linked to assumptions, models, and scenarios. One huge assumption made in such circumstances is that the past is a predictor of the future. Unfortunately, there are many circumstances in which that has not proven true, and important deals involving the sales of businesses or licensing of products have created adverse outcomes for one party or the other. The purchase of the Snapple business by Quaker Oats and NCR by AT&T, both of which were later sold off, cost shareholders more than $1 billion. In each case the future was not accurately predicted by extrapolating the past. Similar though less spectacular examples exist for product licensing. Alas, we know less about the future than we often think we do.

Also, many key factors in a valuation are not really knowable. Management goes bad. Competition gets good. Customers change their minds. New technology emerges. Government interferes with commerce. Such things happen all the time. In the case of technology licensing, these uncertainties and risks are compounded with others. The solution is not despair but good judgment. Develop the best model possible, use appropriate methods, exercise judgment (fro-KNEE-sis). The result is much better than guesswork, and in many cases provides a surprisingly good answer for both the seller and the buyer.

NOTES

1. Budkely, William M. "Missing the Boat: Yachtsman Bill Koch Lost His Golden Touch with Kendall Square." *Wall Street Joural*, October 27, 1994, p. 110.

2. "Everything Must Go," *The Business Journal,* Portland, Oregon, January 27, 1992.

3. The irony, of course, is that the patents could be worth much more than the $10 million investment if, for example, the claims covered significant commercial practice by third parties even in products unrelated to the original venture. However, if the patents only protect a product and process that has no commercial value the patents by themselves will have no value, regardless of the cost incurred.

4. Mack Hanan and Peter Karp, *Competing on Value*, AM Acom, 1991.

4

Method One: Use of Industry Standards to Determine Valuation

In this chapter we begin our study of the six valuation methods with the use of industry standards to determine valuation. We will first consider what is meant by industry standards and how they can be helpful in valuation efforts. We will also examine their important limitations. Then we will review different possible sources of industry standards data. Finally we will characterize the limitations of this method and introduce the complementary method presented in Chapter 5, the Rating/Ranking Method.

THE CONCEPT AND LIMITATIONS OF "INDUSTRY STANDARDS"

The term "industry standards" is used to designate the existence of a database of previous deals in a sufficient number and specificity that buyers and sellers can, by reference to such data, agree upon a fair transaction price. The concept conveys the idea of norms or standards that can serve as a guide, somewhat like a complex price book.

Such norms do exist in many contexts: used cars, corporate bonds, office floor space, peaches, and collector baseball cards. Before considering the utility and limitations of such norms for licensing valuation purposes, it is helpful to understand the circumstances where industry standard norms are usefully applied.

In general, industry standards work well when the item being sold or rented can be characterized by two simple factors—the category and the quality—and when a sufficient number of publicly available, similar transactions that comprise a market history can be determined.

As an example, in the case of used cars, "category" could mean 1993 Ford Taurus with the "quality" represented by: four-door, leather interior, all power, 240,000 miles, runs well. In the space of one sentence, it is possible for the prospective buyer to have a reasonably accurate understanding of what is for sale: probably something that looks pretty bad, but with the possibility of some high-maintenance miles left in its life. With a brief telephone call or email exchange, a prospective buyer can rapidly and accurately decide whether this is indeed a purchase of potential interest subject to subsequent due diligence (test drive, mechanic's inspection, etc.) to confirm what is already believed to be true.

The second key aspect of the utility of industry standards is that there also exist a sufficient number of similar transactions and that such information is generally available to buyers and sellers. Continuing with the Ford Taurus example, it is unlikely that any car fitting this exact description has been sold. However, there have been so many Ford Taurus's sold that the database is sufficiently large enough to enable characterization of the effect on value of 240,000 miles even though no one car sold in the database exactly matches this specification. Further, a small industry has emerged which tracks such information and publishes it in various colored "books" and on the internet. So, both seller and prospective buyer can have a reasonable understanding of what the specific car is worth based upon the agreements reached by many thousands of previous sellers and buyers.

Another example is office space. For the metropolitan New York area there is one firm (Newmark, *www.newmarkre.com*) that publishes quarterly what amounts to a pricing book for all kinds of office space designated by Manhattan neighborhood. How about "Grand Central?" The weighted average asking rental rate is $33.56 per square foot per year in the fourth quarter 1991, up from $29.82 a year earlier—you can look it up. Are you more a "Sixth/Rock" (New York for Rockefeller Center area) company? Then it's $41.01, up from $39.13. Do you want to rent on "Park Avenue?" You're talking $45.68.

An example closer to the subject of this book is the selling and buying of corporate bonds, a debt instrument. For simplicity, consider one class of bonds known as "zero coupon" bonds or "zeros." A zero is simply the obligation of the issuing company to pay the owner of such a bond the face value at the face due date, say $100,000 on January 1, 2010. If the current owner of the bond wants cash now, the owner becomes a seller looking for a buyer. Like the Taurus example, the category here is, simple: a $100,000 zero due January 1, 2010. And, just like the used car example, there exist groups whose business it is to publish market information on what previous sellers and buyers agreed upon for like purchases, depending upon the quality of the bond. An added feature in this example is that there are also groups who provide objective quality measures, called rating agencies, in accordance with established criteria, such as "AAA" or "B" by which the buyer can assess the risk of default. Again, the key elements are present: published market information, large number of deals, and standards by which quality can be assessed.

This is all very nice for bonds and square feet and used cars. The level of specificity enables an efficient market to exist where bonds can be traded with little due diligence. Unfortunately, no such simple "book" or "AAA" rating system exists for the selling and buying of technology. Why not? With certain exceptions, technology transactions cannot be managed like used cars and bonds. One problem is simply that technology almost by definition is unique or at most has few pre-existing examples. (There are exceptions to this limitation: A new catalyst material used in a conventional chemical process can be unique of itself but it still belongs to a readily describable category). Another problem is that of describing the quality of the technology in simple, economically-relevant terms; the dimensions of technology performance tend to be so numerous and detailed that there is no parallel to "runs good" or "AAA." (Again, a new catalyst material can serve as a counter-example). Finally, the number of published similar or "like" transactions is almost always very limited and without such a database of information no "book" can exist.

For business or product licensing, there may be sufficient performance data in which there exists some possible classification and valuation standards such as those expressed in multiples of revenues (such as $1\times$ revenues) and/or multiples of after tax earnings (such as $20\times$, also known as the P/E, price/earnings, ratio) and/or multiples of the free cash flow (such as $10\times$). However, even in such cases and with such metrics, the tumultuous and unpredictable world of business still requires substantial specific due diligence and judgment to create a specific valuation. Even on the public stock market, there are huge variations in the P/E multiple based on the market perceptions of future value.

For technology licensing, there is by definition no "standards" for multiples of free cash flow (there is no cash flow, free or otherwise), of profits (none), or of revenues (not yet, but maybe one happy test customer).

Therefore, one should not expect this chapter to present a notebook of numbers that can be used in every technology valuation. No such all-inclusive notebook exists here or elsewhere. Yet, there is important value in obtaining and understanding market-based data on technology transactions. In almost all technology licensing situations there exists some discoverable previous transactions which can provide useful insight into value, based on what such previous buyers and sellers agreed to. In almost all cases some significant interpretive work will be needed to apply the data to the present circumstance. This will be the focus of the next chapter and Method two, the Rating/Ranking Method.

SOURCES OF INDUSTRY STANDARD DATA

There are many different sources of technology licensing "industry data." There are individuals, organizations, and even countries that have surveyed license transactions and published the results. Some companies have published what amounts to standard pricing terms for certain of their technology licenses. Court cases can be another source as some license agreements are actually made public. Additionally, there are firms that have developed databases which can be accessed under various arrangements. Finally, there is the opportunity for one to develop one's own industry data book over time.

In each of the subsequent sections we will consider these various sources and show examples of data that are available. It should be emphasized that these samples are not intended to create a data book on previous licensing deals; this would be a massive undertaking well outside the scope of this book, and when complete it would still not replicate what is available for corporate bonds, office space, or used cars. Rather, the point of the cited examples is to show illustrations of how such information can be found and used for the specific valuation sought.

SURVEY INFORMATION AS A
SOURCE OF INDUSTRY STANDARDS

There exist numerous surveys of technology license agreements. Some of these have been government sponsored, some gathered by associations, some by companies, and some by individuals. Like all surveys, such "data" have numerous inherent limitations relating to the nature of the respondents (biased? statistically significant?), the raw data (survey data accurately acquired? relevant to a valuation? sufficient detail?), and the summarized presentation (bias in summarization and statistical analysis? useful information?).

As discussed in Chapter 2, there is a rich mosaic to most licensing transactions involving many different kinds elements of what is provided by the seller and paid by the buyer. However, most licensing surveys have focused on a single financial parameter: the royalty rate. There are many dangers in thinking of royalty rate as being the determinant of value. As will be discussed in Chapter 11, there are many variables in structuring licensing payments. The parties may agree to a substantial upfront (or other period) payment and, in compensation, will arrive at a lower royalty. There can be cross licenses back from the buyer to the seller that offset an initial royalty valuation so the reported number is very low or even zero. There can be other aspects of the transaction, such as a supply agreement, that have significant enough value to the seller as to warrant low or no royalties.

Further the royalty *rate* by itself has a dangerously ambiguous meaning. Sellers and buyers care not about the rate but the payment *amount.* The conversion is simple: royalty amount = rate × base. The key element is the "base" against which the royalty rate is applied. Take, for example, a computer chip that embodies a commercially significant and patented functionality. If a large manufacturer makes both the chip and the board on which the chip sits and the box into which the chip breathes life and the system that operates only because said chip functionality exists, what is the royalty base? The buyer will suggest the chip itself, which may be a few dollars[1]; in which case the buyer might gladly accept even a 20 percent royalty on even a $100 chip.[2] But the seller could argue that the board and the box have no functionality but for the patented technology on the chip. Compared to the fair market value of the chip alone, the box can be much more valuable: 10 times as much, even 100 times as much or more. Even system solutions based on the patented technology could be subject to an argument that such sales be part of a royalty base. So, what would a 2 percent or 20 percent royalty mean without sorting through such critical matters? It is important to keep in mind that even when royalty rate information can be usefully extracted from published sources, there is more work to be done to complete a valuation.

License Survey Data from Japan

For many years the Japanese government gathered and published license royalty information. These data were obtained because for a period of time, the approval of the Japanese government was needed for any license entered into between a Japanese company and a non-Japanese company. An example of such data is shown in Exhibit 4.1.

As with any survey, (at least) three questions should be asked: Does the survey contain source bias? . . . data coherence? . . . utility? Clearly this survey has significant bias just by its scope: the data are solely for licenses with Japanese companies. It is also limited in time; these surveys ended many years ago so it does not reflect current market conditions. Another aspect of bias is not distinguishing between business, product, and technology licensing. All other factors being comparable, product licensing generally would be expected to be more valuable than technology licensing because the subsequent investment required is less, the time to profits is less, and the risk is reduced. Grouping such agreements with technology licenses is like performing statistical averages on a

Exhibit 4.1 Key Financial Terms of All License Agreements Filed with the Japanese Government in 1975

Terms of Payment	Classification of Technology	Chemical	Metal	Machinery	Electrical	Others
Initial Payment	Required	100	54	223	119	231
	Not required	65	37	187	119	220
	Less than 2%	5	6	16	32	28
	Over 2% and less than 5%	42	24	119	55	126
Running Royalty	Over 5% and less than 8%	12	8	112	24	119
	Over 8%	7	4	24	11	17
	Others	48	28	80	54	69
	None	51	21	59	62	92
Minimum Payment	Required	38	19	116	35	186
	Not required	127	72	294	203	265
Sub-total		165	91	410	238	451
No Fee, Royalty		16	4	11	2	15
Total		181	95	421	240	466

Source: Science & Technology Agency, Japan. Class A Technological Assistance Agreement for the year 1975.

combined population of men and women; clearly it is possible to do this in some aspects, but leads to misleading results when extended to averaging of height and weight or other matters. Although technology is not as subject to trends as, say, clothing fashions, one should be careful when comparing valuations across significant time spans. It is widely accepted that patents are more highly valued in the 1990s than they were in the 1970s, due in large part to a trend toward higher probability of enforcement. There can be other factors. In the case of licenses to Japanese companies in the 1970s, it is likely that the technology being transferred was, on average, less advanced and thereby less valuable than technology being licensed today.

On the issue of data coherence, it appears that no attempt was made to characterize the subject matter licensed in terms of business importance (or potential), patent protection (strength, extent, life), or the existence of other forms of consideration (supply agreements, cross-licenses, grantbacks). The information that is available does not quantify the magnitude of the initial or minimum payments, only their existence.

Finally on the issue of utility, how might such information be used to perform a valuation? As an example, consider Exhibit 4.1 as a tool to prepare a valuation of a technology for making a new laser. One immediate limitation is that these data do not contain a "laser" category. The closest one can get would be to examine the data for "electrical" licenses which could include electric power generation and distribution, radios and TVs, and who knows what else; the category may not even include a single laser license. However, assuming our way past these questions, let us examine the "electrical" column of data. Provided is a histogram of data for royalty rates: namely, 32 out of 240 total agreements provided a royalty of less than 2 percent, 55 between 2 and 5 percent, 24 between 5 and 8 percent, 11 over 8 percent, 54 with "other" royalty rate, and 62 with no royalty. Which was the most-common rate? Zero royalty!

If one considers upfront payments, Exhibit 4.1 discloses that there were 119 electrical agreements which had such payments and 119 which did not; when one considers that two agreements (the next to last row) had no fee or royalty, one would conclude that actually 121 had no upfronts.

So, by this analysis, the most common upfront payment was zero, and the most common royalty was zero! This is not a comforting outcome for a prospective seller trying to use such industry data to price a laser technology license.

Further studying the reported data, what does one conclude? In Exhibit 4.1 under "electrical," the next most common royalty rate was 2 to 5 percent, essentially tied with "other." That is not a particularly helpful statistic. Finally, when one considers all the data, one finds that there were agreement examples for each of the royalty segments from zero to more than 8 percent, including "other." Such a broad spectrum with a gross collection of agreements has so smeared out the original, potentially-valuable data that using such a table with our laser example is fruitless.

The root of the immediate difficulty is that there does not exist a small enough category of agreements that can be used to compare with the specifics of the laser.

Even if one considers another category such as "machinery," which does show a majority of agreements with upfront payments and a royalty (in this case between 2 and 5 percent), what does one do with such information in terms of preparing for technology valuation? How would one know whether the subject "machinery" technology warranted more, the same as, or less than the most common 2 to 5 percent royalty range? Furthermore, even within such range there is a significant variation: a royalty rate of 5 percent is two and half times as valuable as one at 2 percent.

For such data to have the utility of a used car, office space rental, or corporate bonds "book" it would have to have a much more structured and detailed presentation of information. Gathering and publishing such data would not only require a massive effort, it would jeopardize the proprietary status of such agreements.

Voluntary Surveys

Two more recent surveys are examples of voluntary surveys: McGavock, Haas, and Patin[3] and Degnan and Horton[4]. Both involved mailing out survey instruments to several thousand licensing professionals and tabulating and summarizing the findings. Although the number of respondents was modest (118 in the McGavock survey, and 428 in the Degnan survey), both of these papers provide useful insights into various aspects of licensing practices.

Although the goal of the McGavock survey was to assess the factors that affect value in license agreements, a subject dealt with in Chapter 5, the survey did report certain royalty data. Exhibit 4.2 shows a summary of the licensed-out royalty rates by industry from the McGavock survey.

By examining the category of "general manufacturing" it can be seen that every column of royalty rate category contains a numerical value (based upon 21 respondents). Any attempt to use such data to value a specific opportunity within this category (which itself is a broad term) is limited because there is reason to believe that the "market" value could be as low as 0 percent and, at the other extreme, over 25 percent. In order to understand how the market might value a subject technology it would be necessary to go through a population these surveyed agreements and perform an agreement-by-agreement analysis to extract specific guidance. It should be noted that the reported data for "telecommunications," namely 100% between 10 and 15 percent royalty, is a consequence of only one

Exhibit 4.2 Licensed-Out Royalty Rates as Determined by a Voluntary Survey

	Royalty Rate Category						
	0-2%	2-5%	5-10%	10-15%	15-20%	20-25%	OVER 25%
Primary Industry							
Aerospace		40.0%	55.0%	5.0%			
Automotive	35.0%	45.0%	20.0%				
Chemical	18.0%	57.4%	23.9%	0.5%			0.1%
Computer	42.5%	57.5%					
Electronics		50.0%	45.0%	5.0%			
Energy		50.0%	15.0%	10.0%		25.0%	
Food/Consumer	12.5%	62.5%	25.0%				
General Mfg.	21.3%	51.5%	20.3%	2.6%	0.8%	0.8%	2.6%
Gov't/University	7.9%	38.9%	36.4%	16.2%	0.4%	0.6%	
Health Care Equip.	10.0%	10.0%	80.0%				
Pharmaceuticals	1.3%	20.7%	67.0%	8.7%	1.3%	0.7%	0.3%
Telecommunications				100.0%			
Other	11.2%	41.2%	28.7%	16.2%	0.9%	0.9%	0.9%

Source: McGavock, et. al., "Factors Affecting Royalty Rates," *les Nouvelles*, June 1992. p. 107. Reprinted with permission from *les Nouvelles*.

respondent. It should be noted that there is a great deal of useful information in this survey, which will be referenced in Chapter 5; it is just not
reasonable to expect surveys by themselves to provide the kind of information that one can use directly in support of a valuation.

The Degnan survey likewise provides useful information that will be
referenced in Chapter 5. However, one example cited here is this survey's
efforts to link royalty rates to an innovativeness scale. The authors designed the following three-level "Innovativeness Scale:"

> *Revolutionary*: Satisfies a long-felt need or creates a whole new industry
> *Major Improvement*: Significantly enhances product superiority in an
>   existing product, process, or service
> *Minor Improvement*: Creates an incremental improvement in an exist-
>   ing product or service

The authors then used these distinctions to survey and report royalty
ranges. Their findings are summarized in Exhibits 4.3. and 4.4 for licensing-out and in, respectively.

It appears that the licensing "out" rates are higher overall than the "in"
rates; this suggests that the licensing "in" data more closely correspond to
technology, or at least earlier-stage technology. The high end of the "average" values exceed that of the "median"; this is a result of one or a few
very large values acting almost as outliers pulling up the average royalty
rate. The key distinction based upon the "Innovativeness Scale" shows
what would be expected: revolutionary > major > minor. However, the
overlap in ranges is notable.

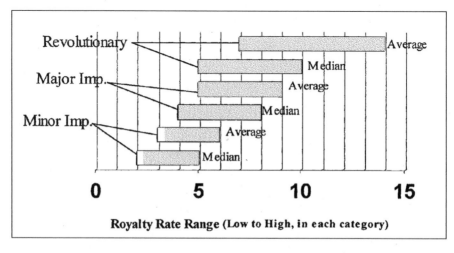

Exhibit 4.3   Licensing-Out Royalty Range

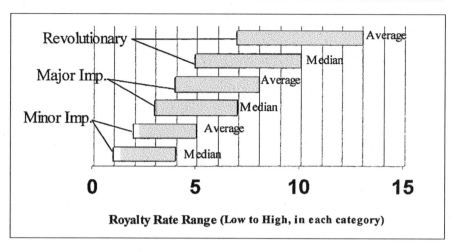

Royalty Rate Range (Low to High, in each category)

Exhibit 4.4   Licensing-In Royalty Range

The Degnan survey also contrasted the median royalty rates for pharmaceutical licensing versus non-pharmaceutical licensing. They found that pharmaceutical licensing showed royalty rates approximately double that of non-pharmaceuticals. The reader is referred to the paper for the details.

Considering again our hypothetical valuation situation for a new laser device, the lack of a specific category of laser licenses or closely-related subject matter, the lack of information on all the other important business dimensions, and the wide range of reported royalties all reveal inherent limitation in the use of such survey data, by itself, in determining a valuation. If one uses the licensing "in" table and reasons that the technology is somewhere between "minor" and "major" and focuses only on the median data, these data suggest a royalty range of perhaps 2 to 5 percent. However, recognize that there is no connection between such data and the specific licensing opportunity.

Summary of Survey Data Limitations for Aiding Valuation

As discussed, such surveys do provide various forms of useful information. However, their capacity to provide guidance in determining a valuation is limited. The primary reasons this is so are as follows:

1. These data frequently cite a wide range of possible royalties within each technology category.
2. There may be limited characterization available that connects the royalty rate data to the extent and value of the IP: i.e., patents only, many patents, new patents, strong patents, patent suitable to

make high margin product for a large market, for a large market, etc.

3. The royalty base in some cases may not be clear. Without understanding the base it may be impossible to determine the significance of a royalty rate (royalties based upon the entire selling price of a large assembly, say an automobile, or upon a small component).

4. The upfront and other fixed payments may not be defined or correlated to the specific royalty rates.

5. Overall there may be lacking a characterization of the many other important terms of a license such as exclusivity, term of the agreement, right to sublicense, improvement rights, etc.

6. There may be inherent vagueness in product categories: "electrical" would presumably cover an integrated circuit and a curling iron. "Mechanical" could cover everything from a complete automobile engine to a staple remover.

7. There is usually an inadequate number of segments of data (because of the scarcity of data). For instance, there are multiple important areas within telecommunications, entertainment/media, pharmaceuticals and medical products, software, and e-commerce. Generally these are omitted entirely or subsumed within very different types of technology licensing.

8. Surveys by their nature contain dated information, which may not be relevant to the present time. Also it is not usually clear how far back in time the data reported by respondents was gathered.

9. Surveys tend to be biased by the nature of the survey segment, membership in a particular society, trans-national licensing to a specific country, and so on.

10. Many of these agreements likely had other commercially significant provisions that affected the numbers. One of the common elements of licenses between companies is a supply agreement provision; often this takes the form of the licensee agreeing to supply the product to the licensor for use or resale. The pricing of such a supply agreement can be such that it influences the valuation of the license; one extreme would be a licensor's willingness to provide a license for no upfront money or royalty in exchange for favorable pricing under a supply agreement. Without a specification of such terms, it is impossible to interpret the meaning of a table of negotiated royalties. Another example would be the existence cross licenses.

11. There is no characterization of the stage of development of the technology licensed. In some cases the licenses were surely for fully-developed products with an already proven market; in other cases, the licenses may have been for unproven inventions still at an early R&D stage.

The observations are not intended to be critical of such surveys. Valuation of technologies is a challenging and important assignment, so every scrap of information is appreciated. However, it is important to understand that such broad surveys have, by themselves, limited usefulness in preparing a valuation.

EXPERT JUDGMENT TABLES AS A
SOURCE OF INDUSTRY STANDARDS

Another source of industry valuation data is that published by experts. Most licensing practitioners tend to focus on certain technology areas and compile data according to their own experience, by networking with colleagues; and by absorbing published information, develop a formal or informal database of what something might be worth. From time to time various experts are willing to publish their opinions at meetings and in journals. These valuation opinions are generally unscientific (that is, unstatistical) but insightful. They exhibit many of the same limitations discussed in the previous section, but they have the advantage that there is a natural segmentation because of the experience and judgment of the expert.

In this section, four examples of such expert judgments are provided. These examples by no means exhaust those available nor are they to be taken as firm and fixed opinions. One of the dangers of publishing anything is that one's opinion may change, but the publication remains throughout the ages. In general be cautious because expert opinions may be dated and may no longer be held by the expert. They are highly contextual (they are judgments based upon the expert's experience however broad or narrow that might have been), and they are subject to interpretation (what an expert meant by a categorization or characterization may not be easily interpreted and applied by others to other contexts). However, obtaining such expert opinion is a useful addition to a database of industry standard information.

Multimedia Licensing Expert Example

The first example is borderline as to whether it should be included in a discussion of technology licensing. It has to do with multimedia royalties in the context of developers licensing context of producers. It is included here because in at least some cases it has the unproven, higher risk nature of technology licensing.

Patricia Martone made a presentation at a Licensing Executives Society meeting that summarized royalty rates in the industry for four kinds of multimedia: text, still images, motion pictures, and music.[5] A summary of her presentation is given in Appendix 4.1, and some example values are given below:

> Text Royalties: 5–20 percent for books; $500–$1500 for small segments
> Still Images: generic photos $50–$75, unique photos $200–$650
> Motion Pictures: $3,000–$10,000 per minute
> Music: 5–13 cents per song.[6]

Again, remember that this judgment was expressed in 1995, and in the context of the expert's experience. Thus, these values should be cautiously considered.

What was particularly useful about Ms. Martone's paper is that she provided background in the industry dynamics including risks, costs, and profitability. Such context provides additional insight into the situation "behind the numbers" and greatly assists valuations because one can compare contexts.

Drug and Diagnostic Expert Examples

Because drug and medical diagnostic licensing has been such an important and active area for universities, there have been numerous publications of licensing experiences including valuation. Exhibit 4.5 gives an expert opinion by Tom Kiley who proposed normative royalties in certain pharmaceutical applications (rDNA designates recombinant DNA, and MAb monoclonal antibody).[7]

Again this is presented not for the purpose of providing authoritative values, but as an example of the availability of published expert opinion. In particular, it should be noted that the 1990 publication date of Mr. Kiley's paper dates the information and, in the rapid pace of this industry, may no longer be reflective of his present thinking.

Another example of expert judgment in this technology area is shown in Exhibit 4.6A based upon a publication by George Korey and E. Kahn.[8] The context for this table was early stage licensing from universities to industry. This example illustrates how such expert opinion can also in-

Exhibit 4.5   Another Proposed Table of Industry Standards

Proposed "Standard" Royalties	Exclusive (%)	Non-Exclusive (%)
Developmental rDNA drug	7–10	3–4
Approvable rDNA drug	12–15	5–8
Therapeutic MAb	5–7	3–4
Diagnostic MAb	3–4	1–2
Drug delivery component	2–3	0.5–2

Source: © 1990 by Thomas D. Kiley. IPH Newsbrief. Reprinted with permission.

clude other important dimensions of an agreement such as upfront payments and minimum payments.

A useful adjunct to Exhibit 4.6A is the specification of the underlying assumptions; these are specified by Korey and Kahn and provided in Exhibit 4.6B.[9]

In Chapter 9, an example will be given of the licensing of an early-stage drug compound for an upfront payment of $20 million. One needs to be reminded that expert opinions deal with normative, common situations—events that have occurred with sufficient frequency and regularity that it is possible to make generalizations. However, by definition, generalizations do not cover all examples.

Exhibit 4.6A   More Tables of Royalty Rates (for the Medical Industry)

Technology/Industry	Earned Royalty	Up-Front Payments	Minimum Payments
Reagents/Process	1–3%	Patent Costs	$2–10K
Reagents/Kits	2–10	Patent Costs	2–10
Diagnostics In Vitro	2–6	$5–20K	2–60
Diagnostics In Vivo	3–8	5–20	2–60
Therapeutics	4–12	20–150	20–150
Medical Instrumentation	4–10	5–150	5–20 (Yr 1)
			10–25

Exhibit 4.6B   Underlying Assumptions for Table No. 1 [Exhibit 4.6A]

1. Up-front payments may be combined and such terms are deal dependent.
2. The high end of up-front payments is usually associated with a "hot" technology in a developing field.
3. Exclusive world wide licenses; anything else diminishes the royalty rates.
4. Licensee holds no equity in licensor. If equity is held or is part of the transaction, then the rates are reduced.
5. There is no claim of infringement by the licensor against the licensee. If a claim exists then the up-front payments can be significantly increased to recapture presumed royalty payments that may have been owed.
6. Terms regarding crediting of any up-front payments toward running royalties are negotiated on a deal-by-deal basis.
7. No significant sponsored research agreements are involved, otherwise the royalties are usually reduced.
8. Overseas licensing rates sometimes command a slightly lower set of rates.
9. Up-front payments are based on 1989–90 dollars.
10. The technology which is licensed may or may not have been issued a patent, but the patent has been applied for and a reasonable opinion exists that the technology is patentable under the laws of the United States and at least one other country.

Adapted From G. Corey & E. Kahn, *Genetic Engineering News*, July–August 1991, p. 4; Also published in *Licensing Economics Review*, December 1990, p. 13.

Major University Expert Example

As a final example of expert judgment, Lita Nelsen of MIT presented her approximate characterization of what buyers where willing to pay sellers such as MIT in a paper presented to AUTM in 1989 and summarized in Exhibit 4.7. In this case, the royalty rates all correspond to early-stage inventions, protectable by patents (because of the need for universities to retain the right to publish).

Repeating aforementioned caveats, these figures are more than 10 years old. Further, they were based upon experience and expert judgment but were in the context of MIT and the level of technology that was being licensed under the licensing perspectives then in place. Put in succinct terms: your results (and experience) may differ.

What is special about expert opinion is its subjectivity. Experts, like everyone else, are captive to their experience and perspectives. However in such captivity experts see patterns and can extract generalizations that can be very valuable, particularly for fields such as technology licensing which cannot be easily characterized by statistical means.

COURT CASES/JUDGMENTS AS A SOURCE OF INDUSTRY STANDARDS

Another source of industry data are technology licenses that are the subject of a lawsuit. Many cases settle before final judgment and are thereby usually secret. However, when a judgment is rendered there is the oppor-

Exhibit 4.7   Example Table of Royalties Developed by Experience by a University Licensing Office

Product	Royalty	Comments
Materials		0.1–1% for commodities; 0.2–2%
processes	1–4%	for processes
Medical Equipment/Devices	3–5%	
Software	5–15%	
Semi-conductors	1–2%	Chip design
Pharmaceuticals	8–10%	Composition of Materials
	12–20%	With clinical testing
Diagnostics	4–5%	New Entity
	2–4%	New Method/Old Entity
Biotechnology	0.25–1.5%	Process**/non-exclusive
	1–2%	Process**/exclusive

**Expression systems, cell lines, growth media/conditions.
Source: Lita Nelsen (MIT), "University Patents", 1989 AUTM Annual Meeting.

tunity to study in some detail the specific circumstances that led a court to a subject valuation.

One legal text gives an extensive summary of court imposed "reasonable royalties" ranging from *GM v. Dailey* for supporting rods for automobile curtains (15 cents per car; 1937 case), to a machine for making paper cups (5 percent of selling price; 1948), to a vitamin (10 percent of gross sales; 1960), to CRT oscilloscopes (10 percent of gross sales, 1977), to vehicle suspension systems (30 percent of net sales; 1986).[10] Another example of a survey done by Mike Carpenter of legal judgments is given in Exhibit 4.8.[11]

Such data represent the opposite extreme from the survey and expert judgment examples considered earlier: whereas those surveys and judgments were averages and general, sources from legal cases are specific, narrow, and exact. However, legal disputes more frequently pertain to product licensing rather than technology licensing. It is difficult to find a dispute on a directly comparable situation, particularly within a recent time frame. Also one needs to be careful in the interpretation of the finding because there are many factors argued and considered that may or may not be relevant to a pure technology licensing situation.

Some other issues involving the use of court-originated royalty data include:

1. The patent or know-how involved has been judged as valid and infringed which tends to make the license more valuable than the customary case where the validity of patent is unknown and in some cases the patent has not yet been issued.
2. The data is very situation specific.
3. The data can be old because litigation often starts after manufacturing by an infringer has begun and can take many years. By the time it is available to the public it can be 10 years after the R&D stage.

Exhibit 4.8   Case Law Sources of Royalties

Product	Royalty	Date	Cite
Rotary Wing Aircraft	2%	1976	192 USPQ 612
Sleeping Bag	5%	1967	156 USPQ 403
Digital Data Transmitter	7.50%	1978	200 USPQ 481
Oscilloscope	10%	1977	193 USPQ 385
Computerized Teaching Aid	12%	1978	199 USPQ 178
Toilet Paper Perforator	20%	1977	195 USPQ 125
Airline Baggage Cart	100%*	1977	196 USPQ 129

*of profit
Source: Mike Carpenter, Workshop at the 1979 LES Annual Meeting.

4. The biggest limitation is simply that there are very few cases in which the royalty rates (or other financial information) become publicly known.

Despite these limitations, court cases should be considered as a possible source of industry standard insight.

PRICE LISTS AS A SOURCE OF INDUSTRY STANDARDS

Another source of industry standards data can be price lists prepared by offerers of technology rights. Such price lists, or more-accurately pricing tables or pricing categories, arise when a seller is in the fortunate position of having to deal with many different buyers and users. Rather than attempt to negotiate individual agreements, the seller in such circumstances prepares a form agreement with financial terms. Although buyers can still seek "exceptions," the seller normally takes the position that it is bound to keep the same terms for all buyers and cannot thereby enter into reduced payment arrangements without having to rebate or renegotiate with all previous licensees.

One use of price lists occurs when a university has developed a technology that it expects to be widely used on a non-exclusive basis. This could occur, for example, as a result of an invention of a fundamental and widely needed diagnostic tool. Another example would be a software technology, such as a speech recognition algorithm. Although such pricing begins to look like right-to-use licenses commonly employed for selling products, in the context of the approaches described here are for *technologies*—and lack some combination of packaging, documentation, commercial data, technical and product support, warranties, etc. The buyers in such technology licensing understand that what they are obtaining will require further development and adaptation to be usable.

Another context where price lists arise is under the threat of patent enforcement. Such licensing involves numerous other issues which are outside the scope of this book.

In both opportunity and enforcement licensing situations, one should be cautious with the use of pricing "data" because the seller may have had many other considerations in mind when deciding on a value (such as pricing at a very low level to create momentum to develop the approach as a de facto standard). Nonetheless, the existence of price list values can create an expectation in the mind of buyers that such are "industry standards."

One very detailed example is from an actual licensing program for two related patents, one for a digital display and one for LCDs. A price list was widely produced that specified the royalty rates in each of seven categories of products with a different rate for each patent for each category. Example categories included: (1) vehicles, (2) VCRs, CD players, microwave ovens, (3) meters and gauges, and (4) wrist watches, clocks, timers. The royalty rates quoted per patent ranged from a low of 0.125 percent to a high of 7 percent, depending on the product category (this was in the late 1980 time frame). It appears that the distinction in rates was partly a result of the royalty base, and partly the seller's perception of the relative value of the technology rights to the buyer's product.

Another example was IBM's practice in the early 1990s of licensing essentially all its portfolio on a nonexclusive basis for 1% per patent up to a maximum of 5 percent for all the patents in its portfolio in the field of information handling systems (which did not include manufacturing apparatus).[12] Further such licenses provided an initial payment of $25,000 unless only a single patent was licensed, in which case the payment was $5,000. Although an approach of 1 percent per patent, regardless of patent or particular application, can appear to neglect opportunities to value specific licenses more highly, IBM at that time had a portfolio of approximately 10,000 living U.S. patents, and this apparently was a cost-effective way of dealing with such numbers and complexity. When a large and important industry player such as IBM creates such pricing, regardless of the rationale or intent, it can broadly influence prospective licenses in other negotiations within the same field, and licensees can, thereby, develop an expectation of paying not more than 1 percent per patent and 5 percent in aggregate for a nonexclusive license.

Although not in the category of a "price list," business publications regularly cite royalty rates as part of a story. Some examples follow:

- Rodime was reported as having established a royalty rate of 7 percent on disk drives covered by its patent, and IBM took out a license but under unknown terms.[13]
- Microsoft was reported as collecting a royalty of $33 a copy for Windows 3.1, $43 for Windows 95, and between $80 and $90 a copy of Windows NT Workstation.[14]
- Texas Instruments was reported seeking royalties of as high as 10 percent on the price of semiconductor chips ("triple the usual level"), and for licenses applicable to PC royalties in the range of 2 to 3 percent of the PC selling price.[15]

As with other sources of industry standard data, some precautions should be noted:

1. Price lists may not reflect final negotiated values (i.e., the licensor may have been willing to take less than the published list).

2. Other business issues may drive price lists. For example, in the IBM case, such practice may have been influenced by IBM's interest in trying to find a cost-effective way of licensing such a numerous portfolio.
3. Stories citing rates may simply be uninformed or speculative, and may not reflect actual values. (Companies cited in such stories often decline to confirm or deny the values.)
4. As previously stressed, the rate depends on the basis, and the overall deal economics depend on many factors besides just the royalties themselves.

Nonetheless, gathering such information can provide useful additional insight into market-based pricing.

PUBLISHED LICENSE AGREEMENTS AS A SOURCE OF INDUSTRY STANDARDS

There are a variety of circumstances whereby a license agreement becomes publicly available. In some states, it is mandated that license agreements become published under "sunshine" laws. The author was able to obtain a summary of one such agreement covering Dupont's license from the University of Houston for a certain type of superconductor material. This agreement provided that Dupont would pay as much as $5.5 million plus royalties for the patent rights to Professor Chu's invention.[16] Because it may be useful to the reader in other respects, these license terms are summarized in Appendix 4.2.

Just as in the circumstance of the legal judgments, published license agreements can be extremely valuable because they provide the complete agreement which conveys a detailed enumeration of all the elements offered by the seller and paid by the buyer.

On the other hand, this superconductivity agreement shows some of the limitations of this approach as well. The inventor was, at the time of the agreement, one of the premier superconductivity researchers and the subject matter of the license was believed to be among the most promising superconductor opportunities. The licensee was highly motivated to branch into what was believed to be an extremely exciting new market. Without comprehending the context of the negotiation, one could easily be misled into thinking that such terms were and are commonplace. Nonetheless, this is a concrete example of the result of a willing buyer and a willing seller reaching an arm's length agreement.

Another circumstance whereby license agreements become public is when the licensee is a publicly traded company. Under SEC rules, such companies are required to disclose transactions that can have a "material" effect on the value of the company as protection for its shareholders. Because of the concern for shareholder suits, some companies interpret "material" quite broadly and so are more likely to publish license agreements. The smaller the company, for any given size license, the more likely the company will be to deem it as "material." There are SEC depositories where such agreements are filed and available to the public. Frequently there is redaction present in such agreements, but even in these cases there can be some important business terms inferred. With the explosion of small startup companies in biotech and internet/e-commerce, there is a surprisingly large population of license agreements available.

PUBLICATIONS, DATABASES, AND CONSULTANTS AS SOURCES OF INDUSTRY STANDARDS INFORMATION

There are several publications that regularly contain articles citing technology licensing financial terms: *les Nouvelles* (published by the Licensing Executives Society), and the *Journal of the Association of University Technology Managers.*

There is a publication that is dedicated to licensing economics: *Licensing Economics Review,* published by AUS Consultants.

There are various consulting firms that specialize in the valuation of intellectual property that maintain proprietary databases on published or available agreements and track and collect information for such purposes. Recombinant Capital (Mark Edwards) has presented papers regularly on its study of published agreements, mostly in the biotech area. IPC Group (such as the McGavock survey) also publishes regularly and maintains a proprietary database of license agreement valuations. There are numerous other firms offering such consulting and data gathering services.

ONE'S OWN DATABASE EVOLVING INTO A PERSONAL INDUSTRY STANDARD

One should not neglect an obvious source of industry standards: one's own experience over time. An active licensing professional will eventually develop a record of first-hand valuation experience based upon deals done as well as deals that could not be consummated. This personal database can be expanded through long-term professional relationships and experience sharing that develops through active participation in societies such as the Licensing Executives Society (www.les.org). Always consider the value of fresh insight from third parties, published and consultative, but remember, there is also great value in one's own first hand deal-making experience.

CONCLUDING OBSERVATIONS AND CAUTIONARY NOTES

The power of the method of this chapter is that the valuations are based on market outcomes: real live buyers and sellers reaching agreements by acting in their respective self-interest. This can be very valuable when the point of reference is relevant to a subject valuation.

However, be aware that there is an inherent time lag to historic information, that in many cases there were other unknown terms and conditions that affected the valuation numbers, and that there is an uniqueness associated with each technology license that makes the translation from reference agreement to subject opportunity a matter of judgment.

The search for the holy grail of an industry standard "pricing book" is not likely to bear fruit (nor does it need to for the search to be valuable). A wide variety of published information is available that will increase the likelihood that examples exist that are reasonably close to your deal. When used cautiously and judiciously, they can usefully contribute to the consideration of value.

In the next chapter we will consider the use of rating/ranking as a semi-quantitative method of making comparisons between a reference (or comparable) agreement and the opportunity being valued. It is a natural extension of the subject addressed in this chapter.

NOTES

1. Buyers characteristically play a game I've called the "Where's Waldo™ of Licensing?"—shrinking the domain of the licensed technology down to the most microscopic scope possible so that almost any royalty rate, even 100 percent, does not constitute a significant payment.

2. For the moment we are ignoring the issue of how one would determine the appropriate "price" of the base, as in this example the manufacturer is "selling" the chip to itself.

3. "Factors Affecting Royalty Rates," Dan McGavock, David Haas, and Michael Patin, *les Nouvelles*, June 1992, p. 107.

4. "A Survey of Licensed Royalties," Stephen Degnan and Corwin Horton, *les Nouvelles*, June 1997, p. 91.

5. Patrica A. Martone, LES Multimedia Licensing Seminar, Copenhagen, Denmark, September 17, 1995.

6. Ibid.

7. Tom Kiley, *IPH Newsbrief*, April 1990, and published *in Licensing Economics Review*, September 1990, p. 4.

8. George D. Corey and Edward Kahn, "Biomedical Royalty Rates: Some Approaches," *Genetic Engineering News*, July-August 1991, p. 4; also published *in Licensing Economics Review*, December 1990, p. 13.

9. Ibid.

10. *Patent Licensing*, Harold Einhorn, Section 3.03, Royalty, 1990, p. 3-11ff.

11. Mike M. Carpenter, "Traditional Royalty," presented at the 15th Annual Meeting of the Licensing Executives Society, 1979.

12. This information is based upon a one page summary prepared by IBM in 1993 entitled "IBM Worldwide Patent Licensing Practices." This practice was also cited in a paper by David Guenther and John Wills, "A Survey of PC Technology Royalty Rates," *les Nouvelles*, December 1995, p. 200. It is the author's understanding that this does not constitute IBM's current licensing practices.

13. "IBM to Make Patent Payment in Rodime Case," *Wall Street Journal*, Nov. 2, 1990, p. B2.

14. "Microsoft's Earnings Hot Streak Cools," *Wall Street Journal*, July 18, 1997, p. B6.

15. "A Chip Maker's Profit on Patents," *New York Times*, October 16, 1990, p. C1.

16. "Dupont Stakes Claim on Superconductor Rights," *Science*, Vol. 241, p. 1156.

APPENDIX 4A

Negotiating Licenses from Developers

Exhibit 4A.1 Multimedia Royalties & Business Context of "Producers" Negotiating Licenses from Developers"

1. Producers have the most financial clout and the greatest financial exposure (including substantial distribution costs).
2. Producers want to limit advances and milestone payments and to recoup them as quickly as possible.
3. Producers want to own as many rights as they can, and license only the remainder.
4. Producers want royalties to developers based upon "adjusted gross receipts."
5. Producers are historically unwilling to pay a total royalty (including for development) of more than 10–15 percent. [becomes a "standard"]

Created by: Patricia A. Martone (Fish & Neave, 1995) for the LES Multimedia Licensing Seminar, Copenhagen, September 17, 1995. Reprinted with the permission of Patricia A. Martone, Fish & Neave.

Exhibit 4A.2   More Business Context re: Multimedia Royalties

1. High distribution costs—50 percent to 75 percent** of sales (est.)
2. A lot of CD-ROM titles in typical software store (300–500) but few sales (as few as one copy/month*).
3. Average CD-ROM costs $383K to produce and generates $20 in wholesale revenue. Must sell 19,000 copies to break even.*
4. Consumer pressure for low retail prices for products containing digitized information.
5. Current problem: out of 912 developers in one survey, 96 percent were unprofitable.*.
6. Growth of sales in CD-ROM players provide hope for future—about 27 million CD-ROM players worldwide as of 1994; expected to increase by 80 percent in 1995.**

Created by: Patricia A. Martone (Fish & Neave, 1995) for the LES Multimedia Licensing Seminar, Copenhagen, September 17, 1995. Reprinted with the permission of Patricia A. Martone, Fish & Neave.
*Source: Don Clark, "Slipped Disks," *Wall Street Journal*, March 1, 1995.
**Source: James M. Kennedy et al., "Structuring Multimedia Transactions," University of Southern California Law Center Sixteenth Annual Computer Law Institute, Sect. I, May 1995.

Exhibit 4A.3   Typical Multimedia Royalty Rates

Text (usually separate licenses for North America and Europe)

- small segment (up to several pages), $500–$1500, nonexclusive use
- majority of books, 5–20 percent royalty. (National Writers Union paper recommends no less than 50 percent of list price!)

Still Images

- unique photographs, $200–$650 ("editorial" use, per Timestream, Inc.)
- multiple generic photographs (50 to 100), $50–$75 each
- for more information, see "Licensing Still Images," Timestream, Inc., http//www/timestream.com/web/, September, 1994.

Motion Pictures

- $3,000 to $10,000 per minute
- Often need to license publicity rights through screenwriters and Screen Actors Guild

Music

- each, as appropriate, get a royalty of $.05–$.13 per song
  - recording company (not needed if developer creates its own recording)
  - publisher of musical work

Created by: Patricia A. Martone (Fish & Neave, 1995) for the LES Multimedia Licensing Seminar, Copenhagen, September 17, 1995. Reprinted with the permission of Patricia A. Martone, Fish & Neave.

APPENDIX 4B

Outline of Agreement Between Du Pont and University of Houston (UH)

1. Important Definitions
   a. "Patent Rights"—(1) rights in any patents which the U.S. or any foreign country might grant covering claims to superconductive materials applied for by UH as of execution date, and (2) any certain filed applications.
   b. "Licensed Products" and "Licensed Processes"—products and processes covered by an allowed or issued claim included in any of the Patent Rights. Also includes products, the sale of which would result in contributory infringement.
   c. "Net Sales"—the amount invoiced on sales of Licensed Products or Licensed Processes less certain discounts, return credits, taxes, transportations costs, and insurance premiums.
   d. "Field of Commercial Interest"—any commercial field in which Du Pont can demonstrate financial commitment to research, capital expansion, marketing plans, and so forth.
   e. "First Commercial Sale"—can include a sale to U.S. government pursuant to a contract awarded without a competitive bid by a third party.

2. Grant of License
   UH grants Du Pont an exclusive, world-wide license to make, use, and sell Licensed Products and Licensed Processes, subject to the following:
   a. UH may make materials for its own research.
   b. Du Pont will use its best effots to introduce Licensed Products and Licensed Processes into the commercial market as soon as possible.
   c. Includes the right to sublicense; all sublicenses will include a "best efforts" clause.
   d. U.S. government rights.

3. Sublicenses
   Du Pont may grant sublicenses under the following conditions:

a. At UH's request, Du Pont will grant a restricted sublicense to a TCSUH (Texas Center for Superconductivity at the University of Houston) consortium member, who shall pay a reasonable royalty therefor. Du Pont will pay UH 75% of sublicense royalties in fields of no commercial interest to Du Pont and 50% of royalties in fields of commercial interest to Du Pont.

b. At UH's direction, Du Pont will grant a sublicense to a third party, regardless of TCSUH membership, in any field of no commercial interest to Du Pont. Du Pont will pay UH 75% of royalties in such cases.

c. After the earlier of (i) three years after Du Pont's first commercial sale (unless Du Pont is proceeding diligently toward commercialization) or (ii) eight years after date of patent issuance, UH may direct Du Pont to grant a sublicense to a third party in a field of commercial interest to Du Pont at a royalty rate no less favorable than Du Pont is paying in that field. Du Pont will pay UH 50% of royalties so received.

[NOTE: These features, i.e., 2(d), 3(a), (b), and (c) render the license, in some respects, a "non-exclusive" license.]

d. Du Pont may grant sublicenses on its own initiative and will pay UH 75% of all royalties received by Du Pont.

4. Payments
In return for the grant of license and rights associated with it, Du Pont will pay UH:

a. $1.5 million upon execution of the agreement

b. $1.5 million upon the issuance of a U.S. patent covering the "1–2–3" phase material claimed in the patent applications.

c. At Du Pont's option, $1.5 million two years following the date of patent issuance. If Du Pont does not execute this option, the agreement terminates with no obligation by UH to refund any previously-paid money.

d. Du Pont will pay royalties on net sales as determined by agreement between UH and Du Pont at the time of commercialization, or in the event UH and Du Pont cannot agree, by a third-party arbitrator experienced in the field of industrial licenses and royalty arrangements. Added value-in-use by licensed technology is to be a prime factor in determining royalty rates.

e. In the event of cross-licenses, trades, single-payments, or receipt of property, UH and Du Pont will agree on the appropriate royalty value, or, failing agreement, submit to arbitration.

f. Du Pont will pay the greater of earned royalties or a minimum royalty of $100,000 per year. The minimum is not required until the earlier of (i) the expiration of three years following the first commercial sale (but not before patent issuance), or (ii) five years following patent issuance.

g. Despite U.S. government rights, if Du Pont is the supplier to the U.S. government of Licensed Products, based on a contract awarded without Du Pont's having to match or overcome a competitive bid, Du Pont will pay UH a reasonable royalty.

h. Du Pont will require sublicensees to pay royalties on sales even before the grant of patent, provided there is no third-party competitor who is not paying a royalty.

i. Du Pont is entitled to credits against earned royalties due UH, but only for the third $1.5 million payment and for reimbursement of legal expenses associated with patent filing and prosecution.

5. Patent Filing and Maintenance

   UH will prepare, file, and prosecute patent applications. UH will cooperate with, and consider the opinions of, Du Pont with respect to such applications. Du Pont will pay all expenses relative to such applications, retroactive to the filing of the first application. In the event Du Pont decides to cease paying expenses (after the expenditure of $1,000,000) with respect to particular applications, its rights in such applications will terminate.

6. Records and Reporting

   Du Pont and its sublicensees will keep accurate records and permit a UH-designated CPA to inspect them upon demand. To the extent permitted by law (e.g., Texas Open Records Act), UH will keep confidential information obtained from such inspections. Du Pont will submit semiannual of sales and royalties due.

7. Improvements
   a. Any inventions which are "improvements" of the licensed technology will be included in the Patent Rights. For purposes of the agreement, "improvements" are considered additional filings or new applications that would be dominated as matter of patent law by the existing applications.
   b. UH will continue to file patent applications on inventions resulting from Chu-directed work. For three years, Du Pont will have a right of first refusal on new patent applications (as opposed to "improvements") covering superconductive materials resulting from Chu-directed work. Other research and researchers at UH are not covered by this right.
   c. Du Pont and UH will encourage and promote exchanges of information between Chu and Chu-directed researchers and Du Pont's Wilmington Experimental Station. Any contribution of a UH researcher at Du Pont will be subject to Du Pont's right of first refusal.

8. Infringement

   Both parties have the right to pursue legal action against infringers or to otherwise protect the Patent Rights, and either may bring action in the name of the other if the other is an indispensable party. Funding of legal expenses may be derived partially from royalties, and recoveries will reimburse such expenses, then cover royalties, then be shared equally. Royalties may be partially reduced during the period of an infringement if it has not been successfully abated within six months after it is discovered.

9. Termination
   a. Unless earlier terminated, the agreement will automatically terminate on the expiration of all Patent Rights.
   b. If either party defaults, the other party may terminate by giving notice and the defaulting party does not initiate action to cure the default within 90 days.
   c. Du Pont may terminate if it decides not to make the payment provided in 4(c) above.
   d. Du Pont may terminate without making the payments provided in 4(b) and (c) above if the patent is not granted in 10 years. UH need not refund the initial payment, and all rights revert to UH. Du Pont is relieved of any remaining obligations to pay legal costs.

e. UH may terminate without refunding any payments and all rights revert if Du Pont does not make a royalty-bearing sale with eight years after grant of patent and Du Pont is not proceeding diligently toward commercialization.

f. After Du Pont makes all of its payments required by 4(a), (b), and (c), it may still terminate by giving 30 days notice. All rights revert to UH.

10. General

a. UH warrants that all interest in the Patent Rights have been assigned to it, and that UH has the authority to license those rights. UH does not warrant that the Patent Rights are valid, that they have any particular scope, or that Du Pont may exploit them without infringing other patents.

b. Du Pont indemnifies UH from personal injury and products liability claims.

c. Du Pont may not assign the agreement without UH approval.

d. UH and Du Pont agree to attempt to settle all disputes, claims, etc., amicably between themselves. If they fail, they will submit the matter to binding arbitration.

R18/18.11.03.1,2

5

Method Two:
The Rating/Ranking Method
to Determine Valuation

In this chapter we will consider the second of six valuation methods, that of Rating/Ranking. This method requires the pre-identification of a reference or comparable agreement or cluster of agreements. For this reason this method is closely associated with Industry Standards, the method described in the preceding chapter.

INTRODUCTION: WHAT IS MEANT BY
RATING/RANKING AND WHY IS IT HELPFUL?

Rating/ranking approaches are one of the most widely used tools when dealing with hard-to-quantify issues. They regularly appear hidden behind newspaper stories of "the best city in America" or some other "best of..." story. How could such a "best" determination be made? Within the body of such stories is usually embedded a description of how the results were obtained. Generally, a series of criteria (or issues) was prepared by an individual or panel together with some form of a prescribed numerical scoring scale for each criterion. This information was then supplied to a panel of experts who solely or in committee fashion developed scores for each of the criterion; the purveyors of the survey then tabulate the scores and rank the winners.

A variant of such an expert panel scoring system is using a prepared look-up table, such as: if the city has one or less libraries per 10,000 people, then the score on this criteria is "1," if two to four libraries then it is

"2," and so on; usually in such instances, an expert panel was initially used to create the look-up table.

Another example of a Rating/Ranking method is Benjamin Franklin's "decision algebra." He is reported to have developed this decision-making tool over his life and used it in many contexts. When faced with a decision he would create two columns, one for the "yes" outcome and one for the "no" (he lived in simpler times). Then in each column he would list every reason or argument that would support the respective outcome. (Presumably he did some compression so that he did not end up with the same reason expressed multiple times in different ways). Then he would select one idea from, say, the "yes" column and cross it off and at the same time cross off as many "no" entries as needed to be of equal "weight" to the "yes" entry crossed off. He would continue to cross off equal weights of reasons until one column had no more reasons left. Then he would examine the other column to find at least one good, un-crossed-off reason supporting that decision (say, "yes"), unbalanced by any entries supporting the opposing decision ("no"), and chose "yes". In these times of "paralysis by analysis" one can truly appreciate Mr. Franklin.

The five elements that comprise the Rating/Ranking Method are as follows:

1. Scoring criteria
2. Scoring system
3. Scoring scale
4. Weighting factors
5. Decision table

Scoring Criteria

Examples of criteria that are used in licensing valuations are market size, patent protection, and stage of development. A further discussion of useful criteria is given later in this chapter in the section entitled, "Developing Criteria for Using Rating/Ranking for Valuation of Technology."

Scoring System

Many different kinds of scoring systems are used, and the choice is a matter of taste and experience. Perhaps the most common system is the 1 to 5 point system, with 5 as the best, 1 as the worst, and 3 representing equivalence to the reference condition or standard. Its appeal may be related to people's familiarity with college GPAs. It is also very simple as there are only two levels "better" and two levels "worse" than the reference condition.

For those preferring more distinctions or levels, there is the 1 to 7 scale, sometimes known as the Likkert Scale. Here a 4 represents equivalence to the reference condition, 5 is "better," 6 is "much better," and 7 is "outstanding" (and vice versa for 3, 2, 1), thus permitting three levels of "better" and "worse."

Others, more digitally inclined, seem to prefer the 0 to 10 point scale. For obsessive compulsives, a 0 to 100 point scale is a possibility.

Right-hemisphere people seem to lean toward non-numerical methods. The simplest such approach used is H/M/L for high/medium/low (i.e., better, same, or poorer) which forces the decision to one level better and worse. A variant of this approach is to use symbols such "+" for "better," "++" for much better, "=" for comparable, and similar negative signs for worse and much worse; this has the same effect in terms of levels as the 1 to 5 scale but avoids attaching numerical significance to the outcome. A finding with the "+" approach would be expressed as "somewhere between a + and ++" whereas in the 1 to 5 scale the result would be "4.5."

For the Crayola regressives there is even the possibility of colors: green for "better," blue for "much better," yellow for "worse," and red for "much worse" (no color, or white, for equivalence to the standard). Colors can be useful when presenting findings to either young children or management (there's a Dilbert cartoon yet to be written here).

Although there is some arbitrariness about the choice of a scoring system, it is actually important and serious to select one and to standardize it. The power of rating/ranking increases with experience and a database of previous determinations. It would defeat some of the value of the method to make ad hoc selections of scales.

Although every scoring system has its advocates and is a matter of personal style and preference, the 1 to 5 point system is recommended and illustrated later in this chapter.

Scoring Scales

Two types of scoring scales can be used: subjective and objective. Subjective scales merely ask an expert or expert panel to consider the described circumstance through the "eyes" of each of the criteria and assign a score based upon the selected scoring system (i.e., 1 to 5). Objective scales can be created when enough experience has been gained with predicting values using rating/ranking and comparing such predictions with actual outcomes. After numerous experiences, it is possible to estimate (or in some cases derive) numerical scales; when derived scales can be created they are commonly known as influence coefficients. It is possible to use a mixture of subjective and objective scales for any given rating/ranking valuation.

When subjective scales are used, an expert panel of some sort has to be established. Setting up such a panel requires some thought and planning. If the number of people on the panel is small, say two to four, the panels tend to operate by consensus rather than by vote. This seems to work best when all the parties are in the same room and participate in an active discussion and debate before proposing scores and reaching consensus. If a large number of people are involved, then voting and averaging seems to work better. In such cases it may be difficult to assemble everyone in the same room and commit the time to hear all opinions and debate. However, when voting remotely, it is possible, even likely, that such voters will not have considered important aspects of certain matters, calling into question how much weight to attach to their vote. Sometimes political necessity requires the larger panel. Decision-making in large groups has been the subject of much research, though none known in the context of technology valuation. The recommended approach would be a panel of three to five persons, at least half of which (two to three) are regular participants in such technology valuation processes, and the balance are other needed experts and stakeholders. The optimal result is a weighted opinion of the "regulars" over the experts and stakeholders.

Weighting Factors

The weighting factor is used as a means of assigning a higher importance to some criteria and a lower importance to others. For example, one could choose 10 criteria to be scored and deem that one particular criterion (say, market size) is twice as important as any of the other nine; in this case, the score for the market size criterion would be doubled, effectively (but intentionally) counting it twice. What should be carefully avoided is unintentionally counting the same idea or criteria multiple times. This might happen if one criterion was "market size," another was "projected sales," another was "likelihood of use for other applications," and another was "likelihood of sales in other countries"; this is tantamount to scoring "market size" four times.

Decision Table

The end result of a rating/ranking process is a column of raw scores entered by the expert(s) next to each criterion, which is then multiplied by the respective weighting to obtain a weighted score, and then all the weighted scores are added to determine the rated/ranked score. For convenience, often the rated/ranked score is normalized so that, for example, on the 1 to 5 score system, an "average" score would yield a "3.00." This simply makes interpretation easier.

The issue then becomes this: How does one actually put a result to use and aid a valuation? It is helpful to consider what is being accomplished by the Rating/Ranking Method. In essence, we can visualize the process as creating an "industry standard" in the following sense. The method requires a comparable or reference agreement or cluster of agreements in order for the scoring to take place because each score is always in the context of a point of reference. A comparable deal could be one specific technology which was licensed under known terms, or a general understanding of population of related (in the sense of belonging to a category) technologies licensed. In effect, this method assumes that the technology being valued "belongs" to the category of the comparable deal. The scoring and calculations are means of creating quality or value differences from the comparable deal. The result is similar to saying the technology being valued is "like" a 1995 Ford Taurus, but its overall quality differs from the norm of that category by the rating/ranking score.

At one level, this approach can appear to be so ad hoc and so subject to intentional and unintentional biases that it is a pointless exercise. However, this is how decisions need to be made in many highly complex situations. In Chapter 4, some New York City office rental rates were quoted, which might seem a comparatively simple decision domain but how would one decide whether to pay $33.56 for "Grand Central," or move up to $41.01 for "Sixth/Rock," or go for $45.68 on "Park Avenue?"[1] There is no differential equation or computer program that can answer such a question.

Here are some reasons why the Rating/Ranking method is used and valued:

1. It causes one to prepare for negotiation by thinking through the relevant factors that make up licensing value.
2. It facilitates discussions with other valuation experts as it focuses on the key components of value and what is known (and not known) and good (and not good) about the subject technology.
3. It can be useful in explaining to non-expert stakeholders how the valuation was reached.
4. With experience, the method increases in value. As one sees more and more outcomes and develops more experience with rating and ranking, the structure of the method enables one to make more insightful comparisons. The method becomes a tool for creating a storehouse of one's own licensing experience.
5. It is easy to use and can, with a good benchmark(s) and appropriate criteria, yield useful results.
6. For all its subjectivity, it is a tool in the toolkit of the licensing professional and no tool should be ignored (and, in this regard, it complements the more quantitative methods considered in Chapters 7 and 8).

7. It can lead to strategies for increasing the value of the technology by identifying important missing components of a potential deal, or reducing the risk (uncertainty) by further research or inquiry to improve a low score on a particular criterion.
8. During or after negotiations, an already-completed Rating/Ranking valuation can be useful in assessing the need for a re-valuation, or a "Plan B."

DEVELOPING CRITERIA FOR USING RATING/ RANKING FOR VALUATION OF TECHNOLOGIES

One of the critical steps in employing the Rating/Ranking Method is selecting appropriate criteria. Like other aspects of this method, the identification of such criteria is a matter of judgment. For the method to be effective, one needs at least five criteria.

A set of criteria widely cited in legal context is the 15 "Georgia Pacific Factors."[2] These were developed by a court for the purposes of determining a reasonable royalty. These factors are presented in Exhibit 5.1 below. Bob Goldscheider has written an extensive review article on the use of such factors in litigation contexts.[3]

Factors 1 and 2 are expressions of the first method considered, the Industry Standard Method. Factor 8 is applicable to rating/ranking and will be also considered in the Discounted Cash Flow Method and the Monte Carlo Method (Chapters 7 and 8, respectively). Factor 11 is primarily relevant in the context of a litigation matter. Aspects of Factors 12 and 13 will be considered in Chapter 6 under the Rules of Thumb Method, although these are also legitimate matters for use in the Rating/Ranking Method. Factor 14 is itself a summary statement of the use of this Rating/Ranking Method. Factor 15 is the outcome of the valuation process and so can for our purposes be considered as the objective, not a criterion. From this perspective, that would leave 10 of the 15 Georgia-Pacific Factors that could be directly applied in a rating/ranking approach: numbers 3, 4, 5, 6, 7, 8, 9, 10, 12, and 13.

In the Degnan and Horton survey cited in Chapter 4,[4] one of the surveyed questions was directed toward the use of such Georgia-Pacific Factors in performing valuations. The respondents were asked to rank each factor on a 1 to 5 scale with "5" designating very important and "1" not important; this in itself was a rating/ranking exercise. The results are shown in Exhibit 5.2. The two columns deal with the two licensing situations: selling and buying. The factors are ranked from highest to lowest, so the numbers do not correspond to the numbering of Exhibit 5.2.

The McGavock survey discussed in Chapter 4[5] also asked its participants similar questions. The findings on this matter are presented in Exhibit 5.3.

Exhibit 5.1 *Georgia-Pacific Corp. v. U.S. Plywood Corp.* **Factors Applicable to the Determination of Reasonable Royalties**

1. The royalties received by the patentee for the licensing of the patent in suit, proving or tending to prove an established royalty.
2. The rates paid by the licensee for the use of other patents comparable to the patent in suit.
3. The nature and scope of the license, as exclusive or non-exclusive; or as restricted or non-restricted in terms of territory or with respect to whom the manufactured product may be sold.
4. The licensor's established policy and marketing program to maintain his patent monopoly by not licensing others to use the invention or by granting licenses under special conditions designed to preserve that monopoly.
5. The commercial relationship between the licensor and licensee, such as, whether they are competitors in the same territory in the same line of business; or whether they are inventor and promoter.
6. The effect of selling the patented specialty in promoting sales of other products of the licensee; the existing value of the invention to the licensor as a generator of sales of his non-patented items; and the extent of such derivative or convoyed sales.
7. The duration of the patent and the term of the license.
8. The established profitability of the product made under the patent; its commercial success; and its current popularity.
9. The utility and advantages of the patent property over the old modes or devices, if any, that had been used for working out similar results.
10. The nature of the patented invention; the character of the commercial embodiment of it as owned and produced by the licensor; and the benefits to those who have used the invention.
11. The extent to which the infringer has made use of the invention; and any evidence probative of the value of that use.
12. The portion of the profit or of the selling price that may be customary in the particular business or in comparable businesses to allow for the use of the invention or analogous inventions.
13. The portion of the realizable profit that should be credited to the invention as distinguished from non-patented elements, the manufacturing process, business risks, or significant features or improvements added by the infringer.
14. The opinion testimony of qualified experts.
15. The royalty that a licensor (such as the patentee) and a licensee (such as the infringer) would have agreed upon if both had been reasonably and voluntarily trying to reach an agreement; that is, the amount which a prudent licensee—who desired, as a business proposition, to obtain a license to manufacture and sell a particular article embodying the patented invention—would have been willing to pay as a royalty and yet be able to make a reasonable profit and which amount would have been acceptable by a prudent patentee who was willing to grant a license.

Source: 318 F. Supp. 1116 (S.D. N.Y. 1970).

Exhibit 5.2   Frequency of Use of Georgia Pacific Factors by Licensing Professions According to a Survey

Importance of Factor	Licensing In	Licensing Out
1. Nature of the Protection	4.3	4.2
2. Utility Over Old Methods	4.2	4.2
3. Scope of Exclusivity	4.1	4.1
4. Licensee's Anticipated Profits	3.0	3.4
5. Commercial Success	3.7	3.7
6. Territory Restrictions	3.7	3.5
7. Comparable License Rates	3.6	3.7
8. Duration of Protection	3.3	3.1
9. Licensors' Anticipated Profits	2.6	3.1
10. Commercial Relationship	2.6	3.6
11. Tag Along Sales	2.1	2.1

Source: Stephen A. Degnan and Corwin Horton, "A Survey of Licensed Royalties," *les Nouvelles*, June 1997, p. 91–96. Reprinted with permission from *les Nouvelles*.

One massive list of 100 factors was developed by Tom Arnold.[6] Although Mr. Arnold did not present his list in the context of employing a formal rating/ranking approach, he did enumerate a comprehensive list of points to consider. Mr. Arnold's paper is provided in Appendix 5.1 and summarized below in Exhibit 5.4. In this author's experience, 100 criteria are simply too many. Such a large number makes it difficult to grasp and adequately characterize a reasonable predictive value. However, the list and article are commended as a reference in the consideration of which criteria are to be selected.

For many licensing situations, the most important criteria include:

1. **Estimated attainable market size and overall product profit margins.** Together, these two factors will determine the earnings (EBIT, as will be discussed in Chapter 7), which has a very strong influence on the value of a license.
2. **Strength of the IP protection (patents, trade secrets, copyrights, and trademarks).** For exclusive licenses, this criterion plays an important role in creating defendable, unique products (and, thereby margins higher than commodity levels). For nonexclusive licenses, buyers consider this criterion because it affects what they would have to do if a license agreement is not entered into.
3. **Breadth of the IP protection.** This criterion addresses the economic impact of working just outside the patent or other IP protection. It is

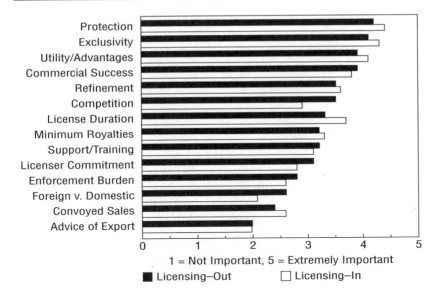

Exhibit 5.3   Importance of Various Factors on Royalty Rates
McGavock, et al., "Factors Affecting Royalty Rates," *les Nouvelles*, June 1992, p. 109. Reprinted with permission from *les Nouvelles*.

Exhibit 5.4   A Checklist of 100 Factors in Setting the Value of a License: A Summary of the 100 Factors

	Category	Example Factors	
I.	Intrinsic Quality	Stage of development Marketability	Significance of the invention Type of license
II.	Protection	Scope of protections Contractual commitments	Enforceability issues
III.	Market	Market size	Distinctiveness of market
VI.	Competition	Scope of protected market niche	Third party alternatives
V.	Licensee Values	Grant-backs	Manufacturing, market, capital
VI.	Finances profit	Manufacturer's margin Degree of design-around possible	Costs of warranty negotiation Expected follow-on sales
VII.	Risk	Exposure to liability suits Exposure to patent validity suits	Technical obsolescence
VIII.	Legal	Force majeure clauses Duration of license	Favored nation clauses
IX.	Requisition	Government restrictions on royalty and other terms	Currency movement restrictions

Source: Arnold, White & Durkee, Houston, Texas; paper presented at workshop at LES U.S.A./Canada Annual Meeting, Los Angeles, California, October 1986; published in *les Nouvelles*, March 1987, p.34. Reprinted with permission from *les Nouvelles*.

important to know, for example, that even in the case of a strong patent, one can operate outside the boundaries of the claims at (say) only a 1 percent performance or cost penalty; such a situation would clearly lower the value of a license in comparison to a circumstance where such a penalty were 100 percent, or practical operation was impossible.

4. **Stage of development.** This criterion addresses three interrelated issues: How long will it be until the licensed invention will be producing profits? How much additional investment will need to be made prior to commercial introduction? What is the overall development risk?

5. **Market environment.** Any invention being developed for commerce enters some kind of business environment. Is it in a generally growing market (or not)? Are there strong and aggressive competitors? Are there existing channels of delivery or will entirely new infrastructures have to be developed (for instance, to create value for a hydrogen burning auto engine technology, one would also need hydrogen "gas" stations, hydrogen mechanics, etc.).

Referring again to the McGavock survey in Exhibit 5.3, although there is some variation in perspective between seller and buyer, overall both sides appear to place the highest importance on "protection," "exclusivity," and "utility/advantages," and lowest importance on "advice of expert," "convoyed sales," and "foreign versus domestic."

The selection of specific criteria, the scoring system, and weighting should be tuned for the particular industry in which the valuation is being made. Thus, there are multiple levels of expert judgment required with the Rating/Ranking method:

1. Selection of benchmark agreement or category of agreements
2. Selection of criteria to be used
3. Scoring system (what warrants a score of "4"?)
4. Weighting factors for each criterion which are used to multiply the raw scores
5. Interpretation of the result (discussed later in this chapter).

This may appear daunting. Yet, with experience and expert help inside and outside the organization, this method can be very useful.

AN EXAMPLE OF APPLYING THE RATING/RANKING METHOD

Consider an instance where one is attempting to value a new laser device for optical communications. The first step is to find a "comparable," or an individual license agreement or group of agreements to which such a device generally "belongs." One would conduct reviews of one's own company files, search for published information (as discussed in Chapter 4), look for SEC filings (also Chapter 4), network with colleagues, and/or hire consultants who have developed license agreement databases or who are expert at conducting searches or finding comparable agreements. By some means, one must find at least one "comparable" in order to begin.

For the sake of this example, let us consider that this search has found an excellent comparable: a different technology for making a comparable laser device was found to have been licensed for $1 million upfront, and 5 percent royalty on the sale price of the entire laser device, with no rights to improvements, no grant-back rights, and no other significant financial factors. Further, let us assume that the criteria selected are as shown in Exhibit 5.5. As shown, it was determined that there were three different levels of weighting, 1, 2, or 3. For this marketplace, the experience and expert opinion was that factors 2, 4, and 5 were notably more important than 1 and 3, and significantly more so than 6. Also as shown, the scoring system used was the 1 to 5 scale. Multiplying the score times the weighting determines the right-hand column, the weighted score.

By adding up all the weighted scores, the result is 47. However, the result needs to be scaled in comparison to the benchmark with all the weightings. Had all the scores been "3," the total weighted score would have been 42. In other words, based on this scale and score, the subject opportunity was perceived to be only a little better than the comparable (12 percent to be exact, though this is not an exact process, corresponding to an average score of 3.36). Allowing for the uncertainty of the process, this finding would suggest that the subject opportunity should be worth only a modest amount more than the reference agreement or category.

ISSUES IN INTERPRETING VALUE FROM A RATING/RANKING SCORE

In Exhibit 5.5, the result of the rating/ranking method was essentially parity with the benchmark. What if the result had turned out to be much higher? Suppose the total score had been 4.0. What should one do with such a value?

One approach is to do a simple linear normalizing ratio: 4.0/3.0 = 1.333. Multiply each of the economic terms of the comparable agreement by the ratio 1.333 to yield a valuation. So, in this example, such an approach would yield a valuation of $1,333,333 as a market-based upfront payment, and 6.67 percent as the corresponding running royalty.

EXHIBIT 5.5   Example Use of Rating/Ranking Method

	Weighting (1–3)	Score (1–5)	Weighted Score
1. Market Size	2	3	6
2. Product Margins	3	5	15
3. IP Strength	2	4	8
4. IP Breadth	3	3	9
5. Stage of Development	3	2	6
6. Market Environment	1	3	3
TOTALS	–	–	47 [1.12]

The reality of using such a ratio as a direct multiplier depends upon the reasonableness of the assumption of a linear scale. Does a score of 4.0 compared to the comparable reference of 3.0 really mean that the subject technology is four-thirds as valuable? What would a score of 1.0 mean? (Remember a score of "1" was effectively a zero; it was the lowest possible outcome). It could be argued that 1.0 scoring technology would be worth nothing, not 33 percent of the comparable. On the other hand, a 5.0 on this basis could only be worth 67 percent more than the comparable license value.

It is often helpful when translating a rating/ranking score to a value to go through each of the criteria that was scored and look at how it affects value. For example, if the total gross profitability of a deal (defined as market size multiplied by average margins summed over the commercial life of the products made from the technology) is estimated to be one-half of the comparable, and if the other criteria are scored as good or even somewhat better than the comparable, then a deal is likely to be doable with an upfront payment of approximately half as much, namely $500,000 and likewise for the royalty. This translation between score and value will be considered in detail in Chapter 7, once discounted cash flow analysis has been introduced. As we shall see, the use of the Discounted Cash Flow Method is a very powerful technique for assessing the impact of market size, margins, timing, and risk upon license value. This is another example where two valuation methods can work well in combination.

However, if one were to try to resolve this question without resorting to other methods, how would one convert a "4" into, value compared to a "3?" Like many of these matters, there is no simple answer. If there had been a benchmark license of a comparable technology that had been a "4" itself, then it would have been used and the subject technology would have shown a parity score suggesting that the value of the "4" benchmark license was an appropriate place to start. However, by definition, the best we could find in this example is the benchmark that led us to score this opportunity as a 4. What is needed is some combination of license agreements in other areas, or equivalent experience and expertise with another panel, that can begin to characterize the sensitivity to the value of such scores. With study and experience, one can begin to grasp, at least qualitatively, how the market reacts to opportunities that are "better" or "much better" in various criteria. A valuation expert panel could be convened to examine a series of published agreements using an established rating/ranking method for the purpose of sorting them out by score from low to high. Then by comparing their rating/ranking scores to their actual valuations (recall that one chooses the benchmarks because one has the data needed), it is possible to develop a correlation, however approximate, between rating/ranking score and value, at least with respect to the selected family. In the absence of other information, such correlation would be a useful place to begin to assess the value of a "4" in the subject case.

A caution is needed on the use of numerical scoring approaches for the special case of a fatal flaw. If one critical rating/ranking factor has a fatal flaw, say patent protection has been irretrievably lost and there are no other forms of protection, then one can obtain a misleading result by assigning a value of "1" to such factor. For this situation, some modification to the approach is needed. One way this can be treated is with a color-scoring system where a "red," for example, eliminates any value to the opportunity being analyzed. Another approach is to multiply the scores, rather than add them so that the effect of a "1" or a "0" can be dramatic. Yet another approach is to discard the analysis when confronted with a genuinely fatal flaw.

CONCLUSION

The Rating/Ranking Method is the most overtly subjective of the six methods we will consider. However, as we shall see, all methods contain a certain amount of subjectivity because they deal with the unknowable future.

Rating/Ranking works best when it is systematized and applied by a panel of "regulars" who develop a history of making such judgments. It is greatly aided by feedback from actual values received (favorable and not). Over time, an organization can develop a very powerful set of enabling tools for expert panels to apply.

It should be recognized that this process is very similar to that followed by focus panels and other formats that companies use to test market acceptance and enthusiasm for new drugs. It is also used with proxy juries in preparation for trial before the actual jury. It is used with prospective voters on issues as well as candidate subjectives. It is even used on odors. It turns out that for many purposes, the human nose is the most appropriate instrument to assess favorable and unfavorable odors. Companies concerned about such matters work very hard to develop an expert "smell panel" that is used again and again to perform similar rating/ranking exercises. So, rather than thinking of the Rating/Ranking Method as a "smelly business," it should instead be considered as a structured way to "scent opportunity."

Because the application of a rating/ranking method must be fact and content specific, it is not possible to identify a universal set of criteria that can be applied in all circumstances.

The method has to commend it three important values: It directly links to market value while characterizing the differences; it is useful preparation for marketing and negotiation by causing one to sharpen thoughts about strengths and weaknesses, and it is a useful way of defending both a valuation and a process to internal stakeholders.

In the next chapter we will consider another powerful technique: the use of rules of thumb. In many respects this method will be based on a subjective judgment because the "rules" are guidelines and need to be applied case-by-case. In this respect, the Rating/Ranking Method will apply in the next chapter as well.

NOTES

1. Apologies to those unfamiliar with New York City. For our purposes all one needs to know is that if money were no object, "Park Avenue" would be the answer, and for those who like the ambiance of industrial parks, they would probably actually prefer "Grand Central."

2. *Georgia-Pacific Corporation v. U.S. Plywood Corporation*, 318 F. Supp 1116 (S.D. N.Y. 1970).

3. Robert Goldshieder, "Litigation Background for Licensing," *les Nouvelles*, March 1994, pp. 20-33.

4. Stephen Degnan and Corwin Horton, "A Survey of Licensed Royalties," *les Nouvelles*, June 1977. p. 91.

5. Dan McGavok, David Haas, and Michael Patin, "Factors Affecting Royalty Rates," *les Nouvelles*, June 1992, p. 107.

6. Tom Arnold, "Factors in Pricing License," *les Nouvelles*, March 1987, pp. 19-22. Adapted from a paper presented at a workshop at LES U.S.A./Canada Annual Meeting, Los Angeles, CA, October 1986.

APPENDIX 5A

Factors in Pricing License

A checklist of 100 important considerations in setting value of technology license

By Tom Arnold
and Tim Headley

There is cost, risk of (i.e. hope for) profit and risk of loss involved,
- in licensing early or concept-only technology vs. matured and proven technology development;
- in scale-up from prototype or pilot plant to production model or commercial plant;
- in commercial manufacture and marketing;
- in patent or know-how litigation and commitments to enforce rights;
- in license nonexclusives and in license exclusions;
- in licensee competition with the licensor;
- in third-party competition and new leap-frogging developments;
- in guarantees of costs, quality or production rates of the licensed operation;
- in favored-nations clauses;
- in the cost and quality of the technology transfer itself;
- i.e. in everything in the license.

The total price for a technology may be structured in the forms of commitments and guarantees plus total or partial payment in equity, debt, front money, postponed sums certain, minimum royalties, running royalties, etc. But in the ultimate sense the total price is primarily a balance in the hope/risk of profit and loss by the two license parties.

Each of the following-listed considerations affecting the setting of the price on a technology, should be reviewed by both sides in the context of hope/risk, in arriving at that balance.

If reviewed before and during a negotiation, these considerations will help a party put his own value on the technology and will forewarn him of the thinking on the other side—thinking for which he should be forearmed when entering the negotiation.

Because many of the considerations are a mixture of intrinsic quality, strength of protection, market niche, financial and other factors, grouping them under headings can

be misleading and beget redundancy. We feel, however, the headings and groupings help
the reader a bit in spite of such inherent shortcomings.

Intrinsic Quality

1. The stage of the technology's technical and market development. Barely
conceived? Reduced to practice? Commercially proven?

2. The intrinsic quality of the technology as a marketable quality, reliable technology.

3. The *perceived* utility by the buyer or user of the technology or its product.

4. The value to the licensee or its country of educating the licensee employees in the
technology. Often developing nations will subsidize a technology-transfer or a licensee-
research clause in a license in order to get their citizens technically trained and gainfully
employed in a technology.

5. Perceived value of continuing access to technical help and ongoing research and
development by the licensor and/or other licensees, including reputation of the seller for
innovation and technical development.

6. The possibility of profiting from the good reputation of the licensor.

7. The need for the licensor's technology in the licensee's operations.

8. Pioneering invention or mere slight improvement?

9. Ongoing technical services by the licensor.

10. Whether the technology arose as a byproduct of other R&D. (This does not truly
change the intrinsic value of the licensable technology, but it seems to have a
psychological influence which, when properly advocated, does sometimes affect what a
licensor will take.)

11. The type of license (patent, know-how, trademark, copyright, mix, etc.).

Protections and Threats of Protection

1. The scope and reliability of the protections of the technology, be it patent, trade
secret, trademark, copyright or chip protection, etc.

2. Whether there is a favored-nations clause.

3. Precedent, the value in money and other considerations being paid by, or offered as
acceptable from, other licensees, particularly if they are likely to be partly competitive.

4. Reputation of the seller for defending its invention and for technology protection.

5. Contractual commitment of either party to protect the technology, or risk of
nonprotection.

6. Can the offered patents or secrets be designed around (and at what cost in time,
money, legal risks or technical risks)?

7. Enforceability of capacity, volume, location, geographic restriction or field-of-use
clauses or other restrictions against competition.

8. Is this license a compromise of a suit for patent infringement or misappropriation of
trade secrets, etc.?

Market Considerations

1. Size of the total relevant market and licensee's likely share.

2. Distinctiveness of the market niche of the licensed subject matter; differentiation
of licensed product (e.g. if 10 companies are making a soft, stretchable quality of
polyethylene as commonly used for garment bags, would a licensee pay more for a
license for a nonstretchable film strong enough for use as shopping and grocery bags?)

3. Demand for the product of the technology in the licensee's potential market at
various potentially available prices and product quality and styles (e.g. the same
invention may have a bigger market in a Cadillac than in a Volkswagen or vice versa).

4. Geographical location of licensee's manufacture or sales base.

5. The importance of a second source of supply in the market. Many is the market where two quality competitors will sell nearly three times as much as one alone.

6. Changing market trends in competition.

7. Dynamism of the market.

8. Trade cycles.

10. General state of the economy.

11. The possible extent to which the demand for the licensed product may be depressed by unemployment, union attitudes, etc. in the primary marketing area of the licensee.

Competitve Considerations

1. The nature and extent of the third-party competition with the licensee.

2. The nature and extent of licensee competition with the licensor and/or reaching markets not served by the licensor.

    a. Will the licensee serve markets the licensor cannot effectively serve or will the licensee serve competitively the licensor's own markets, etc.?

    b. Whether and to what extent gray-market goods of the licensee will compete with the licensor's products.

3. The scope of the market niche which is protected, and the cross-elasticity of the market within and without the protected niche (i.e. the degree of exclusivity of the license of the inherent market niche).

Value Brought to the Table By the Licensee

1. Capital, marketing talent, and other values brought to the table by the licensee.

2. Grant-backs of research and development by the licensee.

3. The possibility of acquiring an equity interest in the licensee.

4. Manufacturing and marketing capability of the technology recipient: Whether the licensee has greater talent and capacity effectively to make or to market the invention in the subject market, or to use the technology, than the licensor.

5. The degree of economic and industrial development, the labor and capital availability and cost, etc. in the licensee's country.

Financial Considerations

1. Manufacturer's margin. For example, a unique agricultural chemical, medical device or pharmaceutical may often be priced in response to value to the customer, independently of cost of manufacture and sale or competitive prices. Perhaps the farmer can be given a three dollars return in increased crop yield for one dollar of cost to buy the product, and the manufacturer can still sell such a chemical, if protected, at eight or eighteen times its manufacturing plus sales costs. A much higher royalty (33% of retail price in one of my cases) is justified in such a case than when the manufacturer's margin is forced to be one or two percent.*

2. Cost of the license negotiation and the technology transfer itself, and profit on that cost. Licenses for small markets often cost more to negotiate than the license is worth.

3. Potential for profits at royalties at X%, Y%, and Z%, each to the licensor and the licensee.

4. Availability and cost of capital and labor.

---

*As with many of the considerations, manufacturer's margin is a mix of the considerations of intrinsic quality, strength of legal protection, uniqueness of market niche, competitive, financial and other considerations, so it could be classified many places.

5. Tariffs.

6. Taxes and related considerations—capital gains vs. ordinary income. But "capital gains" as such seems destined to disappear under U.S. Tax Reform Act of 1986.

7. The amount of the licensor's expected cost savings, risk savings, and other burden savings, which follow from licensing a given market in lieu of developing it himself.

8. A comparison of the projected license net income against the potential for profit by the licensor's service of the same market.

9. Can the offered patents be designed around? Or the secrets be independently duplicated?

10. The burdens on the licensee inherent in its developing the same or competitive technology by its own effort:
- Cost of licensee R&D.
- Time for licensee R&D.
- Quality of licensee R&D result.
- Unresolved infringement, environmental and other legal risks involved in likely licensee R&D result.
- Technological risks in likely licensee R&D result.

11. What did the technology cost the licensor to develop? This should be disregarded except insofar as it helps evaluate the cost of the licensee's competitive development of the same technology.

12. Cost and risks of enforcing patents or trade-secret rights.

13. Cost of warranty service.

14. Cost savings in avoiding litigation to enforce a patent.

15. Costs of obtaining and maintaining local or foreign patent and trademark protection. (Really, not relevant.)

16. Cost of training the licensee's employees; risk that the planned training may prove inadequate.

17. The seller's cost of continually upgrading the project.

18. The nature and type of obligations to be assumed by the licensee under the contract; e.g. books to be audited by the competing licensor, licensor quality control burdens, royalties to be made on sales before goods paid for, force majure clause.

19. Policing costs: accounting audits, quality control tests/inspections.

20. The *probability* of the license being profitable for the licensee.

21. The *amount* of expected profit or saving incurred by the licensee, including any likely monopoly profit.

22. Different costs in the different countries involved,
- of capital (either equity or debt capital),
- of labor,
- of raw materials.

23. Traditional royalty rates in the industry—a factor relevant more to negotiating tactics and psychology than to what is fair or economically reasonable for the subject technology. Be imaginative in developing reasons for departing from tradition. Precedent-priced technology is often wrongly-priced technology.

24. The profit plan; the traditional profit margins in the industry. But again, be imaginative in finding reasons for departure from tradition.

25. Estimated cost of adapting the technology to planned applications like 220-volt power in lieu of 110, etc.

26. The structure and time spread of payments of equity, sums certain, royalty minimums, running royalties, payments to be of large sum certain in spite of market failure by licensee, etc.

27. Accounting simplicity.

28. The potential for and availability of barter and local manufacture arrangements to cover currency control problems and the like.

29. Follow-on related sales, the profits thereon.

31. The buyer's right to duplicate the seller's technology in subsequent projects.

32. Inflation, in some countries running at 400% annually.

33. Varying international exchange rates.

34. The prices (equity, sums certain, royalties) being asked by sellers of competitive or similar technology. Recent industry licensing rates and practices for similar products and processes.

35. Anticipated sales volume of licensed products.

36. Contract administration costs, comfort, and convenience.

37. Division of projected profits, as for example 25% to 50%, which is common for the licensor, and perhaps 50% to 75%, which is common for the licensee who usually has much more at risk.

Particular Risk Considerations

1. Exposure to product liability suits.

2. The licensor's risks and costs of litigation against the licensee, in lieu of license, e.g. risk of loss of royalties from existing licensees if the patent is held invalid.

3. The risk of cost and other burdens upon either party who assumes to police patents and sue infringers.

4. Risk of having to perform uncompensated technical study or training services to verify performance guarantees and specifications.

5. The risk of loss or prior license royalties if the patent is litigated and held invalid. The potential for this risk biases toward an early litigation—which in turn puts at risk all the royalties that might have been collected, usually at lower rates, had the patent never been risked in court.

6. Licensee's credit position.

7. Licensee's willingness to be audited—perchance by a competitor.

8. The risk of a diminished quality of future R&D if the licensor does not manufacture.

9. The reliability of clauses protective against product liability law suits, particularly in connection with trademark licenses.

10. Exposure to charges of infringement of rights of others.

11. The risks of the licensee's developing the same or competitive technology by its own effort.

12. The risks of the licensee's developing the same or competitive technology by its own effort.

13. Uncertainties in cost, time, legal quality and technological quality of licensee R&D result, if independent development is selected in lieu of license.

14. Risk to the licensor and value to the licensee of the licensor's guarantee of performance in

- time of plant erection,
- quality of product,
- production capacity,
- cost of product,
- enforcement of patent and know-how protections and exclusivities,
- indemnity against infringing 3rd party patents,
- etc.

15. Apart from the guarantee (which is often an incomplete remedy for failure of performance), the licensee's perception of the true reliability of the
- time of performance,
- quality of product,
- production capacity,
- cost of product,
- enforcement of protections and exclusivities,
- indemnity against infringements of third-party rights,
- etc.

16. The potential licensee's
- cost of defending an infringement suit,
- risk of damages,
- risk that the license price if any will go sharply up after a litigation.
- risk of injunction with no license available at all.

17. The term of licensee lock-in (as by a plant design frozen in steel and concrete).

18. The risks of technological obsolescence.

19. Can the offered patents or secrets be designed around (and as aforesaid, at what cost in time, money, legal risks or technical risks)?

20. Risk of erroneous estimates of licensee employee training.

Legal Considerations

1. Force majure clauses.

2. Legal enforceability of restraints on competition.

3. Whether the patent value has been or will be enhanced by a judicial reexamination and decree. Patentees frequently should decline to license or price a license very high before the first litigation, hoping to precipitate an early litigation with respect to an infringer suffering poor litigation equities, thereby to enhance the subsequent license value of the patent(s).

4. Duration of the license, of payments of sums certain, of the royalty payments, of the obligation of confidence—all of which commonly should be different terms.

5. Favored-nations clauses.

6. The risk of, or opportunity for, suit by the licensee to invalidate patents at times and forums of his choice—he may not stay hitched.

Government Regulatory Considerations

1. Licensee's government's restrictions and law on royalty rates, royalty terms, etc.

2. Legal restrictions on currency movement.

BIBLIOGRAPHY

T. Arnold, "Basic Considerations in Licensing," in 2 *The Law and Business of Licensing: Licensing in the 1980s* 2A-73 (1984).

Bayes, "Pricing the Technology," 1977 *Current Trends in Domestic and International Licensing* 369.

J. Bowler, "Payments for Technology," 1980 *Les Nouvelles* 241.

D. Cruver, "The International Marketplace" (September 16, 1983) (Handout at The Society for Marketing Professional Services, Tenth Anniversary Convention, Dallas, Texas).

Evans, "Packaging and Pricing Technology," 1984 *Domestic and Foreign Technology Licensing* 77.

Evans, "Pricing the Technology," 1977 *Current Trends in Domestic and International Licensing* 361.

L. Evans, "Turning Patents and Technology Into Money" (Handout at The First Annual Licensing Law and Business Institute. February 26-March 2, 1979).

Farley, "Price Fixing and Royalty Provisions in Patent Licenses," 34*J. Pat. Off. Soc'y* 46 (1952).

Finnegan & Mintz, "Determination of a Reasonable Royalty in Negotiating a License Agreement: Practical Pricing for Successful Technology Transfer," Vol. 1, No. 2 *Licensing Law and Business Report* 13 (1978).

R. Goldscheider, "The Art of 'Licensing Out'," 1984 *Les Nouvelles* 84.

R. Goldscheider, *Technology Management Handbook* (1984) (In particular, see Chapter 9, "Royalties and Other Sources of Income from Licensing").

S.B. Hadji, "Licensing as a Proft Center," 1985 *Les Nouvelles* 193. Interview with Donald R. Cruver, Partner, Blask, Cruver & Evans, Houston, Texas (July 17, 1986).

H. Janiszewski, "Licensee Evaluation of Payments," 1978 *Les Nouvelles* 248.

P. Leprince, "How Evaluation of Process Technology Affects Licensing," 1974 *Les Nouvelles* 182.

R. Marlow. "Matrix Approach to Pricing." 1978 *Les Nouvelles* 11.

Y. Matsunaga, "Determining Reasonable Royalty Rates," 1983 *Les Nouvelles* 216.

McKie, "Pricing and Packaging the Technology," 1984 *Domestic and Foreign Technology Licensing* 93.

G.P. Orleans, "Pricing Licensing of Technology," 1981 *Les Nouvelles* 320.

R.W. Rahn, "Determining the Royalty—What is Done and What in Fact Should Be Done." in 2 *The Law and Business of Licensing* 657 (1980). (Excellent! He lists 46 factors ranked by usage by licensing executives.)

Root & Contractor, "Negotiating Compensation in International Licensing Agreements," Vol. 22 No. 2 *Sloan Management Review* 23 (1981).

P. Scaglione, "Licensor View of Royalty Rates," 1981 *Les Nouvelles* 231.

Source: Arnold, White & Durkee, Houston, Texas: paper presented at workshop at LES U.S.A/Canada Annual Meeting, Los Angeles, CA, October 1986. Reprinted with permision from les Nouvelles.

6

Method Three:
Rules of Thumb to
Determine Valuation

INTRODUCTION

This chapter will consider another approach for using market data to value a technology. The focus will be on identifying and using suitable market-based "rules of thumb" as a tool in value assessment.

The term "rule of thumb" has come to mean a useful guideline for decision-making based on numerous experiences. A simple example used with first-year college students is: two hours of study outside of class for each hour spent in class. There are similar such rules in every walk of life that serve as useful simplifications of complex phenomena and behaviors. They tend to be reasonable approximations, not unbendable laws, so "rules" is probably a poor though well-established term; "guidelines" may be a better word as it more accurately reflects the idea behind the method.

Rules of thumb are closely related to a more formal idea known as a *heuristic*. A dictionary definition of a heuristic is: "involving or serving as an aid to learning, discovery, or problem-solving by experimental and especially trial-and-error methods."[1] The idea of a heuristic as used here is the desire to develop a simple valuation principle that can be conveniently and quickly applied to many different types of specific situations and one that can be flexibly applied to publicly-available data. The origin of such an idea is the belief that negotiations between numerous willing buyers and sellers have some rational, underpinning principle that can be discovered and applied.

The most famous heuristic, or rule of thumb, for licensing valuation is known as the "25 Percent Rule" or, the "25 to 33 Percent Rule." In this chapter such rule, the 25 Percent Rule, will be defined, the rationale behind the rule will be analyzed, specific examples will be considered. Situations that require values other than 25 percent also will be discussed.

FOUNDATIONS OF RULES OF THUMB

The existence and wide use of a term such as the 25 Percent Rule is itself an indication of an important fundamental idea. The undergirding idea of a valuation rule of thumb is that the total value created from a deal (license) should be equitably apportioned between the seller and buyer; the DE of *TR R A DE*™ can also be thought of as *Deal Equity*.

An agreement reached by a willing seller and buyer is a value-creating event. For the moment, without considering who keeps what portion of the value created, it is important to recognize that a deal necessarily creates the expectation of a gain. Were this not so, neither the buyer nor the seller would be willing to enter the agreement. (Presently, we are not considering the case of involuntary licensing, such as in the settlement of a lawsuit, where a gain unjustly realized is being reapportioned between the parties).

How Is "Deal Equity" Determined by Rules of Thumb?

The question arises, is there a general observation, (or rule-of-thumb) that can be made about how sellers and buyers seem to reach agreement on splitting such gain? Put another way, on average what do buyers *and* sellers both agree is deal equity? Clearly cases where either the buyer or seller claims "it's all mine" can be dismissed. We are considering values for which the seller will receive more than 0 percent and less than 100 percent of the total gain resulting from a deal. Well, how about 50 percent, where the seller and buyer split the gain 50:50? Except for some unusual circumstances, this rarely happens. In order to understand why, it is useful to analyze four elements behind the idea of rule of thumb.

- Total value (or gain)
- Apportionment (split)
- Investment
- Risk

Total Value
As a result of the transaction, the buyer will be able to create a product(s) or provide a service(s) that will produce a stream of revenues and a profit.

(The presumption throughout this book is that the "buyer" of the license becomes the "seller" of the products made from the technology and, so, receives all the proceeds from all the sales, a portion of which must then be re-distributed to the licensor/seller.) Generally such profits will occur over a period of many years.

Apportionment

The second element is apportionment, or in colloquial terms, the split. This is the heart of the rule of thumb as applied to valuation. For the 25 Percent Rule, the apportionment is 25 percent of the total gain to the seller, and 75 percent to the buyer. This particular value seems to be arbitrary so it leads to the logical question: on what basis is 25 percent fair? For the moment, we will only assert that enough buyers and sellers believe that this particular value is fair that it has risen in stature to a commonly used guide; a deeper discussion of this issue will take place later.

Investment

The third element is investment. The seller has made the investment in order to bring the technology to its current state. From this state, the buyer alone, or in some circumstances with participation from the seller, must make subsequent investments to create a product and business. When two parties to creating a business begin at the same point, it is common to apportion the rewards in the same manner as the total investment: Whoever does most of the work gets most of the reward—it is a principle as old as antiquity. Because in a licensing transaction the two parties by definition did not begin at the same point, there was a period when only the seller was investing and there will be a period when only the buyer is investing. In addition to the timing of the investments being different, the magnitude of the investments is almost certainly going to be different, as will be the risk undertaken in making such investments. Therefore, it should not be a surprise that a 50:50 split rarely occurs.

Risk

The aforementioned sentiment brings us to the fourth and final element: risk. Not all investments deserve the same return. Although this principle will be examined in quantitative detail in Chapter 7, the relevant point here is that higher risk investments, typically borne by the seller, deserve a greater return in proportion to the magnitude of such investment than the lower risk investments that will be borne by the buyer, all other factors being the same. There is a prevailing failure rate of all new technology projects that begins at conception. Although failure can and does occur at all phases, including after market introduction, it is generally the case that the fallout rate of new ideas is highest during the research and development stage, which normally precedes a licensing event.

Practical Application of the 25 Percent Rule

In order for any valuation rule of thumb to be of use, there has to be a way that both the buyer and seller can compute the first two elements: gain (value created) and apportionment. In general, there are two ways "gain" arises, cost savings and new profits. The cost savings type is realized because the licensed technology enables the buyer to make a product or provide a service more cheaply than without the technology. In the new profits case, the buyer will be able to charge more for a product already being made (because it has some new performance benefit as a result of enabling the licensed technology) or it will create an entirely new product or even product category. We will first consider the cost savings application.

COST SAVINGS EXAMPLE OF THE 25 PERCENT RULE

Although the cost savings situation occurs less frequently than the new profits case, it is easier to understand and apply, so it will be presented first.

Consider a seller offering to license technology that will enable the buyer to operate a factory (or some other business process) at lower cost. For simplicity, let us assume that both the seller and buyer agree that if the technology can be successfully deployed in a factory floor environment, it would save the buyer-manufacturer $100 per unit made.

Setting aside temporarily the issue of upfront payments or other forms of non-royalty compensation, what would be an equitable apportionment of this $100 savings? If the seller argues for receiving 100 percent of the $100 benefit per unit made, the buyer will rightly point out there is zero (or negative) incentive to incorporate the technology. Likewise if the buyer argues for keeping the entire savings, there is no incentive for the seller to transfer a rightful possession. What about a 50:50 split of the savings? From the point of view of the buyer, this is unlikely to appear reasonable as there are numerous costs commonly borne solely by the buyer:

- Making the technology fully design-ready for manufacturing
- Purchasing, installing, and conducting shake-down of manufacturing tooling
- Sample making and test marketing
- Creating and maintaining finished goods inventory
- Creating specialized products for specific customer requirements
- Marketing the product (advertisements, collateral materials, trade shows)

- Selling the product (salespeople, 800-numbers, processing orders)
- Shipping and distributing the product (warehousing, tracking, re-ordering)
- Handling returns and allowances
- Collecting payment (that's why it is called "accounts *receivable*")
- Performing the accounting, paying the royalties

If two parties decided to go into business and split the profits 50:50, it would be expected that they would likewise split 50:50 all the investment, risk-exposure, and day-to-day work to make the business successful. In the above licensing example, it is perfectly legitimate to consider the seller and buyer as going into a business to produce $100/manufactured unit of gain. Thinking of the transaction in this way, are the seller and buyer making equal contributions to creating this new $100/unit? In most circumstances, the situation is that the buyer is recognized to contribute more than the seller to the $100 realization. (Later in this chapter, circumstances will be considered where the seller deserves 50 percent or even more, but these are not common situations.)

The 25 Percent Rule states that an equitable split of the $100 savings is $25 to the seller and $75 to buyer. Thus, in this simple example, the royalty rate would be $25 per item manufactured, with some terms to account for the effects of monetary inflation and perhaps changes in the savings benefit over time.

Before going further in the use of the 25 Percent Rule, it is useful to think through the rationale for the specific apportionment of 25:75. The following are six different ways of looking at why this apportionment could be perceived as fair to both the seller and buyer.

"That's The Way It Is" Perspective

One simple way to look at the 25 Percent Rule is to simply say this particular apportionment is what numerous sellers and buyers have agreed to, or appear to have agreed to, in many different transactions and there is nothing more to be learned by thinking about it. This perspective is exactly the how technical analysts, sometimes called "elves," look at stocks and the overall stock market: The market has spoken, deal with it.

The Going Concern Perspective

As enumerated above, there is a long list of business processes that the buyer must possess and apply in order to realize the benefit from the technology. Many if not all of the processes are business assets that the buyer has developed prior to the transaction and which will be leveraged to create value out of the technology. The 25 Percent Rule then asserts that 75 percent of the work that has to be done to go from a raw idea to the customer's cash in hand will be done by the buyer using extensive business assets it has previously and independently developed, which are also necessary to commercialize the subject technology.

The Golden Rule Perspective

In a famous and light hearted re-statement of the Golden Rule, "He who has the gold makes the rules," there is the recognition that in many transactions a willing buyer can exert considerable leverage in a transaction. This is generally because there are more goods, services, and technologies seeking buyers than there are buyers seeking goods, services, and technologies. The money in the hand of the buyer is readily transformable into many different kinds of assets and opportunities. From this perspective, the deal will have to look attractive or buyers will look elsewhere to make their investments. This perspective suggests that buyers will look for opportunities where they can realize *most* of the gain in their own pocket, and they will continue to scan for sellers until they can find a suitable opportunity in which this will be true. Put simply, if a buyer is considering the subject technology (Plan A) and an alternative (Plan B), and the seller of Plan A insists on a 50:50 split of the future gain, and the seller of Plan B will settle for a 25:75 split, the buyer will have no difficulty in deciding which deal to pursue (all other factors being the same).

The 3-Times Impetus Perspective

Buyers tend to include payback multiple in their decision-making. Buyers (in business) think in terms of every one of their payments resulting in a multiplied return. The more complex the circumstances, the more unclear the timing and likelihood of the return, the higher the multiple has to be in order to be worth making the deal. It has been observed in other contexts that buyers frequently need to be convinced that they will benefit at least about three times the cost of getting the benefit (although the author is not aware of any formal study of this phenomenon). However, it has been observed in diverse settings that to induce buyers to proceed with projects, they need to be convinced (if only by an introspective mental calculation) of a 3-times return on the immediate costs, assuming all goes according to plan. Applied in this context, the commitment to pay a royalty equivalent to 25 percent of the cost savings is another way of saying that the buyer is getting back 3 times what it is committing to pay on each unit being manufactured.

The One-Quarter of the Way Perspective

Yet another way of looking at the 25 Percent Rule is that it is the recognition that "technology" is only about one-quarter of the way to a product.[2]

How might this be? One could assert that creating the technology of a new product or service is one big step. Making it manufacturable is a second big step. From this perspective, then manufacturing and selling the product are the third and fourth big steps. Therefore, creating the technology is one of four big steps to commercialization and, thereby, receives one quarter or 25 percent of the gain. From the perspective of a "33 Percent Rule," the argument is that the technology has already accomplished a portion of the manufacturing component. Therefore, the making and selling yet to be done are two big steps out of three, so the "technology" is actually one-third of the way.[3]

The R&D Tax Perspective

One can think of technology as the "product" of a research and development (R&D) organization. When a company's own R&D department creates technology, normally there is no license payment or royalty made by the manufacturing group or the respective business unit that puts the technology into commerce. However, on average there has been a payment made by all the business units for such R&D technologies. This is commonly done by "taxing" a company's sales in accordance with industry norms and the company's strategy (being the lead innovator justifies more spending; being a follower requires less R&D spending). *Business Week* used to publish an annual "R&D Scorecard." The last such version known was published June 27, 1994 and covered the year 1993. *Business Week's* "all industry composite" covers public companies with annual sales exceeding $75 million and R&D expenses of at least $1 million. The total annual R&D spending for 1993 was $83.023 billion and compared to pretax profits of $129.501 billion. Using a strict interpretation that R&D is usually for long-term benefit, it can be argued that all such R&D spending could have been added to the current-year profit increasing such profits to $212.52 billion. In other words, in aggregate all these many companies elected to spend $83 billion of their potential total profit of $212 billion on the prospect of future economic benefits. The ratio of $83 billion into $212 billion is 39 percent. So in terms of discretionary corporate investment, it appears that companies elected to follow a "39 Percent Rule." However, companies did so because there was the expectation that the current-year R&D spending was going to increase annual profits when such R&D began to be commercialized. Therefore, in forward-looking profit terms, the "R&D Rule" was actually less than 39 percent. Also, some of the R&D was really non-discretionary, such as designing a costly operating process to comply with environmental regulations; so it wasn't all really elective or profit-enhancing. Taking this into account would further reduce the R&D ratio. Without resorting to a research process it is possible to envision that companies choose to invest something in the range of 25 to 33 percent of their profits to acquire the fruits of their own R&D department. Put another way, if an external organization could provide all the technologies otherwise produced by a captive R&D department, management should be willing to pay such an external organization (the seller) approximately 25 to 33 percent of its profits and be in the same financial situation as when funding its own R&D operation.[4]

PERSPECTIVES ON THE 25 PERCENT RULE

Regardless of the validity or weight of the previous arguments as to why 25 percent (or 33 percent) has emerged as a commonly cited rule, the fact is that the phrase "25 Percent Rule" (and the idea behind it) is widely recognized in the licensing community. It appears in almost every article about valuation. It has been cited in court cases: "As a general rule of thumb, a royalty of 25 percent of net profits is used in license negotiations."[5]

Bill Lee has written a very succinct summary of the history of the 25 Percent Rule.[6] It has a long history, with many claimed fathers. His paper summarizes values ranging from 25 to 33-1/3 percent and it is cited in an "authoritative treatise on licensing,"[7] in an article by Larry Evans,[8] and by a Japanese author, Yoshio Matsunaga,[9] and, finally, in an article by Edward P. White who cites the value range as 25–35 percent.[10]

However, it is important to note that there are other points of view. Buyers can argue, especially when dealing with very early-stage, speculative technology that 25 percent is simply too high to make business sense. Such reasoning is this: (1) the seller has not moved the technology even to the end of the R&D stage, and/or (2) the costs (and risk) of getting through "manufacturability" are huge (especially in comparison to the R&D), and/or (3) the costs (and risk) of marketing and sales are large, and/or (4) this is a low margin, competitive business that does not provide the profitability to support a 25 Percent Rule. The net result of such an argument could be a proposal from the buyer that amounts to a split smaller that 25 percent.

On the other hand, sellers can, in some circumstances, argue: (1) this technology is ready to manufacture (or nearly so), and/or (2) there will be almost no incremental costs or risks in marketing and sales, and/or (3) this is or will be a very high margin (high profitability) business in an exploding market. The net result of this point of view could be a proposal that reflects a 33 percent split or even higher.

The key point here is that 25 percent, and to a lesser extent 33 percent, has emerged as a commonly-cited number that appears to be helpful in many negotiations. However, it is not a rigid "rule," despite the use of the word next to "25 percent." The specific circumstances of each valuation should be analyzed to determine whether it deserves more, the same as, or less than that given by the 25 Percent Rule. One useful tool for conducting such an analysis is the Rating/Ranking Method (discussed in Chapter 5). An effective way of using rating/ranking for this purpose is to use as a comparable agreement one which is known (or believed) to have resulted in a valuation and agreement that reflects the use of the 25 Percent Rule. Then by conducting a rating/ranking scoring process, one can develop a perspective as to whether the present valuation is wisely guided by 25 percent or by some other number.

USE OF THE 25 PERCENT RULE
FOR APPORTIONING NEW PROFITS

In the preceding discussion of the 25 Percent Rule, the example used was a cost savings of $100 per unit. In most licensing situations, what is being licensed is more appropriately considered as creating new revenues rather than reduced costs. How would one apply the rule to such a situation? The 25 Percent Rule for this case can be stated as follows: The royalty in percent of net sales price should be one quarter of net sales after deduction of (1) cost of goods sold (including depreciation of relevant plant and equipment), (2) appropriately allocated general and administrative cost, (3) appropriately allocated marketing and sales cost, and (4) any other appropriate costs (but not including interest, taxes or dividends). Let us now consider each of these elements.

Net Sales Price

Why, after all the discussion of dividing profit or gain, does one base the royalty on sales? Rather, it would seem convenient for the buyer and seller to agree that the buyer will simply pay the seller a royalty of 25 percent (or 33-1/3 percent) of its pre-tax profit, as such a figure includes the deduction of the appropriate costs. This actually is a bad idea. Companies pay taxes on their pre-tax profit.[11] So there are (well) paid people at such companies to make every effort to reduce the taxable exposure. Further, companies of any reasonable size create operating groups onto which costs are allocated with wide discretion and such allocations determine profitability for such groups and individual products. Basing a royalty on a number that is calculated "low" (i.e., below the top line, namely that of sales) on the income statement is just not a good idea. For this reason, almost without exception sellers insist that the royalty be based on the easiest-to-measure number: sales revenues. The term "net sales" will be discussed in Chapter 11, but "net" in this context does not refer to net of operating costs but of certain direct costs associated with delivering the sale, such as shipping and insurance.

Appropriately Allocated Cost of Goods Sold

Cost of goods sold (commonly designated COGS) refers to the direct costs of producing the product or service. It typically includes the cost of raw materials, the direct labor of converting the materials to the product, the depreciation cost of the necessary manufacturing equipment, and so forth. A portion of all such costs are unambiguously connected to the making of the product from the technology. Some of the costs are calculations derived from many circumstances, such as two products, one based on the licensed technology and one not, being made on the same machine in the same building. How should the depreciation costs of machine and building be allocated between the licensed product and all other uses? Like all cost allocation issues, there is some degree of interpretation and opinion involved.

The number that results from subtracting COGS from net sales is called the "gross margin." It is a very important barometer of profitability and, as such, is widely reported and studied. However, the reported values for gross margin are not always to be relied upon. It is believed that some companies engage in reporting lower gross margins by finding ways to increase the calculated cost of goods sold so as to dissuade competitors from entering a business because of the attractiveness of high reported gross margins; another example of a rule of thumb is that if your gross margin is more than 50 percent you will be attacked by competitors. Also, upon seeing "juicy" gross margins a company's customers are likely to become more aggressive in their purchase negotiations. Finally shareholders, who always want to see costs minimized, are especially vigilant for overhead (SG&A, discussed below) costs, so some companies interpret certain gray-area costs as being COGS. These are serious complications to valuation because the gross margin is a very useful measure of the profitability of a technology or business. Sellers are at a valuation and pricing disadvantage if they are unable to make accurate estimates of the potential gross margin of a product. Conversely, buyers who are likely to have a much better estimate of their potential gross margins are motivated to understate them.

Two points should be made here: (1) basing royalties on gross margins, rather than net sales, is fraught with accounting (and other) perils and should rarely, if ever, be done, and (2) there is some inherent uncertainly when surveying gross margins data on public companies.

Other Allocated Costs

As one goes lower on the income statement, there is increasing room for, shall we say, "discretion" in allocating costs. Below the gross margin line are the "general overhead" (sometimes known as SG&A for sales, general, and administrative) and other expenses of running a business such as paying loans to lenders of operating capital. Considering an appropriate allocation of sales cost for, say, a drug being licensed, the result can be very different if the drug will be sold through an existing sales force, or whether an entirely new sales force has to be created, or through some combination of the two. Other issues relating to general allocations will be considered in the next section, which covers specific examples.

EXAMPLES OF APPLYING THE
25 PERCENT RULE TO NEW PROFITS LICENSING

Considering first a generic example, let us take the following "data" from the marketplace and apply the 25 Percent Rule. Considering the case where the buyer has revenues of 100, and "profits" of 6.6, what would be an appropriate royalty from the application of the 25 Percent Rule? The specific value of 6.6 is selected because it reflects the average after-tax profits using *Business Week's* "all-industry composite" for the first six months of 1998.[12] This composite is made up of the largest, primarily United States companies. The "profit" number represents that the all-industry average, after-tax profit is 6.61 percent of revenues. We will assume for this example that the appropriate costs have been included in the income statement leading to the reported profit figure.

To apply the 25 Percent Rule, one begins with the revenues, deducts all the direct costs (COGS, as defined above), indirect costs (SG&A), and other costs (such as interest expense and restructuring or other extraordinary costs), and finally provision for taxes (both federal and state/local). The final number, often referred to as EAT for earnings after tax, represents the net gain from operations after all bills have been paid. It is the figure to be distributed to the shareholders (the owners) or to be retained by management for reinvestment in the company, or any combination of the two.

An easier direction to take is to start with the after-tax profit and work backwards. The 25 Percent Rule should be based upon a pre-tax profit which is known by a variety of terms: EBIT (Earnings Before Interest and Taxes), operating profit, even "gross profit;" here we shall use EBIT. The immediate question is why the 25 Percent Rule should be applied to pre-tax profits. The answer is that the royalty is an expense of operations and like any other expense of operations it is a deductible business expense that reduces taxable profits. Further, the seller receiving such royalties will have to pay tax on such moneys (depending, of course, on the kind of entity the seller is and its particular tax situation in any year in which it receives such royalties). In addition, the value "25" (or "25 to 33") in the 25 Percent Rule has evolved because parties used such EBIT value as the basis for the calculations.

To convert from after-tax to pre-tax dollars, one divides by the factor: $1 - T$, where T is the effective tax rate of the reporting organization as a decimal value. Although the value of T depends upon specific circumstances, including the effective tax rate of the respective state/local government, for illustration purposes the factor 0.45 will be used. Thus, dividing 6.61 by 0.55 (which comes from $1 - 0.45$) results in 12 percent pre-tax earnings.

Using the 25 Percent Rule on these data, taking 25 percent or one quarter of the value "12," would result in a royalty of 3 percent of sales. Such payment would become a revenue line to the seller and an expense line to the buyer, reducing the buyer's pre-tax profit to 9 percent (by simply subtracting 3 percent royalty from the 12 percent EBIT) which results (by multiplying 9 percent by 0.45, the assumed effective tax rate) in an after-tax profit of approximately 5 percent (exactly 4.95) all based on the total sales of 100. Thus in this example, the seller would receive 3 percent of sales, and the buyer's after-tax income would be reduced from 6.6 percent of sales to 5 percent of sales for those sales subject to the royalty.

So, what does the 25 Percent Rule teach us by this example? If one assumes that the technology being valued will result in gain to the buyer that is the average gain of publicly-traded, primarily large United States companies of all industries, and that the gain anticipated over the period covered by the license can be characterized by the reported profits of the first six months of 1998, then the royalty should be (per the 25 Percent Rule) 3 percent of sales.[13]

Creating such an all-enveloping category on which to apply the 25 Percent Rule does not produce a very usable result. This is because in this example the gain has included businesses with widely varying profitability, as well as those that do not use technology to any appreciable degree and those that have a high reliance on technology. A much more useful result is obtained when the reference profit numbers are closer to the technology being valued, as will be shown.

Applying the 25 Percent Rule to Specific Companies

In any specific valuation, one should attempt to perform the calculation on an income statement that most closely approximates the expected profitability of commercializing the subject technology. There are two general ways of doing this: "bottom's up" or "benchmark." Bottom's up means that all the terms of the income statement are estimated from first principles. So the COGS would be calculated by considering the actual costs of raw materials required, the labor costs required, the capital equipment and the associated life of such equipment, the number of salespeople and related non-personnel costs, and so on. For new technologies it can be quite difficult to make accurate estimates of such costs. Also, in many circumstances the seller is somewhat unfamiliar with the licensed application, which is why the seller is licensing rather than going into manufacturing.

The other approach is to find benchmark data from published sources. This is very similar to what was done in Chapter 4 to find a published agreement approximating the subject valuation and then using the Rating/Ranking Method of Chapter 5 to estimate valuation differentials based on the particular situation.

Thus, the first task is very similar to what was done in performing the rating/ranking method, namely, finding a benchmark or comparable. Rather than using an "all industry" composite as was done in the preceding section, it would be much better to be focused on the industry and companies that typify those that will be commercializing the subject technology. Using the *Business Week* data for the first six months of 1998 and the "laser" example, consider the following data for two companies, both of which make lasers and many other things:

HP (Hewlett Packard) 6.77 percent (after tax profitability)
AMP 5.72 percent

For reasons to be discussed, it is also useful to examine the industry groups to which these companies belong. These two companies belong to two different industry groups in the *Business Week* data: HP is in "Computers & Peripherals, within "Office Equipment & Computers." Computers & Peripherals composite had a net profit of 1.08 percent. Office Equipment & Computers composite was 3.66 percent.

AMP is in "Semiconductors & Other Components" within "Electrical & Electronics." Semiconductors & Other Components as a composite had 8.72 percent. Electrical & Electronics had a composite of 3.56 percent.

Just considering these two companies and the immediate and larger categories to which they belong results in net profit numbers ranging from 1.08 percent to 8.72 percent. Performing the 25 Percent Rule calculation using an effective tax rate of 45 percent results in a royalty range of 0.5 percent to 4 percent, a range spanning a factor of 8, a very wide variation. If one considers just the two company's individual earnings performance, the range would be narrower: approximately 2.5 to 3.0 percent (exactly 2.6 to 3.1 percent).[14]

So what is the right answer? Unfortunately, there is no easy answer to this question. HP and AMP both make many products besides lasers. Normally companies do not report their profitability by product line. Their reported earnings are the smeared out average on all their products. It is possible then, that their laser profitability could be substantially larger or smaller than the average number used above.

Because the buyer's use of the licensed technology will extend over a period of years, it is important to look at profitability data over a period of time. There could be, and are, "down" years in individual companies and even entire industry groups. So it is prudent to consider trends in profitability over at least several years. Many companies and industries go through regular boom and bust cycles. Unless something extraordinary is happening with a comparable company or its industry, going back five years or so is probably sufficient to capture the important time varia-iabilities. However, since the whole point of the 25 Percent Rule is a prospective calculation, it must be realized that it is the future profitability that is important, not the historical performance. Unfortunately, no data for the future profitability of companies or industries exists so there is a forecast issue involved. This is one good reason to use the 25 Percent Rule on the profitability of industry groups rather than a specific company: because groups are averaged by definition, the historical data will show less dramatic swings and the future will as well. The difficulty with using groups of companies is the same one encountered in the discussion of industry data and benchmarking for rating/ranking: groups include both high performers and low performers.

Should One Just Use the Average Value?

Businesses have upturns and downturns that may or may not be related to the specific technology/product area being valued. In either case one needs to consider several different time periods to appreciate the effect of year-to-year variability.

Another important factor to consider is the maturity of an individual product within the product family. Let us suppose that the profitability of the division that makes lasers and only lasers was identical to the 2.5 percent figure considered earlier. This number is a smeared out average of all the laser products being sold, including some old, low-margin products and some high-margin products.

Analyzing the Profitability of a Benchmark Category

One reasonable way to approach this issue is to decide on a percentile performance of an industry group as the benchmark: Percentile performance is defined as follows: taking the median is taking the 50th percentile performer; taking the highest performer in the group would be taking the 100th percentile performer. Consider the laser example calculated previously. There were four groups identified: semiconductors and other components within electrical and electronics, and computers and peripherals within office equipment and computers. What would be the most relevant category to consider for the making of lasers? There are two other groups that could be considered: equipment and services within telecommunications (because lasers are widely used in telecommunications), and "medical products" within "health care" (because lasers are also used in medical diagnostics and therapy). Lasers are also used in instrumentation for manufacturing and in certain manufacturing operations (such as laser cutting) so companies that make lasers for use in these areas could be relevant as well. The point here is that one needs to identify as closely as possible the business of the technology being licensed. Is this a high-powered laser that will be used (primarily) for cutting steel? Alternatively, is it a highly reliable, high speed monomode laser that would be used in telecommunications? Is it most suited for low power level diagnostics? Or is it a revolutionary new laser method that could be used in multiple industries? The closer one can come to the most likely use, the more accurately one can identify a data set on which to apply the 25 Percent Rule.

For illustration purposes, let us assume that the laser technology being valued would be used by semiconductor manufacturers to create lasing components which would subsequently be used by various manufacturers to create a "box" that has, as one of its devices, a laser. At this stage, it is not known or predictable how the technology will be used beyond these assumptions. In this case, it would make sense to focus just on the industry group "semiconductors and other components." The 14 companies in the *Business Week* index for this category are shown in Exhibit 6.1. Clearly the average profit figure of 8.7 percent (6 months' profits of 2,621 divided by corresponding revenues of 30,052.8) used previously results from a very non-uniform group: four of the 14 companies lost money during the period, a lot of money, losses ranging from 11 percent to more than 16 percent. At the other extreme is Intel which had an after-tax profit of more than 20 percent (2,445/11,928).

No buyer is going to license technology from a seller for the joys of losing money. So the four companies showing a loss should not be used in characterizing this industry group.[15] (One could also argue for deleting TI, which had unusually low earnings because of the same adverse business climate affecting the four companies with losses.) Of the remaining 10 companies, the average profitability was 12.2 percent, significantly higher than the 8.7 percent average. Using this figure as the basis of the 25 Percent Rule results in a calculated royalty of 5.6 percent versus the 4 percent calculated previously with all 14 companies in the equation. If one discards TI, because of its unusually poor performance, and Intel, simply because it is (at the moment) the Michael Jordan of companies making devices, then the 25 Percent Rule for the remaining eight companies results in a royalty of 3.1 percent. (One question is this: Does one compute the average profitability by adding up all the profits and all the revenues or by averaging the profit percentages? The difference is that the former approach weights the calculation to the large companies,

Exhibit 6.1 Semiconductors & Other Components

	Sales				Profits				Margins		Return on Common Equity 12 Months Ending 6-30	Price-Earnings Ratio 7-24	12 Months' Earnings Per Share
	2nd Quarter 1998 $Mil.	Change From 1997 %	6 Months 1998 $Mil.	Change From 1997 %	2nd Quarter 1998 $Mil.	Change From 1997 %	6 Months 1996 $Mil.	Change From 1997 %	2nd Quarter 1998 %	2nd Quarter 1997 %			
Group Composite	**14875.8**	**-5**	**30052.8**	**-3**	**1094.0**	**-54**	**2621.0**	**-49**	**7.4**	**15.1**	**15.0**	**31**	**1.74**
Advanced Micro Devices	526.5	-11	1067.4	-7	-64.6	NM	-127.3	NM	NM	1.7	8.9	NM	-1.20
AMP	1352.8	-8	2747.7	-4	54.8	-49	157.4	-25	4.1	7.3	14.0	16	1.85
Analog Devices (2)	333.1	11	663.8	12	48.4	15	92.7	14	14.5	14.0	15.9	20	1.10
Atmel	288.2	28	548.6	15	44.5	NM	-70.5	NM	NM	12.2	-19.9	NM	-1.37
AVX (9)	292.0	-7	597.0	-3	17.4	-50	47.1	-28	6.0	11.1	13.8	12	1.33
Intel	5927.0	-1	11928.0	-4	1172.0	-29	2445.0	-33	19.8	27.6	26.5	26	3.24
Jabil Circuit (4)	309.6	25	640.3	36	17.3	19	37.4	46	5.6	5.9	30.2	17	1.94
LSI Logic	330.1	-1	655.0	2	32.0	-30	62.5	26	9.7	13.8	8.6	21	0.97
Micron Technology (4)	609.9	-37	1365.3	-26	-106.1	NM	-154.2	NM	NM	10.0	-2.6	NM	-0.36
Molex (6)	398.1	-4	807.3	1	45.8	-3	92.2	2	11.5	11.4	14.4	23	1.15
National Semiconductor (7)	510.0	-24	1160.0	-16	-212.4	NM	-190.1	NM	NM	NM	-5.3	NM	-0.62
Solectron (4)	1278.2	30	2465.0	34	49.2	18	98.0	24	3.8	4.2	17.5	31	1.58
Texas Instruments	2167.0	-15	4353.0	-10	43.0	-81	54.0	-83	2.0	8.8	0.5	NM	0.07
Thomas & Betts	553.3	-5	1054.6	-7	41.5	3	76.8	7	7.5	6.9	15.6	15	2.91

BUSINESS WEEK / AUGUST 17, 1998

Source: Business Week Financial Data for semiconductor industry, second quarter 1998.

whereas the latter calculation averages the performance of the companies regardless of size. Unless there is some particular reason why the technology being valued is better utilized by larger companies, a more representative measure of company profitability is obtained by calculating the average of the profitabilities directly).

A further refinement of the calculation is derived from realizing that most companies do not embark on new business ventures with the goal of replicating their average performance. A key step in the decision-making of the buyer is how much can the subject opportunity *boost* its average performance. How might this be taken into account? One way would be to apply another kind of 25 Percent Rule: use the 75 percentile profitability (25 percent from the top) of the category. Again, referring to the 10 companies in Exhibit 6.1, the profit percentages vary from 1.2 percent to 20.5 percent and the 75th percentile profitability would be 10.5 percent. Dropping TI from the calculation would boost this to 11.0 percent and dropping both TI and Intel (because of its extraordinary performance) would decrease this to 9.5 percent. The corresponding royalties to these three possibilities as computed by the 25 Percent Rule would be 7.1 percent, 7.4 percent, and 5.2 percent, respectively.

Further Refining Benchmark Categories

In the above example, the benchmark category was obtained by selecting the most appropriate *Business Week* grouping. A better benchmark could be obtained by creating one's own grouping based upon an analysis of the subject technology. This could be done by identifying about 10 specific companies that appear to be closely related in technology, industry, and business model to the deal being valued. Start by identifying (1) companies to which the technology is being marketed, (2) competitors of such companies, (3) companies of like SIC code (a government code used to index companies), (4) companies found from Internet or library searches that make products like or similar to those produceable by the technology, and (5) companies from lists such as those compiled by *Business Week* and others.

All such data should consider multiple time periods (if available). Certainly whole years should be used, because there are seasonal effects. Multiple years should be considered to average out unusual fluctuations.

The data should then be analyzed to see if some companies should be dropped from the calculation because, for example, they had losses or their business performance was suppressed because of other factors. There may also be cases where the top performers might be excluded: the "Michael Jordan" effect. Other reasons could include extraordinary performance due to a huge new marketing initiative, or the realization of profits from the sale of a division, and so forth.

The result is a list of at least two or three and ideally five or more companies. The average profitability of the group is one indicator of profitability. A better indicator is to consider the 75th percentile performer, or even higher, because all companies are buying and selling with the aspiration of increasing their profitability performance, not just holding steady (again, perhaps, the extraordinary performance by one company, such as Intel in the previous example, could warrant it being excluded).

All of this can consume a significant amount of time and requires critical thinking. For this reason it is common to employ consulting experts to develop some or all of this type of information or to provide an expert pair of eyes to review an internally-prepared analysis. The economic significance of the valuation in question has to be used to determine how much effort should be expended. If a particular opportunity cannot conceivably be worth more than, say, $100,000 in total, then it is not prudent to spend $25,000 worth of time or consulting to develop a ten-member benchmark category. On the other hand, if the opportunity could be worth $10 million, it is worth making a serious effort to develop a thorough economic framework in preparation for negotiation.

Using a Specific Company's Profitability for the 25 Percent Rule

Another approach to finding a benchmark for the 25 Percent Rule calculation is to identify one single company instead of looking at a category. In this section, two examples will be considered: Raychem and Morgan Matroc.

In Exhibit 6.2, the income statement for Raychem for the year 1991 is presented. In previous examples, the starting point was the after-tax profit numbers. A more accurate method is to look at the income statement and examine how the profitability number was reached. Recall that the definition of the 25 Percent Rule introduces the ideas of "appropriate" deductions from the sales number. In the Raychem example we see the following deductions from sales: COGS (Cost of Goods Sold) of $643 million or 52 percent of sales, SD&A (Sales, Distribution, and Administrative) of $448 million or 36 percent of sales, R&D of $140 million or 11 percent of sales, leaving an EBIT (Earnings Before Interest and Taxes) of just $18 million or 1.5 percent of sales.

Below the EBIT line, there are two other deductions: interest expense (paying lenders of capital employed by Raychem) and "restructuring costs" (presumably non-recurring costs associated with some significant change in business operations). Together, these two additional charges result in a net loss for the year of $3 million, shown as EBT (Earnings Before Tax).

Now, assuming that Raychem 1991 is the appropriate benchmark, how would one apply the 25 Percent Rule? Clearly, applying the 25 Percent

Exhibit 6.2   Example Applications of the 25 Percent Rule

	Raychem Annual Report, 1991			Morgan Matroc Annual Report, 1991 European Company	
	$K	%		£M	%
Sales	1,249,512	100	"Turnover"	454.0	100
COGS*	643,357	52	Other Inc.	2.2	
Gross Margin	606,155	48		456.2	
SD&A	447,607	36	"Operating Costs"	405.0	89
R&D	140,196	11			
EBIT**	18,352	1	EBIT	51.2	11
Interest	8,090		"Investments"	(1.4)	
Restructuring	3,697		"Finance Charges"	8.7	
Other	9,674				
			EBT	43.9	10
EBT†	(3,109)	(0.25)			
			Now what?	2.5%?	
	Now What?	0.25%?			
		(0.06%)?			

*Cost of Goods Sold (all "direct" costs of making the product).
**Earnings Before Interest and Taxes.
†Earnings Before Tax.
Source: Raychem & Morgan Matroc Company Annual Reports. Reprinted with permission.

Rule to the EBT line would result in no royalty at all, which makes no sense. However, one cannot just arbitrarily pick a favorite line on the income statement and take 25 percent of that number as the appropriate royalty calculation.

What about the appropriateness of the interest and restructuring cost deductions? Restructuring costs, like other extraordinary costs, are by their nature not reflective of normal business operations. Although they may be a legitimate deduction for tax computation purposes, it is not reasonable to deduct these costs from the profitability calculation for computing royalties. Adding such costs back increases the EBT line to $10 million or 0.8 percent of sales.

What about interest costs? Generally it is not appropriate to deduct such costs before applying the 25 Percent Rule. The idea is that a company obtains capital from lenders and equity holders in accordance with its financing strategy. However, the corporate financing strategy should not be used to affect the profitability calculation for use with the 25 Percent Rule.

Also shown in Exhibit 6.2 is shown the 1991 financial data for Morgan Matroc, a UK company. This is an example of a sparse income statement. "Turnover" corresponds to sales. "Operating costs" encompasses COGS,

SG&A, and R&D. The lack of detail shows how difficult it can be to use financial reports to analyze the real operating economics.

By studying an income statement, judgments can be reached about the appropriateness of the charges against profitability in the context of the subject valuation. For example, the COGS shown is 52 percent. If estimates can be made of the COGS that will occur for the subject technology, then this figure could be adjusted upward or downward to more accurately reflect the prospective situation. Although adjustments could also be made for SD&A (more commonly termed "SG&A"), and R&D, it is more difficult to rationalize. One could argue that "R&D" costs are really being incurred to develop other products for the company—products which will not be subject to the royalty and so will not benefit the seller. From this perspective, R&D costs should not be deducted. On the other hand, "R&D" covers a bundle of activities associated with keeping products up to date with enhancements, new models, and so forth, and such costs will benefit the seller because they will tend to keep the technology up to date and commercially useful. So, generally speaking, it does make sense to allocate same R&D costs prior to using the 25 Percent Rule. Further analysis could reveal appropriate adjustments in such costs if the company is incurring extraordinarily lower- or higher-than-average costs in those business segments that make products closely related to the technology being licensed.

Likewise, adjustments in SG&A could be made because, for example, the company incurs very large sales costs on average, but will not incur them for the subject technology (or vice versa). Again, a detailed analysis should be performed to determine norms for such costs and to compare them to the specific income statement being analyzed.

If we conclude that the COGS, SG&A, and R&D are appropriate allocations, and the restructuring is not, then the bottom line EBIT is 1.5 percent of sales, so the 25 Percent Rule suggests a royalty of 0.37 percent. However, such a low value of EBIT would not be credible to an opportunity licensing situation: why would a buyer aspire to enter such a low-performing business?

Another factor in income statement analyses is shown in Exhibit 6.3. These data are from a publication by Robert Morris Associates that gives aggregate percentages of SIC coded companies.[16] The data are available by company size, as shown in the left two columns, and by year, as shown in the right three columns. These data tend to be for smaller companies that are seeking commercial loans from banks, so for many purposes they do not accurately reflect profitability for technology-based companies. Using the data as shown is a judgment call. Does one simply take the average of all five data points and take 25 percent of this value to obtain a royalty of 1.5 percent? Generally, this is not a good idea because it completely smears out the beneficial distinction that may be a consequence of exploiting the technology.

Exhibit 6.3   Another Example Application of the 25% Rule

	Minerals and Earths, Ground or Otherwise Treated* (SIC #2395)				
	11 Co's $500K-$2M Assets	17 Co's $2-10M Assets	All 1991	All 1990	All 1989
Net Sales	100.0	100.0	100.0	100.0	100.0
Gross "Profit"	29.9	21.8	25.4	33.8	32.5
"OP-Exp"	21.5	17.7	20.7	26.0	22.1
"Op Profit"	[8.4	4.1	4.7	7.8	10.4]
"Other"	1.2	0.8	1.0	1.8	1.6
"Profit Before Tax"	7.2	3.3	3.0	5.9	8.7
	Now What? 1.5%? ◄—————————— Average				

*Operating witihout a mine or quarry crushing, grinding, pulverizing, or otherwise preparing clay, ceramic, and refractory minerals; barite, and miscellaneous minerals, except fuels. Also includes crushing slag and preparing roofing granules.

The "Pure Play" Analysis

All of the above examples were based upon public data for companies making multiple products. Although some useful information can be obtained by analyzing clusters of related companies, it would be better to find financial data on companies that make essentially only products similar to those being planned under the subject valuation. This is the notion of a "pure play."

The approach is similar to the previous discussion except that the search for benchmarks (comparables) is confined to just the products in question. In many cases this search yields very small companies.

Although such examples exhibit the usefulness of pertinent costs, there are other issues that require interpretation of the data. First, such companies can be rapidly growing which causes significant growth costs of funding inventory, advanced sales and marketing, and so forth. This can bias the profitability to lower values. Also, because they are small, such companies can be subcritical and are thereby incurring a higher percentage of SG&A and R&D than a larger, more established company might incur. Finally, many smaller companies are privately held and their financial data can be harder or impossible to find.

Nevertheless, even with these cautions, it is a good idea to find some examples of pure plays to supplement the analysis.

The Use of a Bottom's Up Income Statement Estimate

All of the approaches to finding EBIT values and applying the 25 Percent Rule rely on data available from existing companies. Another, more complex approach is to prepare an income statement for a hypothetical business unit (or company) created solely to make products from the subject technology. This process is sometimes referred to the making of a pro forma, that is, a forward-looking estimate of business performance.

Preparing such a pro forma would require a mature understanding of how manufacturing, marketing and sales, R&D, and overall administration of such a new business would operate. If the technology is at an early stage, there may need to be substantial assumptions about how the product would be manufactured. Often this leads to a scenario approach to financial modeling: namely, two or three different models are developed (such as optimistic, pessimistic, and most likely) based upon different manufacturing approaches and efficiencies. Similar assumptions would likely need to be made about pricing and other elements of an income statement.

Outside experts knowledgeable in the industry are frequently necessary to be able to determine usable numbers. Depending upon the potential significance of the licensing deal, such an expenditure may or may not be warranted. When such an investment is made, it can provide a very useful cross-reference to the EBIT data obtained from industry analysis.

Technology buyers typically have an important valuation advantage as they are more likely to have good estimates on the costs of making the technology into a business, although they may likewise have to use a scenario approach because of substantial uncertainties.

One potential benefit of both buyers and sellers performing this type of analysis is that it can lead to creative ways of structuring a license so that the royalty rate could be adjusted based upon future events. For example, this can happen through the use of a royalty or lump-sum "kicker." A baseline royalty (fixed payment sums) is calculated assuming a more conservative outcome for manufacturing cost (for example). Then, if it happens that the more optimistic manufacturing costs come true, because the yield is higher or the process is faster or the raw materials are cheaper, then there is an additive royalty (or payments) known as a "kicker." Thus, an agreement could be structured with a 3 percent royalty on all sales providing that the product is made in accordance with Scenario A (the more conservative scenario); however, if Scenario B results, then the buyer agrees to pay a "kicker" royalty of an additional 2 percent (making it a 5 percent royalty) to reflect the added profitability resulting from the more favorable outcome.

Such approaches can be creative ways of dealing with highly uncertain situations by sharing risk. However, to avoid subsequent disputes it is critical that the provisions are carefully specified so that it is clear when the "kicker" becomes effective.

OTHER PERCENT RULES

The 25 Percent Rule, though widely cited, may not be appropriate in many licensing situations. One can easily conceive of circumstances where the technology being sold is very far from commercialization, in terms of investment and time required, for an outcome that is not predicted to be commercially significant; it is unlikely that a buyer, under such conditions, would be willing to pay as much as the 25 Percent Rule computation. The Rating/Ranking Method could be used to scale the 25 Percent Rule downward.

On the other hand, there are also circumstances whereby the seller deserves and should receive more than the 25 Percent Rule (or the 25 to 33-1/3 Percent Rule). Software licensing can easily involve significant contributions by the seller in creating something more akin to a product. Further, a seller could agree to completing the software that expresses the technology (invention) complete with documentation and training manuals and activities, and provide ongoing telephone hot line support for the buyer, and perhaps, even commit to providing upgrades. Such seller-buyer relationships can approximate wholesale-retail sales: the wholesaler provides the finished product and the retailer owns and manages the storefront and the direct one-to-many retail selling environment. Under these circumstances, the appropriate split of the gain may be a 50 Percent Rule, or even more than 50 percent.

The Rating/Ranking Method used on one or more benchmark agreements, or clusters of agreements, can guide both the seller and buyer in determining a fair split of the gain. The closer the benchmark agreement is to the subject valuation, the more accurately the Rating/Ranking Method can be used. In Chapter 7, an additional tool will be presented.

SUMMARY POINTS ON THE USE OF THE 25 PERCENT RULE

Some cautions in the use of the 25 Percent Rule:

1. The appropriate number is not always 25 percent.
   The figure "25" (and 33-1/3) has emerged as a common generalization and is almost always a useful initial calculation. However, one should always consider whether more or less than 25 percent of the gain is the appropriate reward for the seller.

2. The base against which the 25 percent is applied is subject to interpretation.

   The idea of the base against which 25 percent is applied is that
   the gain (profit) should be divided 25:75 between seller and buyer.
   However, determining the "gain" requires analysis. In the cost savings approach, it is important to determine the costs of operations
   without the benefit of the subject technology, and the costs with the
   technology or as compared to the next best alternative.

3. A pro forma income statement needs to be created.

   In the case of new sales, the result of the 25 Percent Rule should
   be expressed in terms of a royalty against sales so as to create an
   auditable system. Likewise, in the case of cost savings, some conversion is necessary so that the royalty can be paid on something
   that is counted in an accounting sense and adjusts for inflation.

4. The 25 Percent Rule does not provide guidance on upfront payments.

   The 25 Percent Rule suggests how future savings or profits
   should be divided between seller and buyer. In normal circumstances there is an upfront license fee paid by the buyer. In order to
   determine what an appropriate upfront figure should be, some additional methodology is needed. In Chapter 7 some tools for doing
   this will be reviewed.

Some positive aspects of the 25 Percent Rule that make it popular and
worth using are as follows:

- It gives a feeling of fairness. Because it is based on apportioning anticipated gain, it creates a basis for considering the respective contributions of the seller and buyer.
- It is based directly on resulting benefits. The 25 Percent Rule is focused on the EBIT line in the income statement, which is an appropriate measure of the direct benefit of the subject license (subject to
  potential adjustment in allocated costs).
- It can be the basis of an early agreement. Parties beginning a negotiation can sometimes agree to agree that their negotiations will be
  governed by the 25 Percent (or some other) Rule. This can be helpful in determining mutual expectations at any early stage and in
  reaching closure.

CONCLUSION

Rules-of-thumb and specifically the 25 Percent Rule are widely used in
valuation situations. Like the previous two methods, Industry Standards
and Rating/Ranking, it requires judgement in its use and is situation specific. The next chapter continues the analysis of the income statement but

with more sophistication. Estimates of the actual cash flow of a business will be made. Then, by using certain simple accounting equations, such future cash flows will be discounted to reflect their timing and risk.

NOTES

1. Merriam Webster's Collegiate Dictionary, Tenth Edition, 1994.

2. Duke Leahy has made this point in talks he has given.

3. This discussion should not be confused with relative magnitude of investment made at these various stages. The timing and risk of investments need to be weighted along with magnitude.

4. This example leads to the same definitional ambiguities encountered in Chapter 1 as to what is "R&D." Because this discussion is intended to be only illustrative, one should not attempt to be precise on the appropriate fraction of R&D that corresponds to early stage technologies.

5. *W.L. Gore and Associates v. International Medical Prosthetics*, 16 USPQ 2nd, p. 1257.

6. William Lee Jr., "Determining Reasonable Royalty," *les Nouvelles*, September 1992, p. 24.

7. "The Basics of Licensing," *The Licensing Executives Society*, 1982.

8. Larry Evans, "Turning Patents and Technology into Money," *Licensing Law and Business Report*, Clark Boardman Company, 1979.

9. Yoshio Matsunaga, "Determining Reasonable Royalty Rates, *les Nouvelles*, December 1983.

10. Edward P. White, *Licensing—A Strategy for Profits*, Licensing Executive Society, 1990.

11. An exception occurs when there are losses from previous years being carried forward, a frequent situation with startup or early-stage companies. Although even in these cases companies prefer not to consume the tax credit any faster than necessary. There can be circumstances where such companies are positioning themselves for other investors and actually want to increase their taxable profitability because it can dramatically increase the value of the company for sale. However, as a seller, it is advisable not to base the royalty on a number which can be computed in different ways for different purposes.

12. *Business Week*, August 17, 1998, p. 89.

13. It should be noted that interest expense and extraordinary and non-operating costs should be added to the pre-tax profit to create EBIT valvues. This important refinement will be covered in the next section.

14. As noted before, to apply the 25 Percent Rule correctly, the interest expense and other non-operating or inappropriately allocated costs should be added to such pre-tax figures to produce the predicted EBIT value. Throughout this section, this adjustment will be ignored to simplify the analysis for illustration purposes.

15. The procedure followed in this example is using expert judgment to determine an appropriate benchmark population. Another approach is to include all the data available, the money losers and extraordinarily profitable cases, and deal with population as a whole. The issue boils down to this: Is the use of expert judgement improving the data set or simply biasing it? When there is reason to believe that expert judgements leads to valid insight into profitability, then there is every reason to do so. When uncertain of the situation, it may be better to be cautious and use all the available data. The decision is comparable to that faced by every interpreter of experimental data: When do I discard "outliers?"

16. Robert Morris Associates, *Annual Statement Studies*, Philadelphia PA.

7

Method Four: Discounted Cash Flow Method to Determine Valuation

INTRODUCTION

This chapter has two objectives: (1) to aid in the development of financial tools and perspectives that can be used in support of all valuation approaches, and (2) to apply such tools to the fourth valuation approach, "Discounted Cash Flow."

Underlying all of the discussion in this chapter is the issue of computing the value of money that becomes available at various times and with varying degrees of certainty. Considering one's own personal finances, when transferring control of $1,000 to an institution for five years one must consider the relative value of the $1,000 today and what will be returned, or paid back, five years hence. As a result of inflation, which appears to be a permanent fixture, it would not be reasonable to expect to get back the same $1,000 investment in five years, because by then $1,000 will be less valuable than it is today, even though the face value of the currency is unchanged. Therefore, an invester must seek a return that is large enough to cover this diminished value caused by inflation.[1]

In addition to covering the cost of inflation, there are a variety of investment options. Suppose a person could pay down a home mortgage with an interest rate on the unpaid balance of 7 percent. With such an option, one would ordinarily conclude that this hypothetical five-year investment should return at least 7 percent compounded; the basis of this perspective is simply that one has an alternative investment yielding such return.

In addition to inflation and returns on alternative investments available, one must consider the risk that either the increase above $1,000 might not occur, or that some or all of the $1,000 itself might be lost.

This kind of assessment is what buyers go through when valuing an investment opportunity in commercializing a technology. In this chapter some very simple but powerful equations will be developed that will aid such assessments. They will be used in conjunction with discounting future cash flows for valuation purposes and in combination with the 25 Percent Rule discussed in Chapter 6.

BASIC FINANCIAL CONCEPTS

The key concept required to use the Discounted Cash Flow Method is the means of converting future cash payments into their present equivalent, taking into account the time such payments would be made and the risk associated with their being paid. A very simple derivation provides useful insight.

If one lends an entity "A" dollars (such as the $1,000 example), and expects a "k" rate of return (such 7 percent), then after one year, one expects to receive the following:

Money received a year from now = A + k * A, where A is the amount given at the beginning of such year, and k the annualized rate of expected return. Using the $1,000 and 7 percent example:

$$\text{Money one year from now} = \$1,000 + 0.07 * \$1,000$$
$$= \$1,000 + \$70 = \$1,070.$$

Calculating the money due two years from now utilizes the following formula:

$$\text{Money two years from now} = \text{Money one year from now}$$
$$+ \text{ the additional benefit of another year}$$
$$= \$1070 + 0.07 \times \$1070 = \$1070 + \$74.49 = \$1144.90.$$

Expressing this equation in more general terms, we have:

$$\text{Money two years from now} = (A + k * A) + (A + k * A) * k =$$
$$A * (1 + k) + A * (1 + k) * k = A * (1 + k) * (1 + k) = A * (1 + k)^2,$$

where A is $1,000 and k is 7 percent (or 0.07 when used in equation form). So, using this formula,

$$\text{Money two years from now} =$$
$$\$1,000 * (1 + 0.07)^2 = \$1,000 * 1.1449 = \$1144.90,$$

which is the same value obtained by doing the calculation one year at a time.

Now, extending the formula to three years adds another factor of $(1 + k)$ or, in this example $(1 + 0.07)$, so the formula reads:

$$\text{Money three years from now} = A * (1 + k)^3$$
$$= \$1000 * (1.07)^3 = \$1000 * 1.22504 = \$1225.04.$$

The generalized formula then can be expressed as follows:

$B = A * (1 + k)^n$, where A is the money invested at the beginning of the analysis period, B is the money received after "n" years, and k is the expected rate of return (or return on investment, in any case always expressed as a decimal). In finance textbooks, "A" is usually presented as "PV" for "present value" (i.e., money now), and "B" as "FV" for "future value" (i.e., money returned after "n" years)[2].

As used in valuation, this same equation is re-expressed as follows:

$A = B/(1 + k)^n$, which is obtained by solving for "A."

When used in this fashion, "B" is the money in year "n" and "A" is the present value of that money for the chosen value of "k." Normally the term used for "A" is "DCF" for Discounted Cash Flow, "B" is simply the value of the money in year "n," and "k" is the risk factor or, more formally, the "risk-adjusted hurdle rate." The reason these terms are used is as follows. The normal valuation situation is that the buyer agrees to pay to the seller a prescribed amount of money at a defined date. So, rather than calculating the future value of the present $1,000, one is calculating the present value of a future payment of $1,000, as follows:

$\text{A or DCF} = B/(1 + k)^n = \$1,000/(1 + 0.07)^5 = \$1,000/1.40255 = \$712.99.$

Expressed in this way, the idea is simply that in today's dollars, the value of receiving $1,000 five years from now is $712.99 if the "k" value is 7 percent. The reason the $712.99 is called the "Discounted Cash Flow" is that one has reduced or discounted the value of the future $1,000 payment by virtue of the fact it will not be received for five years and the belief that there was a 7 percent loss of value in money each year either through inflation alone, or (more commonly) through a combination of inflation and opportunity cost, given alternatives for investing the money.

With this single simple equation, $DCF = B/(1 + k)^n$, and a computer spreadsheet software program such as Excel, one can perform some very complex financial models as will be shown in the next sections. However, before doing so an in-depth understanding of "k," more generally known as the Risk-Adjusted Hurdle Rate (RAHR) is needed.

CONSIDERATION OF THE
RISK-ADJUSTED HURDLE RATE (K OR RAHR)

In the opening paragraphs of this chapter, "k" was considered from three points of view: (1) inflation, (2) alternative available rates of return, and (3) risk of return. In the following subsections further consideration of these points of view will be developed.

Inflation and "k"

Essentially with no exceptions, money in all countries of the world for the last 100 years has suffered from inflation and is expected to continue to do so indefinitely. Inflation simply means that it will take more dollars to buy in the future what less dollars could buy today. Presently in the United States, inflation is running at approximately 3 percent. What that means with the DCF equation is as follows:

A or $DCF = B/(1.03)^n$, where B is the value of money to be received at the end of "n" years, and (A or) DCF is then the resulting equivalent value of such money in today's dollars. So, considering the example of $1,000 to be received five years hence we have:

$$DCF = \$1,000/1.03^5 = \$1,000/1.15927 = \$862.61.$$

To put this in words, providing inflation continues at 3 percent, which is by no means certain, then someone promising to pay $1,000 five years from now is really promising $862.61 in terms of value in today's dollars. (Note: we can perform the calculation the other way around and say that $1,000 today is equivalent to $1159.27 five years from now using exactly the same factor of 1.15927 obtained from calculating 1.03^5). Another term used to describe the $862.61 is "Present Value " or "Net Present Value" (or NPV) which means that today, the perceived value of $1000 five years from now is exactly $862.61. When considering a *single* future payment, DCF and NPV are exactly the same concept and equation. When dealing with multiple future payments, then the *sum* of *all* the DCF values is exactly the NPV of the opportunity; examples later in this chapter will make this clear.

A key idea with DCF and NPV is the following. If a company is considering conveying a right, such as a license, in return for a promised future payment, and the appropriate RAHR (i.e., k-value) is used, then it is assumed that the promise to pay "B" in year "n" or the present payment of the DCF are exactly equivalent. In the previous example, if it is perceived that the 3 percent value of k is appropriate, then there should be no preference between $1000 five years hence or $862.61 now. The test of this perception is a buyer offering the seller the choice of these two situations and being indifferent to the election made.

The DCF concept is crucial in licensing transactions. The buyer will experience the commercial benefit of the license over a period of years and must characterize that benefit in terms of a willingness to pay a lump sum on closing or and royalties or annual payments over time in order for the project to be worth doing. When a license is being granted for a single lump sum (so called "paid ups," a useful short-hand for "paid up licenses"), then the entire future benefit to the buyer is being consolidated into one single, "present day" number. However, even when there is no upfront license payment, the buyer typically performs a spreadsheet calculation of the prospective income including anticipated royalty payments. This will enable the buyer to determine whether the overall returns, net of royalties, will be sufficiently attractive to make the additional, needed development investments, given the perceived risk.

Alternative Available Rates of Return and "k"

The inflationary value of k, 3 percent, reflects no real gain (or loss) in value given the *assumption* that the inflation rate will remain constant over the period. Thus, $862.61 is actually identical to $1,000 five years hence, under the circumstances of 3 percent inflation. However in business circumstances, there are numerous investment opportunities that provide greater-than-inflation returns and such returns are used to calculate the value of money for various times and risks.

One standard value of k used is the interest rate on a Treasury Bill (commonly termed a "T-Bill"), which is a short-term debt instrument used by the U.S. Government to fund its deficit and debt. Historically, the rate of return on a T-Bill has been approximately 7 percent, although in 1998 the rate was approximately 5 percent. This value is generally considered the "risk-free" rate of return that every owner of cash would expect. Put in other terms, if one had $1,000 that could be committed for five years, a risk-free investment would be a T-Bill at 7 percent (using the historic value) which would yield the following result:

$$B = \$1,000 * (1.07)^5 = \$1402.55.$$

That is, an owner of $1,000 today would expect to receive no less than $1402.55 in five years. Of course nothing in life is "risk free" or "guaranteed"; however, a T-Bill is backed by the full faith of the U.S. Government so barring default of the United States, the T-Bill will be paid at the face value return rate (7 percent in this example). Of all investments available, T-Bills are considered to be the most secure (one would be tempted to say a "gold standard," however, the United States no longer bases the value of its currency on the value of gold). Another investment opportunity that may be considered equally secure to a T-Bill is the repayment of existing debt; assuming one is able to do so without penalties for early repayment and ignoring any tax benefit associated with debt payment, then the investment value of such payment is exactly the interest rate of the debt being paid off.

Staying with the T-Bill example, a payment of $1,000 promised five years in the future would be considered to have the present value as follows:

$$DCF = \$1,000/(1.07)^5 = \$712.99.$$

Remember that earlier, the present value (DCF) of $1,000 five years hence was deemed to be $862.61, for a k of 3 percent, and here, with a k of 7 percent it is deemed to be $712.99, or $149.62 less. Why would $1,000 five years from now be worth $149.62 less than the previous inflation-based calculation? The answer is because there exists a means of investing money risk-free at a k of 7 percent, so that it is possible to produce $1,000 in face value five years hence by the present investment of $712.99, not $862.61. In other words, the larger the investment opportunity that's available, expressed in terms of k, the smaller the amount of money required today to produce specified value in the future (such as the $1,000 in these examples).

Consider another investment opportunity. Corporations borrow money just like the U.S. Government and, like the government, they issue bonds that pay interest. However, because the guarantee of payment is the promise of the issuing corporation secured only by corporate assets, investors correctly perceive a higher risk. This then requires corporations to pay a higher rate of return than a T-Bill in order to persuade investors to take that risk and lend the corporation money. The premium that corporations must pay in order to attract investment depends upon the financial soundness of the corporation. Historically, when T-Bills have yielded 7 percent, corporate bonds have yielded 12 to 18 percent, or a premium of 5 to 11 percentage points above the T-Bill rate. The lower rates are obtained by "blue chip" companies such as IBM and Coca Cola and the higher rates, sometimes called "junk bonds," are paid by companies in high-risk situations and even sometimes in bankruptcy. In 1998, a period of low inflation and low perceived overall economic risk, corporations with strong credit ratings offered what is known as "investment grade" bond instruments in the sub-10 percent range. When one considers the total rate of return a corporation must pay back to its investors, it is necessary to account for the bond (or debt) capital and the stock (or equity) capital—equity investors rightly expect a higher rate of return because they own a less secure right of return than a bond-holder. Accordingly, the weighted average cost of capital is typically higher than 10 percent, depending upon overall rate of inflation, the perceived risk of the corporation's bonds, and the proportion of debt and equity funding the corporation's operations.

Consideration of all these factors is beyond the scope of this book. For purposes of illustration, a value of 15 percent will be used as this has been a reasonable figure during higher inflation periods. With this value, the present value of $1,000 five years hence is as follows:

$$DCF = 1,000/(1.15)^5 = $1,000/2.0133 = $497.18.$$

Compared to the DCF value of $712.99 obtained for a T-Bill rate of 7 percent, this calculation shows that from the point of view of an investor in debt used by corporations, the present value of $1,000 five years hence is $215.81 less (or $497.18).

Essentially, the value of $1,000 five years from now is, to an extent, in the eye of the beholder, who has available various other means of converting money today to money tomorrow. The higher the available alternative returns (k value), the lower any fixed future amount appears to be worth today. In mathematical terms, the DCF of a fixed, future sum declines with increasing k.

Although this seems to trouble people, the rationale behind it is very straightforward. If George is a business person who considers investments solely in T-Bills (at a k of 7 percent), then George will correlate money now with any future year by the factor $(1 + 0.07)^n$ whether George is borrowing or lending. This factor is simply the way of creating monetary equivalence between now and year "n" from the point of view of George, who does business buying and selling T-Bill investments at 7 percent returns. If Sally is a business person who considers investments solely in corporate bonds at a k of 15 percent, then Sally correlates money at different time periods with the factor $(1 + 0.15)^n$ simply because to Sally that is how future money "looks" today. Because licenses typically involve a business either on the selling or buying side (or both) a k value of 15 percent, plus or minus a few points, is typically the way money is viewed by the parties. Stated more accurately, corporate borrowings are commonly 5 to 11 points above T-Bills, so in the mid-1998 economy this means typical rates are in the 12 to 13 percent range although historic values were more like 15 percent.

Risk-Adjusted Hurdle Rates and Corporate Rates of Borrowing

The previous consideration of corporate rates of return which yielded DCF factors of $(1 + 0.15)^n$ is derived from what corporations have to pay investors for the use of their money. It must, therefore, represent the floor of the overall rate of return of a corporation if it is to be able to pay back all its lenders in the future. However, when an individual project is considered, the risk of that project is normally higher than the overall risk and return of the corporation (15 percent in this example).

Why is this the case? The answer turns out to be essentially the same reason that a mutual fund is less risky than an individual stock. The corporation borrowing money invests it in many different kinds of projects: energy efficiency to reduce utility bills, opening a new sales office overseas to increase sales, building another plant to increase production volumes (and consequently revenues) based upon anticipated higher demand, and R&D projects that will produce entire new products that will be sold at a profit. A large company could easily have thousands of investments of all types being made in any given year. Even though each of these investments might have been made with the expectation that they would succeed in returning an investment of 15 percent, it can be expected that some of these investments will turn out to perform more poorly than expected—in some cases returning 10 percent, in others perhaps 5 percent, in others 0 percent (i.e., zero net gain), and in still others the entire investment will be lost (i.e., a 100 percent loss). If money is lent to a corporation at the individual *project* level, then the risk of the investment is higher than if the money is lent to the *corporation* to be applied to all its projects, because in investment of diversified projects it is highly unlikely that all of them will turn out poorly. Another way to look at this is as follows: If one wants to make a consevative $1,000 investment in corporate bonds, one could invest $100 in each of 10 different companies all in different industries rather than invest all the money in just one company.

However, in a technology licensing situation, a corporation would logically conclude that the overall risk of creating a profitable business is higher than, say, the risk of investing in insulation to reduce its utility costs. Accordingly, corporations typically consider each investment as belonging to a risk category and require higher risk investments to exhibit higher rates of return. For the purposes of illustration, consider the case where a corporation has concluded that investments in R&D require a RAHR (k value) of 30 percent. Therefore we have:

$$DCF = \$1,000/(1.30)^5 = \$1,000/3.71293 = \$269.33.$$

In other words, for a k of 30 percent, an upfront investment of $269.33 must show a return of $1,000 in five years. Conversely, a return of $1,000 in five years based upon an investment in projects that can be counted on to have a RAHR of 30 percent should be thought to have a present value of only $269.33, because the risk of bad things happening over the next five years is relatively high in comparison to T-Bills or typical corporate bonds.

Summarizing Four Points of View of "k" (RAHR)

The values calculated in the preceding sections are summarized in Exhibit 7.1 below.

The interpretation of the values shown in the third column is as follows: $1,000 five years hence under the corresponding risk perspective (k-value) should be considered to be worth the shown amounts in today's dollars. For this reason, when expressed in this way, the k-value is known as the discount rate because it is used to discount future payments.

In the remainder of this chapter, extensive use will be made of this DCF calculation using the $(1 + k)^n$ factor. However, it is first important to consider risk issues in more detail.

FURTHER CONSIDERATIONS OF RISK

The present value of future payments, known as the DCF, is dependent on three factors: the timing, magnitude, and risk of such future payments. In the DCF equation, the timing shows up in "n," which is normally the number of years from the present for such future payment, the magnitude is value in the numerator (symbolized by "B" or "FV"), and the risk is embodied in "k."

Getting back to the *TR R A DE*™ acronym where, "*TR*" designated Technology Rights, and "*DE*" Deal Economics or Equity, now we are prepared to consider formally "R^k" as "Risk expressed in k." Critical to translating Technology Rights into Deal Economics is an understanding and judgment of the risk associated with converting the technology rights conveyed into a stream of profits from which royalties can be justified and paid.

Exhibit 7.1 The Effect of Various Points of View of Discounted Cash Flow

Point of View	k-value	DCF of $1,000 in 5 years
Inflation	3%	$862.61
T-Bill	7%	$712.99
Corporation	15%	$497.18
R&D Project	30%	$269.33

In the eyes of the seller, especially in the eyes of the inventor-seller, the risk associated with obtaining a profit from such rights can appear to be very low. This can be attributed to two primary factors. First, the seller has an intimate understanding of all the difficulties that have been overcome in bringing the technology to its present state (and in many cases it has been a multi-year or even decade-long trail of tears interspersed with transitory joys). Secondly, it is human nature to underestimate the complexities that await the recipient of one's work product. This is particularly true in high technology contexts because the science embodied in the "TR" can be extraordinarily complicated while the seller's expectations of the buyer amounts to "all they have to do is make it and sell it." Although making and selling may not involve differential equations (although sometimes it does), even simple process steps involve risk

Buyers who are too optimistic in valuing technology quickly find themselves providing very low returns on investment and unable to attract capital to make subsequent investments. The purest example of such a situation is the venture capital industry. Venture capitalists, commonly known as VCs, raise money in "funds" from high net worth investors and from high-risk segments of large, traditional investment pools. Typically such "funds" are raised during a recruiting period. If a VC firm is raising "Fund I," then, as the joke goes, their track record is in front of them. Potential investors would examine the performance history of the individuals raising the money and the business model for its subsequent investment and reach a judgment on whether to take the risk. When a VC firm is raising "Fund IV," investors tend to look at the financial performances of "Fund I" and "Fund II" and some preliminary results from "Fund III." From such examples, investors make a judgment on what kind of return might be expected from this new fund and how such return compares with all the other VC firms also seeking investors. Although the volatility of returns in the VC industry is high, investors appear to expect a return of at least 20 percent from the portfolio of investments made by any given fund. In some recent cases, there are funds that have returned more than 40 percent.

In this context, when VCs look at startup deals, they will need to see projected returns on their investment well above 20 or 30 percent because (1) there are VC management costs which dilute the returns to their fund-investors, and (2) it will happen that not all their investments will pan out as planned. (There is a rule of thumb in the risk capital industry that says: "all surprises are negative." It's a pessimistic outlook, but people who have been managing such investments over many years attest to its general validity.) Accordingly, when a technology seller is negotiating a license with a VC buyer, the VC may required a RAHR of 50 percent or more in order to attract their investment. Using such values on the example of $1000 in five years results in the following expression:

$$DCF = 1000/1.5^5 = \$131.69$$

Compared to the DCF of inflation ($862.61) or of a T-Bill ($712.99) or even of a corporate bond ($497.18), this $131.69 seems like an extra-ordinary low valuation for the promise of $1,000 five years hence. However, what a VC is likely to claim is that, based upon (often painful) experience, using a RAHR threshold of 50 percent is needed to produce investment portfolio returns which, after VC costs, are ade-quate to induce investors to make such risky investments. There is an-other factor at work in such high-risk situations: there is almost zero probability that any investment of $131.69 will yield $1000 in five years. Unlike the T-Bill example, or even the corporate bond example, what will happen is unknowable to any human. The technology-based startup could easily fail completely consuming all the original invest-ment (in this example, $131.69). There is some chance that it could be wildly successful producing a 40-times return (known in the art as a "40-bagger"); Microsoft, for example, is presently a 400-bagger from its initial public offering (IPO) date to mid-1998. The above calculation yielding a DCF of $131.69 is a 7.6-bagger in five years (1000/131.69 = 7.594). Risk capital investors expect that a reasonable number of their startup investments will be 10-baggers and more. Given that some in-vestments will be totally lost, some must be 10 or more baggers in order to yield, on average, an attractive return.

Exhibit 7.2 presents, in the author's experience, how various cate-gories of investment/licensing opportunities are viewed by technology investors. These RAHR estimates are very approximate values based upon buyers' general perceptions of the required rate of return, or the associated risk, of commercializing the technology. These values are not hard and fast numbers, but reflect commonly-used values. This in-formation can be useful in negotiations between buyers and sellers to share perceptions of risk and the associated RAHR. Such discussions can help parties understand why they look at the same opportunity and see different values and, in some cases, may aid by removing some of the uncertainty and lowering the RAHR, thereby increasing the per-ceived value to the buyer. This subject will be discussed in more detail Chapter 11.

A 1987 case study on hurdle rates used by venture capitalists provides another persepective.[3] Looking at the opportunity to invest from startup to IPO, these authors suggest the following RAHR values at "seed stage" (raw idea, pre-business plan) > 80 percent, "startup" 50 to 70 per-cent, "first stage" (existing company but with limited or no customers) 40 to 60 percent, "second stage" (to fuel growth) 30 to 40 percent, "bridge" financing (to carry to an IPO) 20 to 35 percent. It should be re-membered that these rates reflect the added risk of creating a startup

Exhibit 7.2   Approximate Values of Risk-Adjusted Hurdle Rate Used in License Negotiations

Characterization of Risk	Approximate RAHR (k value)
"Risk-free," such as building a duplicate plant to make more of a currently made and sold product in response to presently high demand.	Approximates the corporate rate of borrowing, which can be in the range of 10–18%
Very low risk, such as incorporating a new but well-understood technology into making a product presently made and sold in response to existing demand.	15–20%; discernibly above the corporation's goals for return on investment to its shareholders
Low risk, such as making a product with new features using well-understood technology into a presently served and understood customer segment with evidence of demand for such features.	20–30%
Moderate risk, such as making a new product using well-understood technology to a customer segment presently served by other products made by the corporation and with evidence of demand for such a new product.	25–35%
High risk, such as making a new product using a not well-understood technology and marketing it to an existing segment or a well-understood technology to a new market segment.	30–40%
Very high risk, such as making a new product with new technology to a new segment.	35–45%
Extremely high risk (sometimes known as "wildcatting," borrowing an expression from the oil exploration industry), such as creating a startup company to go into the business of making a product not presently sold or even known to exist using unproven technologies.	50–70% or even higher

company, which approximately corresponds to the this situation for the bottom two entries of Exhibit 7.2.

The reader is cautioned that the phrase characterizing each risk category in Exhibit 7.2 is a simplification for purposes of illustration of what must be a case-specific analysis. There are many dimensions to risk; the characterization of Exhibit 7.2 is focused on just two: the technology risk and the target market segment. A buyer could ascribe a low k value to a potential opportunity because it perceives that the risk of *not* adopting the subject technology or entering the target market is significant relative to the long term well being of the company. In the other situations, the buyer may possess inside information from known customers on the high value already placed on potential products or have valuable insights as to how the technology can be scaled commercially.

A summary of the DCF values as a function of RAHR is portrayed in Exhibit 7.3. The present value of $1,000 five years hence is highly dependent on the perceived risk of the investment. Unless one understands how the buyer or seller perceives the risk it is not possible to appreciate how they would create a DCF.

Expressing the same concepts in terms of future returns for a given present investment, we use the following form of the DCF equation:

$$B = A * (1 + k)^n,$$

where A is the present investment (at time equal to zero), and B is the future value; when this equation was solved for "A" previously, "A" was replaced by the more commonly known term: DCF.

By expressing the equation as a ratio of B/A, we obtain a very useful form because it is independent of any particular dollar (or currency) value:

$$B/A = (1 + k)^n.$$

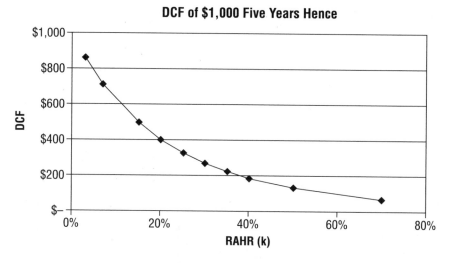

Exhibit 7.3   Discounted Cash Flow (DCF) of a Future Payment of $1,000 Five Years Hence as a Function of the Risk-Adjusted Hurdle Rate (k)

When the values substituted for k and n result in a value equal to or greater than 2, the result is sometimes referred to by the "bagger" term introduced above. So, for instance, a "5 bagger" (that is, a five times return) in five years is obtained for a k-value of 38 percent (i.e., 0.38), namely:

$$B/A = (1 + 0.38)^5 = 5.0$$

When used in this way, the k-value or RAHR can be thought of as that rate of return, given the risks of the specific valuation, required to attract investors to contribute "A" with the reasonable potential, but not guarantee, of obtaining "B" in "n" years. Risk capital investors, VCs and some corporate managers think in terms of "payback" (B/A ratio as used here) or, more colloquially, "baggers." Exhibit 7.4 shows several such "payback" or "bagger" curves.

Exhibit 7.4 shows an important interaction between "n" and "k." For short periods of time, such as three years, the impact of different values of "k" is small. If one is debating whether the appropriate "k" value for a particular investment is 20 percent or 30 percent, the impact on B/A is small: 1.73 for 20 percent, versus 2.20 for 30 percent, an increase of a little more than 25 percent. However, if one is doing this same comparison for a period of seven years, then the impact on

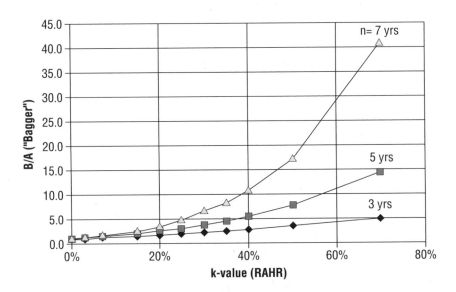

Exhibit 7.4   Effect of k-Value and Time (n) on the Ratio (Known as "Payback" or "Bagger") of the Return (B, the Future Value) to the Investment (A, the Present Value)

B/A is large: 3.58 for 20 percent, versus 6.27 for 30 percent. The 30 percent value of "k" results in a 75 percent larger value of B/A than the 20 percent value of "k." What this means is simply this: when dealing with short investment periods, the uncertainty in appropriate "k" is not highly significant in determining the value of an opportunity, but when the investment periods are longer, say seven years or more, then the value of "k" plays a critical role in the perception of value. This observation is what makes the prediction and assessment of returns associated with inherently long term projects, such as a new pharmaceutical, a challenge.

AN EXAMPLE CASH FLOW PROJECTION FROM A LICENSE

The previous sections of this chapter considered simple situations; the present value of one future payment, or the converse of one future payment derived from a single initial investment. One simple formula was used to make such present-to-future (or vice versa) dollar conversions requiring only two other factors: the time to the future payment (n, usually expressed in years) and the RAHR or k-value.

The bad news is that such single-payment calculations are not sufficient to treat most real-life license valuations. The good news is that with the one trusty equation $\{DCF = B/(1 + k)^n \text{ or } B/A = (1 + k)^n\}$ and spreadsheet software such as Microsoft Excel or Lotus 1-2-3, it is relatively simple to deal with as many future payments and upfront investments as necessary.

First, let us consider why multiple payment calculations are necessary. In a typical licensing transaction, the buyer performs (and the seller *should* perform) a calculation of the future economic benefit of obtaining the subject license agreement. The buyer does this by creating a prospective income statement, known as a *pro forma* because it is being projected into the future and is, by necessity, somewhere between a wild guess and a well-founded and reasonable estimate. The *pro forma* income statement provides a year-by-year cash stream to the buyer over the projected life of the technology being licensed. In order for the buyer to rationalize the present value of such future cash flows, it is necessary to use a RAHR. Further, to compute a royalty payment to the seller, such payment must be reflected as a year-by-year cost of business in the *pro forma*.

The way this is handled is to compute each year's revenues in that year's dollars, for example, the calculation for the year 2005 estimates the revenues for 2005 in 2005 dollars and all the costs in 2005 dollars so the net cash produced by the business also is expressed in 2005 dollars. Then, in a separate calculation, those 2005 net cash dollars are converted back to current dollars using the DCF equation with the appropriate k-value and "n." Finally, all the DCF values for each year are then added resulting in the total present value of the future benefit of commercializing the technology. As part of such calculation the investment costs in the early years need to be considered; any upfront or progress payments to the seller are also included as part of such costs. When all the projected cost outlays and revenues have been estimated and converted to present value (that is, all the DCF values positive and negative have been added), then the result is known as the "NPV" for Net Present Value. Incidentally, there are embedded NPV formulas in spreadsheet programs that can perform this calculation in one step, although this is not recommended because it is useful to see the year-by-year DCF values and, computationally, the use of computer spread sheets make it easy to perform.

Shown in Exhibit 7.5 is a hypothetical example of cash flows that would be experienced by a buyer as a result of commercializing a licensed technology. This exhibit assumes that the buyer invests a total of $10 million by the end of the sixth year from the date of the license, and then receives a total of $136 million from the end of the seventh year through the end of the twentieth year, netting $126 million (136 less 10). The $10 million invested is assumed to be: $1 million in one lump sum at the end of Year 1, $1 million at the end of Year 2, $2 million at the end of Year 3, and so forth. Similarly, incoming net cash flow begins at the end of Year 7 in the amount of $1 million, then at the end of Year 8 an additional $4 million comes in, and so on.

Each year's cash flow can then be discounted by the value of "k" to determine the *present* value of such future payment. The first row of Exhibit 7.5 considers the simple case of k = 0%, for which the Discounted Cash Flow (DCF) is identical to the Gross Cash Flow (GCF). Such an example would correspond to a world of zero inflation where no alternative investment opportunities were available that could produce a greater than zero return, clearly an impractical example.

The second row of Exhibit 7.5 shows the effects of k = 7%. This assumes world money decreases in value by 7 percent per year, and no alternative investments greater than a 7 percent return exist. As discussed previously, 7 percent corresponds to the historic level of a risk-free return such as a T-Bill. From such a perspective, the *present* value of the $10 million in net cash flow projected for the seventeenth year is worth only $3.2 million. The $10 million in net cash flow projected for the ninth year is worth more, namely $5.4 million. The cash outflows projected at the end of years one through six are treated in exactly the same way, so, the $1 million spent at the end of Year 2 is only $900K in present dollars, and the like amount spent at the end of Year 6 is even less at $700K. The net effect of this perspective is that the buyer will enjoy the net benefit of $49 million in present dollars, taking all the projected DCF inflows and subtracting all the DCF outflows. This $49 million is known as the NPV, for the Net Present Value, which is simply obtained by adding all the DCFs.

Exhibit 7.5   Discount Cash Flows as a Function of Year & k

Year	k	1	2	3	4	5	6	7	8	9	10	11	12	13	14	15	16	17	18	19	20	Net
GCF	0%	–1	–1	–2	–3	–2	–1	1	5	10	13	14	15	15	15	14	13	10	8	3	0	126
DCF(k)	7%	–0.9	–0.9	–1.6	–2.3	–1.4	–0.7	0.6	2.9	5.4	6.6	6.7	6.7	6.2	5.8	5.1	4.4	3.2	2.4	0.8	0	49.0
DCF(k)	15%	–0.9	–0.8	–1.3	–1.7	–1.0	–0.4	0.4	1.6	2.8	3.2	3.0	2.8	2.4	2.1	1.7	1.4	0.9	0.6	0.2	0	17.3
DCF(k)	30%	–0.8	–0.6	–0.9	–1.1	–0.5	–0.2	0.2	0.6	0.9	0.9	0.8	0.6	0.5	0.4	0.3	0.2	0.1	0.1	0.0	0	1.568

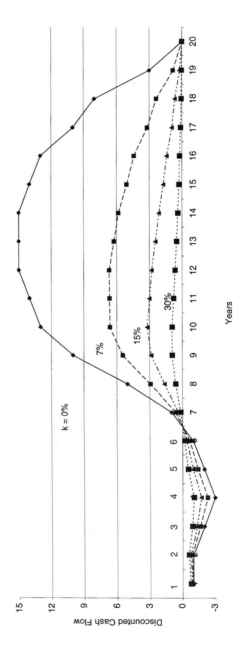

Discount Cash Flows as a Function of Year & k

The third and fourth rows of Exhibit 7.5 show the effect of higher values of k: 15 percent and 30 percent. Such values reduce the NPV of the opportunity from $49 million (for k = 7%) to $17.3 million (k = 15%) and to $1.6 million (k = 30%). Because the projected cash inflows occur far into the future, peak GCF does not occur until the end of the twelfth year, and the discounting effect of larger values of "k" is huge. From the buyer's perspective, the cash outflows occur early and are certain, whereas the inflows occur late and are not at all certain. Assuming this value of k is appropriate to the opportunity (i.e., 30%), then the seller is entitled to 100 percent of the $1.6 million. From the seller's perspective such a small figure does not seem fair given that the buyer should have $126 million in the bank after the project is completed. The buyer's response to the seller is likely to be, "You, instead receive all your return in the form of royalties paid on the inflow GCFs starting at the end of Year 8 and continuing through the end of Year 19."

Computing Royalties from a Rate of Return Perspective Using DCF

There are several perspectives possible on the splitting of the NPV resulting from the use of the DCF Method. The most straightforward perspective is that the buyer and seller reach a common understanding of the rewards, the timing of such rewards, and the overall risk of receiving the rewards as would occur if the parties agreed on a DCF table shown in Exhibit 7.5 with an appropriate "k" value. Continuing with this example, if it is assumed that the buyer contends and the seller agrees that the appropriate "k" value to be used to determine the buyer's justifiable return is 30 percent, then *all* of the $1.6 million NPV shown in Exhibit 7.5 (resulting from using k = 30 percent) belongs to the *seller*. This is built on the assumption that the buyer concluded that it is entitled to all the benefits of a Risk Adjusted Hurdle Rate of 30 percent. Exhibit 7.6 is based on the model given in Exhibit 7.5. Starting just below the row of "years," the first row is simply a repeat of the

Exhibit 7.6   Value of the Opportunity Shown in Exhibit 7.5 as Apportioned Between Buyer and Seller (Assuming k = 30%)

Year		1	2	3	4	5	6	7	8	9
GCF		−1	−1	−2	−3	−2	−1	1	5	10
Royalty	28% (on basis of GCF)							0.28	1.39	2.78
Net GCF		−1	−1	−2	−3	−2	−1	0.72	3.61	7.22
DCF Buyer	30%	−0.8	−0.6	−0.9	−1.1	−0.5	−0.2	0.1	0.4	0.7
DCF Seller	30%							0.04	0.17	0.26

Gross Cash Flows (GCF) paid to the buyer by its customers for sale of products made by the licensed technology. The next row is a calculation of the GCF amounts to be paid by the buyer to the seller as a royalty. The way this royalty payment is calculated involves an iteration between the second, third, and fourth rows. The third row shows the GCF retained by the buyer after payment of the royalty to the seller. The fourth row shows the DCF of such net buyer's GCF using k = 30% as the hurdle rate, which in this instance can be thought of as the buyer's rate of return.

Because the underlying assumption of this example is that the buyer has proposed that it is entitled to a 30 percent return on investment and the seller has agreed, the fourth row discounts the net GCF of the third row. The iteration takes place by adjusting the royalty rate used in the second row so that the sum of the DCFs of the fourth row, i.e., the NPV to the buyer, is identically zero. Such iteration can be done by hand by substituting trial values of the royalty rate until the NPV becomes zero or, much more easily, by using the "Goal Seek" function of the spreadsheet usually available under the "Tools" menu option.

What this example shows is that for a royalty of 28 percent on the basis of the GCF received by the buyer, the net cash flow retained by the buyer produces a return on investment of 30 percent. The buyer will net (if the plan comes true) in GCF terms $88.16 million, $10 million in investment, offset by $98.16 million in cash inflows. Using k = 30% for all the gross outflows and inflows results in an NPV of $0, which means the seller obtained 30% return on investment (ROI). The seller will receive a total of $37.84 million in royalties paid out in Years 7 through 19 as shown. If the seller's perspective of the risk of such payments is also reflected by k = 30%, then the seller perceives the present value of these royalties as shown in the fifth row: namely $1.6 million, just as was determined previously. Put another way, if the buyer counter-proposes to the seller that instead of paying royalties yearly and a single, upfront payment is made, the seller should be entirely indifferent as to whether it re-

Exhibit 7.6 *(Continued)*

10	11	12	13	14	15	16	17	18	19	20	Sum
13	14	15	15	15	14	13	10	8	3	0	126
3.62	3.90	4.17	4.17	4.17	3.90	3.62	2.78	2.23	0.83	0	37.84
9.38	10.10	10.83	10.83	10.83	10.10	9.38	7.22	5.77	2.17	0	88.16
0.7	0.6	0.5	0.4	0.3	0.2	0.1	0.1	0.1	0.0	0.0	0.00
0.26	0.22	0.18	0.14	0.11	0.08	0.05	0.03	0.02	0.01	0.00	1.57

ceives the royalties shown over time or the $1.57 million upfront payment (providing the seller's perception of k is 30%).[4]

The royalty rate in this example is based upon the gross cash flows received by the buyer. Such cash flows result from taking the sales revenues and subtracting all the seller's costs in producing and selling the products. Royalties should normally be based upon sales not on cash flows; therefore in any agreement between the parties, there would need to be a separate calculation that would convert the royalty rate from 28 percent based on cash flows to an amount based on sales. Although this will be discussed later in this chapter, for illustration purposes let it be assumed that gross cash flows of this example were 20 percent of the sales: that is, 80 percent of the total sales dollars were consumed in expenses, taxes, and the like. This means that a royalty of 28 percent based upon cash flows that comprise 20 percent of sales revenues is exactly equivalent to a royalty of 5.6 percent based on such sales revenues (which is normally how royalties are expressed). A quick demonstration makes this clear:

Sales Revenues = 100
Cash Flow = 20 (for the assumption that cash flow
is 20% of sales revenues)
28% royalty based on Cash Flow = 5.6%
Alternatively, a 5.6% royalty based on sales also = 5.6.

Exhibit 7.7   The Effect of a $100K Upfront License Fee on Example Given in Exhibit 7.6

Year	0	1	2	3	4	5	6	7	8	9
GCF	−0.1	−1	−1	−2	−3	−2	−1	1	5	10
Royalty	26% (on basis of GCF)							0.26	1.30	2.61
Net GCF	−0.1	−1	−1	−2	−3	−2	−1	0.74	3.70	7.39
DCF Buyer	−30% −0.1	−0.8	−0.6	−0.9	−1.1	−0.5	−0.2	0.1	0.5	0.7
DCF Seller	30% 0.1							0.04	0.16	0.25

Exhibit 7.8   Using the 25 Percent Rule to Apportion the NPV (k of 30%)

Year	0	1	2	3	4	5	6	7	8	9
GCF	−0.1	−1	−1	−2	−3	−2	−1	1	5	10
Royalty	5% (on basis of GCF)							0.05	0.26	0.51
Net GCF	−0.1	−1	−1	−2	−3	−2	−1	0.95	4.74	9.49
DCF Buyer	30% −0.1	−0.8	−0.6	−0.9	−1.1	−0.5	−0.2	0.2	0.6	0.9
DCF Seller	30% 0.1							0.01	0.03	0.05

Incorporating Upfront and Royalty Payments in a DCF Model

Other variations of royalty payments can be similarly calculated. For example, suppose the parties agree that the seller should receive an upfront license fee of $100K. Now the costs to the buyer would increase by $100K at time zero (at the beginning of Year 1) and so the royalty payments would have to be reduced in order to provide the same 30 percent return on investment to the buyer. This case is shown in Exhibit 7.7.

In the first row (below the "Year" row) the column for "Year 0" (representing the date of execution of the agreement) a $100K expense to the buyer is shown in rows 2, 3, and 4, and a $100K revenue to the seller appears in row 5. The royalties paid by the buyer will need to be reduced in order to provide the same 30 percent ROI due to of the initial $100K payment. Performing the "Goal Seek" function results in a royalty of 26 percent corresponding to the cash flow basis, which is two points less than the 28 percent for the no-upfront payment case in Exhibit 7.6. As shown in row 5, the NPV of the seller is also unchanged in this example because both the seller and buyer are using the same "k" value of 30 percent to calculate DCFs.

Computing Royalties from a 25 Percent Rule Perspective

In Exhibits 7.6 and 7.7, it was assumed that the value of k = 30% provided a fair return to the buyer so that all the excess DCFs, i.e., the NPV, was

Exhibit 7.7 *(Continued)*

10	11	12	13	14	15	16	17	18	19	20	Sum
13	14	15	15	15	14	13	10	8	3	0	126
3.39	3.65	3.91	3.91	3.91	3.65	3.39	2.61	2.08	0.78	0	35.43
9.61	10.35	11.09	11.09	11.09	10.35	9.61	7.39	5.92	2.22	0	90.47
0.7	0.6	0.5	0.4	0.3	0.2	0.1	0.1	0.1	0.0	0.0	0.00
0.25	0.20	0.17	0.13	0.10	0.07	0.05	0.03	0.02	0.01	0.00	1.57

Exhibit 7.8 *(Continued)*

10	11	12	13	14	15	16	17	18	19	20	Sum
13	14	15	15	15	14	13	10	8	3	0	126
0.66	0.72	0.77	0.77	0.77	0.72	0.66	0.51	0.41	0.15	0	6.95
12.34	13.28	14.23	14.23	14.23	13.28	12.34	9.49	7.59	2.85	0	111.95
0.9	0.7	0.6	0.5	0.4	0.3	0.2	0.1	0.1	0.0	0.0	1.18
0.05	0.04	0.03	0.03	0.02	0.01	0.01	0.01	0.00	0.00	0.00	0.39

the value attributable to the seller and that this value could then be provided in royalties only, in an upfront payment only, or in an infinite number of lump sum payments and royalties as long as NPV for the *buyer* was $0 with a k of 30 percent.

Another perspective on this approach is that the value of k = 30% (or whatever final value is deemed appropriate) be "neutral" to the buyer, and not reflective of an adequate rate of return. In other words, the buyer could argue that the 30 percent is simply that value of "k" for which the project is just worth doing, and if the buyer does not obtain the benefit of some or most of the excess NPV, then the buyer will not seek the license or undertake the project.

From this perspective the 30 percent is not an adequate rate of return but is the appropriate way of creating a neutral consideration of all future cash flows in the context of the overall perceived risks. From this situation, the logical follow-up issue is how the NPV above 30 percent, namely the $1.57 million in this example (Exhibits 7.5 through 7.7) should be divided between the parties. Here is where the Rule of Thumb Method can be combined with the DCF Method: the $1.57 million could be divided using a 25 percent split or any other split factor.[5] Using the 25 percent split, this would say that the seller's share of the $1.57 million NPV is $393K (25 percent) and the buyer's share is $1.18 million (75 percent). From this perspective, the royalty rates can be recalculated as shown in Exhibit 7.8. Using the "Goal Seek" function and setting the out-

Exhibit 7.9   Same Net Outcome of Two Perspectives of k-Value

Year		0	1	2	3	4	5	6	7	8	9
Allocated Return Perspective: 30% Return on Investment to the Buyer											
GCF		−0.1	−1	−1	−2	−3	−2	−1	1	5	10
Royalty	26% (on basis of GCF)								0.26	1.30	2.61
Net GCF		−0.1	−1	−1	−2	−3	−2	−1	0.74	3.70	7.39
DCF Buyer	30%	−0.1	−0.8	−0.6	−0.9	−1.1	−0.5	−0.2	0.1	0.5	0.7
DCF Seller	30%	0.1							0.04	0.16	0.25
Risk-Adjusted Perspective: 25% Rule Split of NPV between Buyer and Seller											
GCF		−0.1	−1	−1	−2	−3	−2	−1	1	5	10
Royalty	26.0% (on basis of GCF)								0.26	1.30	2.60
Net GCF		−0.1	−1	−1	−2	−3	−2	−1	0.74	3.70	7.40
DCF Buyer	20.4%	−0.1	−0.8	−0.7	−1.1	−1.4	−0.8	−0.3	0.2	0.8	1.4
DCF Seller	30.0%	0.1							0.04	0.16	0.25

come sought to 1.18 results in a royalty of 5 percent on the basis of cash flows in addition to the $100K upfront payment.

To recap, there are two basic perspectives that can be employed in using the DCF Method to provide a valuation:

- A "k" value that includes the effect of risk *and* justifiable returns (given the contributions of the buyer to achieving commercialization) so that the resulting NPV belongs to the seller either in the form of royalties only, upfront only, or a combination, or
- A "k" value that provides only the appropriate present values of all the future benefits, given the risk of the project, so that the resulting NPV should then be *divided* between the buyer and seller in a way that reflects their comparative contributions.

The first perspective, sometimes referred to as an "allocated return" approach, can be grounded by analyzing what the buyer and comparable companies can expect to receive as a return for the deployment of the particular assets involved in the license. For instance, the buyer could deploy numerous kinds of assets such as cash, plant and equipment, design engineers, proprietary design tools and approaches, trademarks, patents and trade secrets, and so forth. For each asset so deployed, one could perform an analysis of the magnitude of such asset and the appropriate market-based rate of return. The outcome of such analysis would be a weighted-average, market-based rate of return. Done in this way, the

Exhibit 7.9 *(Continued)*

10	11	12	13	14	15	16	17	18	19	20	Sum
13	14	15	15	15	14	13	10	8	3	0	126
3.39	3.65	3.91	3.91	3.91	3.65	3.39	2.61	2.08	0.78	0	35.43
9.61	10.35	11.09	11.09	11.09	10.35	9.61	7.39	5.92	2.22	0	90.47
0.7	0.6	0.5	0.4	0.3	0.2	0.1	0.1	0.1	0.0	0.0	0.00
0.25	0.20	0.17	0.13	0.10	0.07	0.05	0.03	0.02	0.01	0.00	1.57
13	14	15	15	15	14	13	10	8	3	0	126
3.38	3.64	3.90	3.90	3.90	3.64	3.38	2.60	2.08	0.78	0	35.36
9.62	10.36	11.10	11.10	11.10	10.36	9.62	7.40	5.92	2.22	0	90.54
1.5	1.3	1.2	1.0	0.8	0.6	0.5	0.3	0.2	0.1	0.0	4.70
0.25	0.20	0.17	0.13	0.10	0.07	0.05	0.03	0.02	0.01	0.00	1.57
											1.57
											0.00

logic of the process would then say that all of the excess NPV should belong to the seller.

Thus, if one used such grounded methodologies for each of the two perspectives, one would expect the resulting value to be the same. That is, if one performed a reasonable "allocated return" analysis and found k = 30%, so that the NPV of $1.57 million belonged to the seller, and then separately did an analysis of the appropriate "risk adjusted" perspective, one would expect that the risk adjusted "k" value would be less than 30 percent. In this way, when the NPV was divided between the buyer and seller (using, for example, a 25 percent split) the seller would still be entitled to an NPV of $1.57 million. Exhibit 7.9 shows how this could develop. The top set of rows shows that for a 30 percent allocated return to the buyer, the seller receives 100 percent of the $1.57 million which results in a royalty of 26 percent (on the basis of the cash flows) plus an initial $100K license fee. In the bottom group of rows, the seller experiences exactly the same return: $1.57 million NPV with a k of 30 percent. However, in this case a RAHR of 20.4 percent provides an NPV which, when split 75:25 (buyer:seller), provides the aforementioned $1.57 million for the seller and $4.70 million for the buyer. Notice that for this latter case the royalty rate remains unchanged, so the payments made by the buyer to the seller do not change. Also unchanged is what the buyer receives and the buyer's perspective of risk (k = 30%). What has changed is that the "k" value that is used as a risk-adjusted hurdle rate has become 20.4 percent instead of 30 percent as in the top table.

From a negotiation perspective, the seller should be indifferent as to which of these perspectives is employed and can tell the buyer. "Either we discount all the GCF at 30 percent and I (the seller) keep *all* the NPV, *or* we discount the GCFs by 20.4 percent and we *split* the NPV 75:25 buyer:seller."

Although either interpretation and use of DCF can be employed, the normal method is the former: the k-value used includes the effect of

Exhibit 7.10   Effect of Discounting Cash Outflows at a Lower k than Inflows

Year	k	1	2	3	4	5	6	7	8	9
GCF	0%	−1	−1	−2	−3	−2	−1	1	5	10
Outflow DCF	7%	−0.9	−0.9	−1.6	−2.3	−1.4	−0.7			
Inflow DCF	30%							0.2	0.6	0.9

the buyer's profit so 100 percent of the resulting NPV belongs to the seller.

ADDITIONAL CONSIDERATIONS FOR CALCULATING DCF

In all the previous examples, a single value for "k" (RAHR) was used to discount both the outflow GCFs and inflow GCFs. When one uses a risk-free value of "k" such as 7 percent, so that dollars tomorrow are made to look like dollars today, then it makes sense to use such "k" value on all the GCFs. However, what about the case when the parties agree that an appropriate "k" value is 20 or 30 percent?

For such cases, there is logic to structuring a model that discounts the outflow GCFs at the risk-free rate (such as 7 percent) and the inflow GCFs at the appropriate risk rate (here 20 or 30 percent). The rationale for this distinction is as follows: from the buyer's perspective, the outflow GCFs are much more certain than the inflow GCFs. This is because it is known that the prescribed outflow GCFs will be required to complete development of the technology, purchase manufacturing equipment, gear up for production, prepare marketing materials, train the sales force, conduct an advertising launch campaign, and so forth. However, the inflow GCFs will depend on the willingness of customers to buy the product, which is considered to be less knowable and subject to far less control than making expenditures. For this reason, outflow GCFs logically could be discounted by a "k" value appropriate to inflation, and the inflow GCFs discounted by a "k" value appropriate to the overall risk of project success. So, in this example, the outflow GCFs could be discounted at k = 7% and the inflow GCFs at k = 20% or 30% or whatever the appropriate number .

In some cases, the outflow GCFs are not even discounted by this lesser amount (7 percent). This is a result of considering how the outflow estimates are made. Consider a simple case where the only investment required is in people and the seller computes such cost as follows: in Year 1, 10 people will be needed at $100K/person in salary, benefits, and sup-

Exhibit 7.10   *(Continued)*

10	11	12	13	14	15	16	17	18	19	20	Net
13	14	15	15	15	14	13	10	8	3	0	126
											−7.822
0.9	0.8	0.6	0.5	0.4	0.3	0.2	0.1	0.1	0.0	0	5.6
											−2.2

plies, for a total of $1 million. If Year 2 requires these same 10 people, then it could be expected that, because of inflation each person would cost the seller $107K. Thus, the estimate of $1 million spent in Year 2 has *already* discounted the cost of the 10 people required. Consequently, to discount or not to discount the outflow GCFs depends upon how such estimates were made.

Despite the logic of this two-valued "k" approach, it leads to unusable results when applied to long-term projects such as shown in Exhibit 7.5. The resulting problem is shown in Exhibit 7.10. Discounting all the Exhibit 7.5 outflow GCFs at 7 percent causes the NPV of all such outflows to be −$7.8 million, with the minus designating that it is an outflow. The gross total outflow was actually $10 million over six years, but discounting all the inflow GCFs at 30 percent causes the NPV of all such inflows to be only $5.6 million, even though the total GCF was $136 million. The reason this effect is so dramatic is the same one as discussed with respect to Exhibit 7.4: When the duration is long, the impact of large "k" values is huge. If one then combines the NPV of the outflows (−$7.8 million) and the NPV of the inflows ($5.6 million), the result is −$2.2 million and therefore not worth doing from the buyer's perspective.

Fortunately, in many cases the outflow GCFs are made over a sufficiently short period of time, such as two or three years, so that the DCF values obtained are reasonably unaffected by the choice of "k." The development of a new pharmaceutical from the license of an initially tested compound would be an example of a very long investment period. In this case, consideration of a different "k" to discount outflow GCFs would be appropriate.

When dealing with long return periods such as in Exhibits 7.5 through 7.8, there are other valuation approaches based on option pricing. These will be briefly addressed in Chapter 8. In most analysis of short-term investments, the parties do not attempt to include the complication of different inflow and outflow k-values. The simplification is justified partly because the k value applied to the inflow is sufficient to account for this effect, and since this estimating process is sufficiently tenuous such attempts at precision are not justified.

USE OF THE MID-YEAR CONVENTION

There is one additional refinement to be considered. As developed earlier in this chapter, the equation $A = B/(1 + k)^n$, where A is the DCF (present value) of any given future gross cash flow and B assumes that the amount "B" occurs all at once at the end of period "n." Normally, payments are made more or less uniformly throughout a year, not just all at once at the end of the year. Accordingly, the outflow GCFs of Year 1 occur monthly during the year, not all at once at the end of the year. Likewise, the inflow GCFs for, say Year 10, occur throughout the year, not all at once at the end of the year. The way this phenomenon is usually handled is by means of the so-called "mid-year" convention. How this works is as follows: all the outflows (or inflows) of a year are assumed to have occurred throughout the year; for purposes of computing a DCF one can consider them to have occurred half-way through the year. Thus, the time period of the outflow GCFs for the first year occurred actually at mid-year, so that n = 0.5 for Year 1. Likewise for Year 2, all the outflows occurred at n = 1.5, and so on. Thus, the DCF equation becomes:

$$A = B/(1 + k)^{(2n-1)/2}, \text{ so for n = 1 for Year 1,}$$
the exponent equals 0.5, for Year 2 (n = 2),
the exponent equals 1.5, for Year 3 it equals 2.5, and so on.

To be even more precise, which is rarely warranted, one could make monthly estimates of outflow and inflow GCFs and discount by a monthly "k." Normally the mid-year convention is as precise as needed, given all the other uncertainties associated with making such estimates.

INCOME STATEMENTS AND CASH-FLOW STATEMENTS

Creating an income statement is a fundamental requirement for performing the DCF valuation method discussed in this chapter. There is some bad news and some good news. The bad news is that done properly, creating an income statement is a daunting task, as it involves numerous assumptions involving future sales, the cost of raw materials

Figure 7.1
DILBERT © distributed by United Feature Syndicate. Reprinted with permission.

and labor, the cost of the manufacturing plant, distribution costs, sales and marketing costs, efficiency of manufacture (yield ratios), administrative costs, product development and "R&D" costs, taxes (federal, state, and local), and any and every cost associated with producing the revenue.

The good news? The good news is that for purposes of valuing technology for a license negotiation, there are so many inherent uncertainties involved that it is often possible with some skill and experience to create a useful business model without resorting to a highly detailed calculation of individual costs.

In the previous examples, the gross cash flows were simply assumed. In order to perform a valuation, it is necessary to make estimates of cash flows. How does one obtain the future cash flows year by year?

Generally this is performed in two steps. Step 1 is to perform a "income statement" projection; step 2 is to use the "net income" obtained at the bottom of the income statement (the origin of the term "the bottom line"), and adjust it in a "cash flow" statement. To review, an income statement is derived as follows:

- Revenues (sometimes termed Sales or, in Europe, Turnover)
- Less "Cost of Goods Sold" (known as COGS)
- Equals Gross Margin.
- Less all appropriate overheads (known as "SG&A," for Sales, General, and Administrative, including relevant R&D)
- Equals "Earnings before Interest and Taxes" (known as EBIT).
- Less interest expense and provision for taxes
- Equals "Earnings after Tax" (known as EAT).

A cash flow statement can be obtained from the income statement as follows:

- Starting with "Earnings after Tax" off the bottom line of the income statement,
- Add back all depreciation expenses which were embedded in COGS and SG&A or other
- Less the increase in working capital or other investments required, and not included in SG&A of the income statement, to sustain the growth of the business
- Equals Gross Cash Flow (GCF).

The income statement is not directly useful for performing DCF or NPV analysis. This is because the calculation of the income statement handles investments in ways that do not reflect cash generated or consumed in the year being considered. For example, assume there is a need to build a physical plant in the first year of the license to be able to manufacture licensed products starting in year 2 and extending until Year 10 when the plant will be obsolete. On the income statement such an investment would be spread out over the ten years of useful life according to a depreciation model. One such depreciation model is "the straight line" wherein the initial investment is simply divided by the number of years of useful life and that amount is deducted each year from the revenues as though it were a current year cost. In order to convert an income statement to a cash flow statement, one would need to "add back" the amount of such year-by-year depreciation because the depreciation is not a current year cash expense. Further, one would also need to account for the cash amount of the investment in the year or years it occurred as a current year expense.

Consult an accounting textbook for background on these terms and concepts and Smith and Parr's book for examples of cash flow statements.[6]

Depending on the significance of the opportunity, there are several levels at which such a cash flow analysis can be conducted. It turns out that there are reasonable benchmark values for COGS, SG&A, and provisions for taxes that can be obtained and expressed as percentages of Revenues. For example, Robert Morris Associates publishes a summary organized by SIC codes of such ratios for companies of various sizes and over various periods.[7] A typical page from this type of source in shown as Exhibit 7.11.

It should be noted that these data tend to have been compiled for smaller companies seeking loans because this is how such data is collected. For that reason, in many cases the values shown tend to underpredict profitability.

In more important cases, a higher level of effort is justified. Consult annual or quarterly reports of public companies that reflect, as closely as possible, the subject license opportunity and from these reports calculate such ratios, as were discussed in Chapter 6. For instance, a company such as Tektronix may be selected to act as a general proxy for a high-tech device manufacturer. Using their reported results for year-ending May 31, 1997, reveals the following ratios:

- COGS = 57%
- SG&A = 25% + 10% for R&D = 35%
- Provision for Tax = 32% (more typical numbers are closer to 40%)

By analyzing multiple companies over multiple time periods, one can make reasonable approximations of such ratios. By further analyzing

Exhibit 7.11 Manufacturers-Electronic Computers SIC# 3571

	Comparative Historical Data			Current Data Sorted By Sales					
	6/30/89–3/31/90	4/1/90–3/31/91	4/1/91–3/31/92	48(4/1–9/30/91)				51(10/1/91–3/31/92)	
	ALL	ALL	ALL	0–1MM	1–3MM	3–5MM	5–10MM	10–25MM	25MM & over
Type of Statement									
Unqualified	66	43	43	1	2	1	4	10	25
Reviewed	7	13	18		9	2	3	1	3
Compiled	12	9	16		1	7	2	2	4
Tax Returns			4	2	1	1			
Other	23	13	18		2	3	5	3	5
Number of Statements	108	78	99	4	21	9	14	18	33
	%	%	%	%	%	%	%	%	%
ASSETS									
Cash & Equivalents	10.4	12.3	10.4		8.0		7.3	8.7	16.0
Trade Receivables - (net)	31.4	31.5	33.9		38.0		32.9	31.9	31.1
Inventory	25.6	25.1	27.4		27.3		29.2	34.4	19.1
All Other Current	3.3	3.1	3.1		3.8		4.4	1.6	3.9
Total Current	70.7	71.9	74.8		77.0		73.8	76.6	70.0
Fixed Assets (net)	19.2	17.7	14.5		11.9		16.8	15.7	17.0
Intangibles (net)	2.6	4.0	4.5		5.0		4.2	2.8	5.5
All Other Non-Current	7.5	6.3	6.2		6.1		5.2	4.9	7.4
Total	100.0	100.0	100.0		100.0		100.0	100.0	100.0
LIABILITIES									
Notes Payable-Short Term	10.6	8.7	10.9		17.6		9.2	10.0	7.8
Cur. Mat.-L/T/D	2.4	2.7	3.1		1.9		3.1	5.0	1.8
Trade Payables	15.7	15.8	16.8		15.4		21.2	19.2	14.8

Income Taxes Payable	1.2	1.2	.8	.8	2.1	.5	.7
All Other Current	11.7	12.0	12.2	10.6	11.4	12.3	14.0
Total Current	41.6	40.4	43.8	46.3	47.0	47.0	39.1
Long Term Debt	8.5	11.7	9.0	10.6	8.1	7.8	7.5
Deferred Taxes	.8	1.5	.4	.3	.2	.3	.8
All Other Non-Current	4.2	4.2	5.1	2.9	2.5	8.9	5.0
Net Worth	45.0	42.3	41.7	39.9	42.2	36.0	47.6
Total Liabilities & Net Worth	100.0	100.0	100.0	100.0	100.0	100.0	100.0

INCOME DATA

Net Sales	100.0	100.0	100.0	100.0	100.0	100.0	100.0
Gross Profit	40.7	39.5	42.8	48.5	32.0	35.5	44.1
Operating Expenses	38.3	36.5	39.5	44.9	28.4	31.9	41.3
Operating Profit	2.4	2.9	3.3	3.5	3.5	3.6	2.8
All Other Expenses (net)	1.3	.8	1.5	2.6	1.3	.4	1.6
Profit Before Taxes	1.2	2.1	1.7	1.0	2.2	3.2	1.3

RATIOS

Current	3.0	2.7	2.5	2.3	1.9	2.3	3.1
	1.8	1.8	1.7	1.6	1.5	1.6	1.9
	1.3	1.2	1.4	1.3	1.3	1.2	1.3
Quick	1.8	1.8	1.7	1.6	1.3	1.4	2.0
	1.0	1.2	1.0	1.1	.9	.9	1.2
	.7	.8	.7	.6	.5	.5	.8
Sales/Receivables	49 7.4	41 9.0	42 8.6	41 9.0	34 10.6	37 9.8	51 7.2
	64 5.7	54 6.7	56 6.5	51 7.2	45 8.1	47 7.8	78 4.7
	87 4.2	76 4.8	79 4.6	73 5.0	59 6.2	72 5.1	104 3.5

(Continued)

Exhibit 7.11 (*Continued*)

Group headers — **Comparative Historical Data** covers the three dated ALL columns; **Current Data Sorted By Sales** covers the six size columns, which are split by period: 48(4/1–9/30/91) and 51(10/1/91–3/31/92).

	6/30/89–3/31/90 ALL 108	4/1/90–3/31/91 ALL 78	4/1/91–3/31/92 ALL 99	0–1MM 4	1–3MM 21	3–5MM 9	5–10MM 14	10–25MM 18	25MM & over 33
Type of Statement									
Unqualified	66	43	43	1	2	1	4	10	25
Reviewed	7	13	18		9	2	3	1	3
Compiled	12	9	16	1	7	2	2	4	
Tax Returns			4	2	1	1			
Other	23	13	18		2	3	5	3	5
Number of Statements	108	78	99	4	21	9	14	18	33
Cost of Sales/Inventory	54 6.8	36 10.1	45 8.2		22 16.3		30 12.1	40 9.2	41 8.8
	99 3.7	69 5.3	83 4.4		76 4.8		58 6.3	91 4.0	79 4.6
	148 2.5	107 3.4	114 3.2		122 3.0		79 4.6	140 2.6	114 3.2
Cost of Sales/Payable	33 11.2	23 15.6	28 13.0		14 26.7		28 12.9	29 12.6	38 9.7
	42 8.6	42 8.7	41 8.9		40 9.2		36 10.1	41 9.0	55 6.6
	69 5.3	63 5.8	69 5.3		85 4.3		41 9.0	51 7.2	87 4.2
Sales/Working Capital	3.0	3.6	4.1		5.3		5.6	4.9	2.8
	5.2	6.0	7.1		9.6		10.7	7.4	4.4
	14.7	16.5	15.1		15.9		22.4	19.4	10.8
EBIT/Interest	9.8	10.4	8.2		2.7		8.2	25.3	15.2
	(95) 3.7	(65) 2.2	(87) 2.0		(19) 1.5		(10) 2.4	(17) 2.7	(29) 2.0
	.5	.8	-.2		-.2		-6.5	1.0	-1.6
Net Profit + Depr., Dep., Amort./Cur. Mat. L/T/D	12.6	11.1	13.0						23.6
	(54) 6.2	(36) 3.6	(38) 3.3						(13) 5.5
	.7	1.3	.9						.6
Fixed/Worth	.2	.2	.2		.2		.2	.2	.2
	.4	.4	.3		.3		.4	.3	.3
	.8	1.0	.7		.6		.7	.9	.7

				Debt/Worth					
Ratio									
Debt/Worth	.6	.7	.6	.6			1.0	.6	.6
	1.1	1.5	1.5	2.5			1.8	1.3	.8
	2.8	4.0	4.7	7.4			2.7	9.5	3.8
% Profit Before Taxes/Tangible Net Worth	(102) 30.8	40.6	36.7	(19) 43.9			38.9	57.0	33.0
	17.0	(70) 20.6	(90) 15.8	7.1			14.1	(15) 17.5	(29) 19.0
	3.7	6.4	.6	-4.1			-22.2	3.1	-4.4
% Profit Before Taxes.Total Assets	13.5	13.4		8.5			21.3	20.7	15.4
	6.0	7.7	5.0	1.5			6.9	6.8	5.0
	-4.4	1.1	-2.9	-3.3			-7.3	-1.9	-4.4
Sales/Net Fixed Assets	23.2	25.0	36.8	54.3			38.3	33.0	15.7
	13.3	12.9	17.1	33.6			16.0	23.5	8.0
	5.1	6.2	7.4	9.6			8.5	7.0	5.2
Sales/Total Assets	2.4	2.6	2.9	3.1			4.8	3.1	1.9
	1.7	2.0	1.9	2.4			2.0	2.2	1.5
	1.2	1.3	1.4	1.9			1.3	1.6	1.1
% Depr., Dep., Amort/Sales	1.3	.9	.9	.9			.7	.8	1.8
	(89) 3.1	(53) 2.6	(68) 2.1	(18) 1.6			(11) 1.7	(11) 2.0	(20) 3.8
	4.6	4.0	3.7	2.9			4.1	2.6	6.6
% Officers', Directors', Owners' Comp/Sales	2.2								
	(20) 5.6								
	9.9								
Net Sales ($)	5167155M	3910447M	5701101M	2431M	41328M	35234M	103986M	260758M	5257364M
Total Assets ($)	4115028M	2639217M	3885095M	988M	28715M	15838M	49770M	123962M	3665822M

M = $thousand MM = $million

how companies prepare their cash flow statements, also part of the public record, it is possible to make some ballpark estimates for the key adjustments to the income statement: depreciation (which is not a current year expense) and increases in investment required (for working capital or other purposes).

With even more effort, one could make estimates from first principles of what it will cost to manufacture the licensed technology. To do so would require domain expertise in manufacturing for the subject area, and in marketing, sales, and general administration. Where the opportunity warrants such increased investment in analysis, such expertise can be found within one's own organization or, more likely, by employing outside consultants.

A final source of such information is the buyer. Because they are in the business of commercialization, buyers normally have the resources, experience, and the need to develop such detailed projections. Although it is not reasonable to expect the buyer to provide the seller complete access to their records and projections (particularly if the seller is negotiating with multiple prospective buyers), it can be in both party's interests to share reasonable projections for the purpose of conducting win-win negotiations.

Once such ratios are determined, then by making an estimate of the total revenues year by year, an estimate of the year-by-year GCF can be obtained. Exhibit 7.12 shows how this can be done. Shown is a model for developing the revenues over time. Normally one has some idea about the selling price range of the prospective product and the size of the market, although each of these variables alone could be the subject of a detailed analysis. Once the revenue line has been calculated, then the ratios developed previously lead one to the Gross Cash Flow (GCF). It is from the GCF that the discounting techniques discussed in this chapter can be applied. Exhibit 7.12 will be the basis for a demonstration of the Monte Carlo Method in the next chapter.

USING DCF TO DETERMINE THE
VALUE OF FIXED PAYMENTS

One of the powerful features of the Discounted Cash Flow Method is that it can be used with any other valuation method or context to move money forward or back in time. For instance, if, using the "Industry Standard Method" of Chapter 4, the parties agree on a royalty of 5 percent but for some reason want to defer or move up some or all of certain royalties, the above DCF equations can be used to convert such moneys into equivalent value but at different times.

Exhibit 7.12   Example Calculation of Gross Cash Flows (GCF) Based on Tektronix Ratios

	A	B	C	D	E	F	G	H
1	Year		1	2	3	4	5	6
2	Number of Units Sold (1)		100	200	300	350	400	400
3	Average Selling Price (1)		$10,000	$10,000	$9,500	$9,000	$8,0000	$8,000
4	Revenues		$1,000,000	$2,000,000	$2,850,000	$3,150,000	$3,200,000	$3,200,000
5								
6	COGS (2)	57%	$570,000	$1,140,000	$1,624,500	$1,795,500	$1,824,000	$1,824,000
7	SG&A and R&D (2)	35%	$350,000	$700,000	$997,500	$1,102,500	$1,120,000	$1,120,000
8	EBIT	22%	$80,000	$160,000	$228,000	$252,000	$256,000	$256,000
9	Provision for Taxes (2)	32%	$25,600	$51,200	$72,960	$80,640	$81,920	$81,920
10	EAT		$54,400	$108,800	$155,040	$171,360	$174,080	$174,080
11								
12	Depreciation (3)	5%	$28,500	$57,000	$81,225	$89,775	$91,200	$91,200
13	Increase in Investment (4)	10%	$100,000	$85,000	$30,000	$5,000	$-	$-
14	GCF		$(17,100)	$80,800	$206,265	$256,135	$265,280	$265,280
15								

Notes

(1) Values which would be developed from market assessment (illustrated here)

(2) Ratios in Col. B are Tektronix annual report May 31, 1997

(3) Assumed increase in working capital based on 10% of increase in year over year sales

(4) Assumed to be 5% of current year COGS

In some agreements, the seller definitely prefers to receive substantial early, fixed payments in lieu of some of its downstream royalties. These DCF equations can be used to restructure equitable financial agreements into equivalent forms with different payment times and amounts.

OTHER ISSUES TO BE CONSIDERED
WITH THE DCF METHOD

One assumption inherent in the examples selected is the zero terminal value. Such a situation is common, though not universal. It arises, for example, when the license is a bare patent license (no trade secrets). The patents all expire on a known date. Another case is when the product life will be short and there will be no existing residual benefit in a succeeding product generation. Another reason terminal value may be ignored is that the k-value used is sufficiently large so that the DCF value of even a significant GCF figure at the end of the forecast period is so low that it is unaccounted for given all the project uncertainties. However, it is always reasonable to ask: Is there a terminal value that should be considered?

Another assumption inherent in the examples considered is an assessment of potential peripheral benefit to the buyer. This effect may be accounted for by the use of an appropriate royalty base. Returning to the laser example, if the licensed subject matter is the lasing element only, the buyer will likely gain the benefit of selling entire laser components as a result of having such new element. By using the selling price of the entire component, and appropriately adjusting the royalty, the seller can be fairly compensated. But what about the situation where the buyer will now be able to sell additional components not directly tied to the laser but bought from the buyer by the same customers? Accounting for such peripheral sales is normally much more uncertain than the products made directly by the licensed technology. As in the case of the terminal value issue, in many instances this effect is deemed too distant or minor to be included. However, it is always a reasonable question to ask: What is the total benefit of the licensed technology?

CONCLUSION

The DCF method requires delving into the origins of expected profit from the use of the licensed technology. If this is done primarily by reliance on ratios, such as EBIT as a percentage of revenues projected by year, then the DCF resembles the Rule of Thumb Method. However, even in this situation, the DCF can provide additional information to enable moving payments in time such as reduced royalties to create a larger upfront license fee. The DCF method can also provide insight into the sensitivity of the value to perceived risk (k).

If the DCF method is implemented by a detailed analysis of each component of the income and cash flow methods, then it can provide significantly more insight than the Rule of Thumb Method if there is a reasonable basis for making such analysis.

For the valuation of significant opportunities, the DCF Method is often used in addition to other methods to increase one's insight into value and confidence in the calculated result.

Summarized below are the equations developed and used in this chapter.

- A or DCF = $B/(1 + k)^n$, where A or DCF is the present value of a future gross cash flow B
- $B/A = (1 + k)^n$, where such B/A ratio is known as "payback" or "baggers"
- $B/A = (1 + k)^{(2n-1)/2}$, using the mid-year convention
- NPV = the sum of all the DCFs (noting outflows offset in flows)

SOURCES OF INFORMATION TO DEVELOP BUSINESS PROJECTIONS

Although details on how to develop pro forma financials are beyond the scope of this book, provided in Appendix A are two references that list numerous available business resources. I am in debt to Michael Odza of Technology Access Reports and my colleague Dan McGavock of IPC Group for permission to include these references.

NOTES

1. Throughout the book we have generally ignored tax issues that may affect a party's decision-making or valuation because such issues are beyond the scope of this book and are situation specific.

2. The value of "k" has to be based on the same time period as "n" in order for these equations to work. In all the examples provided, "n" was expressed in years; so, the value of "k" was given in *annualized* (yearly) values. One could use monthly periods, but in such an instance the "k" value would be interest expressed per month; for example, the future value (B) of a present sum (A) could be:

$$B/A = (1 + k)^n.$$

For k = 12% on an annualized basis and a period of five years, one obtains

$$B/A = (1 + 0.12)^5 = 1.76$$

Equivalently, one could consider this same example as consisting of 60 monthly periods, such that n

= 60. However, in such a case, "k" must be expressed as the monthly interest rate. Here, the equivalent monthly value of "k" is 0.9489 percent or 0.009489, so that

$$B/A = (1 + 0.009489)^{60} = 1.76$$

3. "A Method for Valuing High-Risk, Long-Term Investments: The Venture Capital Method", Harvard Business School Case Study, 9-288-006, published 1987, Rev. 6/89, Harvard Business School, Cambridge, MA.

4. The seller's appropriate k-value is normally different, and lower than the buyers. The buyer is using the k-value to scale risk and reward of a future investment. The seller is moving money expected to be paid in the future to the present. The discussion of such k-values and how they relate to the weighted average corporate cost of capital is outside this book.

5. It should be noted that this is not the same use of 25% as the 25% Rule of Chapter 6. The 25% Rule applies to the split of EBIT.

6 Smith, Gordon V., and Parr, Russell, L., *Intellectual Property, Licensing and Joint Venture Profit Strategies*, 2nd Ed., New York: John Wiley & Sons, 1998.

7. Robert Morris Associates, *Annual Statement Studies*, 1992, Philadelphia PA.

8

Method Five:
Advanced Valuation Methods

INTRODUCTION

Chapter 7 presented a mathematical structure for performing valuation using projected, or pro forma, income and cash flow statements, together with equations and methodology to assess the present value of future sums based upon timing and risk. This Discounted Cash Flow Method is the most mathematical valuation approach considered thus far and can be used in most valuation situations.

However in recent years, more sophisticated methods of valuation have been developed. In this chapter, two such advanced methods will be considered: Monte Carlo (or Probabilistic) Method and Option Pricing Methods.

The Monte Carlo techniques are based upon the Discounted Cash Flow Method. They are similar approaches in that both are based on cash flow models derived from specific assumptions about revenues and costs. However, they do differ. With Monte Carlo techniques, one is not constrained to make single-value predictions of key variables such as revenues, costs, or even the technical risk of success; instead, estimates are made of ranges of outcomes with associated probabilities. Surprisingly, in many cases this turns out to be easier to do than making discrete value projections.

The second method considered in this chapter is option pricing. When dealing with long-lived projects, particularly when the expenses are significant and early, and the projected returns are far into the future, the use of Risk-Adjusted Hurdle Rates (RAHR, or "k") tends to make all such projects look economically unattractive because of the heavy discounting that takes place by the factor $B/(1 + k)^n$ when "n" is large. Option pricing methods evaluate investments and returns in an incremental way that better handles such circumstances.

MONTE CARLO METHOD

Monte Carlo, more generally known as probabilistic, techniques have a long history, primarily in engineering applications. Within the past 20 years, they have been increasingly applied to business modeling in support of decision-making. These methods are very powerful ways to solve equations and situations so complex that a closed form solution is not possible.[1] With the advent of powerful and inexpensive personal computers, such sophisticated tools are now widely available although not yet widely used. However, in most MBA programs, the Monte Carlo method is taught, used, and required. Such method will be increasingly used in license valuation contexts.

There are two personal computer products available that work with PC-compatibles and with Macintosh operating systems:

- Crystal Ball® by Decisioneering, Inc. (*www.decisioneering.com*)
- @Risk by Palisade Corporation (*www.palisade.com*)

They each work with and require a spreadsheet program such as Excel or Lotus 1-2-3 Different MBA programs have standardized one or the other of these products; they each have a prestigious list of university adoptions. Although both products are suitable for use in license valuation contexts, the examples provided in this chapter have been obtained using Crystal Ball.

To illustrate the Monte Carlo method we will use the previous cash flow projection example considered as Exhibit 7.12, repeated here as Exhibit 8.1. In this context, we will assume that Exhibit 8.1 is the projected situation agreed to by both seller and buyer for the purpose of valuing a technology license. Exhibit 8.1 contains an additional Discounted Cash Flow (DCF) calculation, based upon an assumed Risk-Adjusted Hurdle Rate of 25 percent, enabling the calculation of a Net Present Value (NPV) of $452,827 as shown.

This model says that based on the single valued assumptions of the model and the assumed RAHR of 25 percent, both the buyer and seller would conclude that the licensing opportunity was "worth" approximately $453K. As discussed in Chapter 7, the perspective on the RAHR selected (25 percent) determines whether the buyer would be willing to pay as much as $453K. In our consideration of the Monte Carlo Method, we will make certain probabilistic assumptions of the factors in this

Exhibit 8.1 Obtaining DCF and NPV with Revenue Projection Through Ratios

	A	B	C	D	E	F	G	H
1	Year		1	2	3	4	5	6
2	Number of Units Sold		100	200	300	350	400	400
3	Average Selling Price		$10,000	$10,000	$9,500	$9,000	$8,0000	$8,000
4	Revenues		$1,000,000	$2,000,000	$2,850,000	$3,150,000	$3,200,000	$3,200,000
5								
6	COGS	57%	$570,000	$1,140,000	$1,624,500	$1,795,500	$1,824,000	$1,824,000
7	SG&A and R&D	35%	$350,000	$700,000	$997,500	$1,102,500	$1,120,000	$1,120,000
8	EBIT	22%	$80,000	$160,000	$228,000	$252,000	$256,000	$256,000
9	Provision for Taxes	32%	$25,600	$51,200	$72,960	$80,640	$81,920	$81,920
10	EAT		$54,400	$108,800	$155,040	$171,360	$174,080	$174,080
11								
12	Depreciation	5%	$28,500	$57,000	$81,225	$89,775	$91,200	$91,200
13	Increase in Investment	10%	$100,000	$85,000	$30,000	$5,000	–	–
14	GCF		$(17,100)	$80,800	$206,265	$256,135	$265,280	$265,280
15								
16	RAHR [=k]	25%						
17	DCF(k)		$(15,295)	$57,816	$118,073	$117,296	$97,187	$77,750
18	NPV(k)		$452,827					

model to obtain a richer understanding of the NPV value of this hypothetical license.

How the Monte Carlo Method Works

The basic idea behind the Monte Carlo Method is that instead of prescribing a *value* for a cell in a spreadsheet model of a valuation, one prescribes an *expression* for the cell based upon some mathematical model of reality. When the calculation scheme gets to the point where it must ascribe a value to that cell, the Monte Carlo software program conducts a computation using the mathematical model specified to deduce the one specific number that is then used to compute the final result. What makes this approach probabilistic is that the mathematical expressions used to provide the one specific number are structured to provide a prescribed randomness (also known as a "distribution"). This seems peculiar and non-productive, but it turns out to be very useful.

Two immediate questions arise: what is a prescribed randomness (or distribution), and why would the selection of one value within such randomness lead to a useful result?

Prescribed Randomness (Distribution) Expressions

With regard to the first question, the issue of prescribed randomness, it is useful to revisit the idea of predicting the future. Although it is universally accepted that no one knows the future, there are many aspects of life for which we do know the future in practical everyday terms. The sun will rise tomorrow, pretty much in the east. If it is spring, summer will follow. Even in human affairs, much of life is predictable. The stock market will rise, not every day, not every stock, but overall. In 1999, the New York Yankees will win the World Series again and the Chicago Cubs will not.

There are basically three ways that one can have what philosophers sometimes term a "justified true belief" (JTB)[2] about the future: (1) a scientific law, (2) an established historical trend, or (3) a rational argument. Predicting the sun's rising and the change of seasons is an example of scientific law; there are known and knowable facts concerning the motion of the earth with respect to its own axis (rotation) and with respect to the sun (revolution), and of the tilt of the earth, and of the energy emission rate of the sun that enable predicting the "rising" of the sun, for example. In fact everyone's certainty is sufficiently high about such matters that the word "prediction" would emit a laugh: Imagine a local evening news forecast that proclaims "tonight it will be dark, but tomorrow it will be light again."

The second example of a JTB about the future, reliance on an established trend, is similar to the use of a scientific law. Scientific laws, after all, are simply codified experience. It comes as something of a shock to some college students that there is no "proof" of Newton's Laws of Motion or of the First Law of Thermodynamics. After careful study by many people in many different contexts, no exception to these dogmas has ever been observed and so a critical mass of people have declared them "law" and everyone pretty much agrees to stop wondering about them. Reliance on an established trend to predict the future is simply an uncodified way of asserting that what happened before will happen again. Prior to man's understanding of celestial mechanics, the existence and date of the shortest and longest days of the year (in the Northern Hemisphere, December 21 and June 21, respectively) was widely known. It appears certain that Stonehenge, for example, was constructed in such a way that at sunrise on the Summer Solstice the sun would project its light through a special keyway in the stones on that day and only that day. Other cultures many thousands of years ago similarly understood these dates and all of them did so (apparently) with either an inadequate understanding of celestial mechanics or a completely false one. What they were able to do was to capture an observation that occurs once a year, year after year, and communicate it down through a sufficient number of generations such that it was accepted as a law of life. The rising stock market, or the existence of inflation, is this same type of prediction by extrapolation. There exist approximately 90 years of stock market history encompassing two world wars, numerous presidential administrations and policies, countless numbers of new products being introduced and old ones being abandoned, and, yet there has been a surprisingly uniform rise in value, adjusted for inflation, of about 10 percent per year. Underneath such rise, there are "fundamentals" that can be used to explain why stocks as a whole are more valuable now than they were before, and why stocks on an individual basis are more, or in some cases less, valuable than in the past. So, does anyone "know" that the stock market will be higher by 10 percent one year hence? In the philosophical sense of JTB, the answer is "no." In the business sense of PDM (Prudent Decision Making), the answer is "yes." In a business context, certainty is an unaffordable uxury. If there is a historical data, then it is frequently prudent to predict the future and act on such predictions as though the future were known.

The third way of knowing the future is rational argument. As shown in Figure 8.1, Dilbert and his boss are able to use rational argument to make bold predictions: Dilbert predicts that his project will never be completed with the boss's "help," and both Dilbert and his boss surmise what life will be like when the sun stops shining.

When an investment decision is to be made regarding whether or not to develop a new product, business decision-makers frequently have only rational argument as the basis for PDM. Although there may be both historical data for similar products or previous new product introductions

Figure 8.1
DILBERT © distributed by United Feature Syndicate. Reprinted with permission.

and market assessments based upon surveys and trials, in almost all circumstances the commitment is made by the credibility of an argument. Thus, in the 1999 World Series of Baseball example, there is an argument that *because* the Yankees won 1998, and because of off-season trades and acquisitions has made the team stronger than any other team, they *should* win again in 1999. Of course this is by no means certain, which is one reason why they play the game, but if the 1999 Yankees were an investment opportunity, PDM would be to bet on their winning.

When business forecasts are made, the future values selected for cells in a spreadsheet model are some combination of extrapolations of data or experience and a rational argument as to how circumstances should turn out. With traditional, non-Monte Carlo methods, each "best guess" is but one value from a range of reasonably possible guesses. Monte Carlo tools enable the replacement of the single-valued best guess with a *prescribed randomness* that characterizes not only what is believed to be the most likely outcome but also includes treatment of reasonably probable but less likely outcomes. Normally the solution sought is the Net Present Value (NPV) of the total value of the project. Each time the software program performs a complete NPV calculation, it will determine a somewhat different value for NPV because at least some of the cells have the prescribed randomness expression rather than a single value.

Let us consider three classic examples of prescribed randomness: uniform, triangular, and Gaussian (also known as "normal").

Uniform Distribution

A uniform distribution, or "uniform" prescribed randomness, can be used in estimating the effect of the Cost of Goods Sold (COGS, as defined in Chapter 7). In Exhibit 7.12, we used a value of 57 percent based upon data from Tektronics for the year ending May 31, 1997. In modeling a prospective licensing transaction, we will typically use data wherever possible and deal with the uncertainty in the following way: Although we may believe that 57 percent is toward the middle of the most likely range, it may be equally likely that the COGS could be anywhere from 55 to 59 percent. Alternatively, we are sufficiently confident that the value of COGS will not be less than 55 percent that we are prepared to predict that there is zero percent probability for values less than 55 percent, and similarly, zero percent probability for values greater than 59 percent. However, any value between 55 and 59 percent is equally probable. Exhibit 8.2 illustrates how such a distribution is portrayed; it is derived from Cystal Ball 4.0 Pro for a PC.

Such a uniform distribution acts to put the maximum amount of uncertainty possible within the prescribed upper and lower bounds (here 55 and 59 percent) because we are saying that any value within such bounds is equally probable; on the other hand, this type of distribution has the most certainty possible with respect to values outside the upper and lower bounds because it ascribes zero probability to such values. Clearly, if we had set the upper and lower bounds at 56.99 and 57.01 percent, we would have for all practical purposes reduced the prediction to the single value of 57 percent at 100 percent certainty. Uniform distributions work best for those situations where the certainty is bifurcated: it is highly probable that the values will be within a prescribed range but highly uncertain as to exactly where within such a range.

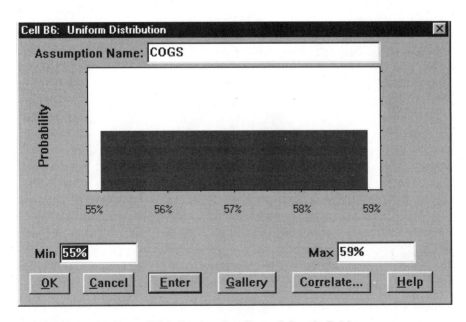

Exhibit 8.2   Uniform Distribution for Cost of Goods Sold
Source: © 1988–1998 Decisioneering, Inc. Reprinted with permission.

Triangular Distribution (Prescribed Randomness)

A variation of Uniform Distribution is the triangular distribution. Triangular distribution is similar to the uniform type in that both types assume zero probability of values below the specified lower bound and above the upper bound. They differ in that the triangular distribution selects a most likely value and constructs a triangle of probability that varies linearly from the maximum probability at the most likely value to zero at the upper and lower bounds. Using a concrete example, consider again Exhibit 8.1. We will use triangular distribution to predict values for the average selling price in any given year, as shown in Row 3 of this exhibit.

The existing model portrays a 5 percent decline in selling price after the second year as a result of price erosion. Looking at the first year only, let us assume that as a result of market studies we are confident that the selling price can be at least $9,000 per unit, but not more than $11,000 per unit, to achieve the 100 units sold projected in Year 1. A triangular distribution would then look as shown in Exhibit 8.3.

Thus, this distribution assumes that the likelihood of the selling price differing from $10,000 declines linearly with price differential from $10,000 until, at plus or minus $1,000, the probability is zero. In comparison to the previously considered uniform distribution, the triangle distribution is appropriate when one has reason to believe that a most-likely value does exist, and that the probability of other values declines with

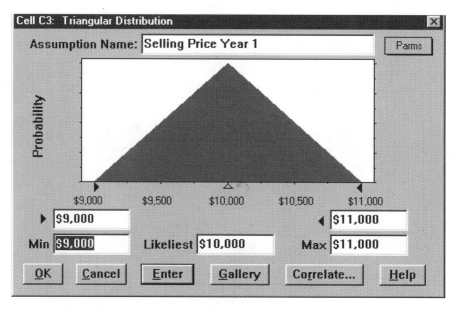

Exhibit 8.3   Triangular Distribution for the Selling Price in Year 1
Source: © 1988–1998 Decisioneering, Inc. Reprinted with permission.

separation from such a most-likely value. Because it is reasonable to hold a "most likely" outcome belief, the triangular distribution is appropriate for many circumstances.

The Normal, or Bell, Distribution

Another commonly used distribution is known by several names: Gaussian, normal, or bell distribution (or bell curve). This distribution, hereafter "bell" or "normal," is similar to the triangular in that the probability peaks at the "most likely" value and declines with distance from the most-likely value. However, unlike the triangle distribution, the bell distribution shows a probability which declines to zero asymptotically, not abruptly, at end points. Further, the probability decline is not a straight line but rather a curve that is described by a complex mathematical formula.

There is another important difference between the triangular and bell distribution: the bell distribution is observed experimentally in many different physical circumstances. If one were to measure the height of a large number of people and then calculated the average height, one would find that most people's height is close to the average. The number of people with heights far from the mean decreases rapidly as one moves away from the mean. For example, if the mean was determined to be 5 feet 6 inches, then one would find many people who stand between 5 feet 4 inches and 5 feet 6 inches, fewer between 5 feet 2 and 5 feet 4, still fewer between 5 feet and 5 feet 2, and still fewer between 4 feet 10 and 5 feet. The distribution of such heights would closely follow a mathematical expression that prescribes the bell curve. The use of such a bell distribution is particularly suited when there exists a natural mean around which there is some randomness and the randomness is equally likely to be higher or lower than the mean. Even for situations where there is no "natural" mean, such a distribution can be used to express a belief that the mean or expected value is highly likely to occur. Essentially, any value is possible, but the probability of values far from the mean is much lower than values closer to the mean.

Considering again the example of Exhibit 8.1, let us assume that the number of units sold each year can be characterized by such a normal or bell distribution as shown in Exhibit 8.4.

The relative slenderness of the distribution is determined by a mathematical quantity known as the standard deviation. One standard deviation, plus and minus, encompasses approximately 68 percent of the total probability of occurrence. That is, in the example shown in Exhibit 8.4, the selection of a standard deviation value of 10 means that the distribution provides that 68 percent of the values selected for the units sold in Year 1 are between 90 and 110 units (plus and minus 10 around the most-likely value of 100). Three standard deviations, in this example plus or minus 30, encompasses 98 percent of all occurrences.

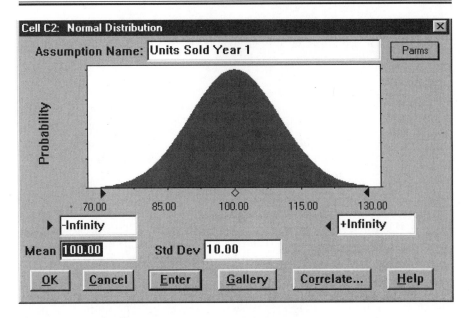

Exhibit 8.4   Example of Bell Distribution for Units Sold
Source: © 1988–1998 Decisioneering, Inc. Reprinted with permission.

Custom Distribution

The Crystal Ball software provides more than a dozen different types of distributions that can be readily modeled and used. In technology valuation contexts, there is usually no basis for identifying a particular distribution from scientific principles because the valuation is driven by business variables. Exceptions can occur. For instance, if the licensed subject matter were a pharmaceutical that was still undergoing trials, then there would be valid reason to select a distribution that accurately represents the rate of patient cures and to use such distributions to model FDA approval, market applications, and size.

In addition to such standard distributions, the Crystal Ball software has the built-in capability of easily creating a custom distribution that allows for the creation of any combination of probabilities at any arbitrary set of values. An example of the use of such distribution in shown in Exhibit 8.5.

This exhibit shows how the probable values of the sum of SG&A (Sales, General and Administrative) plus R&D (Research and Development) can be easily modeled. The original example, shown in Exhibit 8.1, used a value of 35 percent for the single, best assumption. Exhibit 8.5 shows how one can select probabilities at three discrete values: 50 percent probability at 35 percent SG&A + R&D, 30 percent at 34 percent, and 20 percent at 36 percent. Crystal Ball allows one to

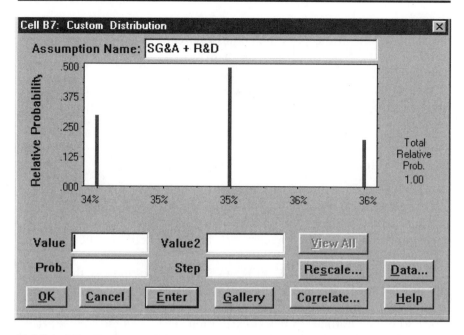

Exhibit 8.5   Example of Custom Distribution to Model SG&A + R&D
Source: © 1988–1998 Decisioneering, Inc. Reprinted with permission.

easily specify any number of pairs and then normalize the entire result so that the integrated probability is 100 percent. This allows one to construct distributions based upon historical experience (data) obtained from previous licensing situations, or other new product development projects.

How Distributions Are Used in Monte Carlo Calculations

The ability to use prescribed randomness is what makes the Monte Carlo Method powerful. It works in the following way. Consider a desire to calculate the predicted value of Net Present Value (NPV) for a new business development opportunity. The various factors that will drive the value are all estimated by using discrete values and distributions as discussed in this chapter. The way Monte Carlo works is that the software performs the calculation for NPV over and over again to create a distribution of outcomes of NPV that can be analyzed and interpreted. Each time the program calculates an NPV, called one "iteration," the result can be thought of as one lifetime of running the business through its entire life cycle. Each new iteration is exactly as though someone else in a parallel universe is able to run the business also through its entire life cycle. Typically one performs 500 to 1000 such parallel universe calculations of

NPV and then all the outcomes are reported and analyzed. By examining the statistics of all the NPV outcomes one can obtain a deeper understanding of the business prospects than from a one-time-through NPV calculation as was done in Chapter 7.

Just as distributions are used for certain of the inputs, the outputs of a Monte Carlo approach are likewise a distribution, rather than a single value. How to interpret such distributions will be discussed later.

Example Valuation Monte Carlo Calculation

Exhibit 8.6 repeats Exhibit 8.1 except the cells affected by the Monte Carlo method in Crystal Ball are highlighted: darker shading are the assumption cells, the ones for which some distribution has been selected, and lighter shading is the forecast cell, the value being predicted by the method.

As shown the shaded cells in Rows 2 and 3, Columns C through H, and in Column B, Rows 6 and 7, are the cells for which the previously described distributions have been provided. The "units sold" in Row 2 is modeled by the normal (or bell) distribution. The "average selling price" in Row 3 is modeled by the triangular distribution. The COGS is modeled by the uniform distribution, and the SG&A plus R&D by the custom distribution. All the other cells are assumed to maintain their single-value as was the case in Exhibit 8.1.

To use the method, the software is set to "run" the iterations. For the first iteration, or "parallel universe," when Crystal Ball needs a value from any of the probabilistic cells (units sold, selling price, COGS, or SG&A plus R&D) it uses the distribution recipe for the respective cell to determine a value that will be used for the remainder of the calculation to determine the first NPV. For the second "parallel universe" the process repeats but a different value will be selected for all the probabilistic cells (those containing distribution expressions rather than single values). Over the course of many iterations, usually 500 to 1000, a sufficient number of selections are made from each of the probabilistic cells that, over the entire set of assumptions, a reasonable approximation of values will correspond to the assumed distribution.

The results from this Monte Carlo calculation can be presented in many ways. Exhibit 8.7 is a frequency chart that shows the number of trials occurring in each of the shown "slices" of NPV values over 1000 iterations.

In Exhibit 8.1, we found that a single-value DCF model produced a single-valued NPV of $452,827. From a visual inspection of Exhibit 8.7, such a value falls in the middle of the results here and appears to be the most probable value. However, what the distribution of NPV values shows is that there are plausible situations where the NPV was in the range of $350,000 to $550,000. Crystal Ball allows us to easily determine

Exhibit 8.6 Monte Carlo Method Applied to Exhibit 8.1

	A	B	C	D	E	F	G	H
1	Year		1	2	3	4	5	6
2	Number of Units Sold		100	200	300	350	400	400
3	Average Selling Price		$10,000	$10,000	$9,500	$9,000	$8,0000	$8,000
4	Revenues		$1,000,000	$2,000,000	$2,850,000	$3,150,000	$3,200,000	$3,200,000
5								
6	COGS	57%	$570,000	$1,140,000	$1,624,500	$1,795,500	$1,824,000	$1,824,000
7	SG&A and R&D	35%	$350,000	$700,000	$997,500	$1,102,500	$1,120,000	$1,120,000
8	EBIT	22%	$80,000	$160,000	$228,000	$252,000	$256,000	$256,000
9	Provision for Taxes	32%	$25,600	$51,200	$72,960	$80,640	$81,920	$81,920
10	EAT		$54,400	$108,800	$155,040	$171,360	$174,080	$174,080
11								
12	Depreciation	5%	$28,500	$57,000	$81,225	$89,775	$91,200	$91,200
13	Increase in Investment	10%	$100,000	$85,000	$30,000	$5,000	—	—
14	GCF		$(17,100)	$80,800	$206,265	$256,135	$265,280	$265,280
15								
16	RAHR [=k]	25%						
17	DCF(k)		$(15,295)	$57,816	$118,073	$117,296	$97,187	$77,750
18	NPV(k)		$452,827					

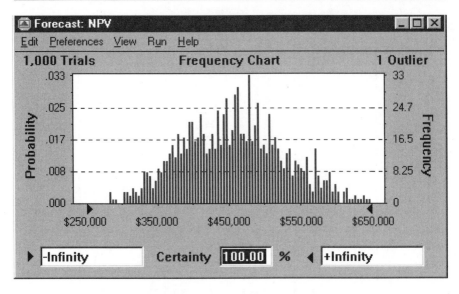

Exhibit 8.7   Monte Carlo Results for the Example in Exhibit 8.6
Source: © 1988–1998 Decisioneering, Inc. Reprinted with permission.

the relative probabilities for any specified value of NPV. So in this example, by moving the cursor or by entering the prescribed range, Crystal Ball provides the following information:

- Minimum NPV = $282K
- Twentieth Percentile NPV (i.e., 80 percent of the NPV results were higher) = $394K
- Mean NPV = $458K
- Eightieth Percentile NPV (i.e., 20 percent of the NPV results were higher) = $518K
- Maximum NPV = $662K

Thus, for the middle 60 percent of the cases, the NPV was bounded by $394 and $518K (i.e., between the twentieth and eightieth percentiles).

There is substantial additional information available from such data. A sample report is provided in Appendix 8.1.

If one repeats the calculations for a new set of 1000 iterations, it is not a surprise that the numbers are different, but yet they yield the same general result. Exhibit 8.8a shows the results of such a second group of 1000 iterations. Looking at the frequency chart one can see that the overall shape is similar to the one shown in Exhibit 8.7 although there are individual differences. Exhibit 8.8b shows a cumulative distribution chart; such a chart makes it easy to isolate the NPV values corresponding to any

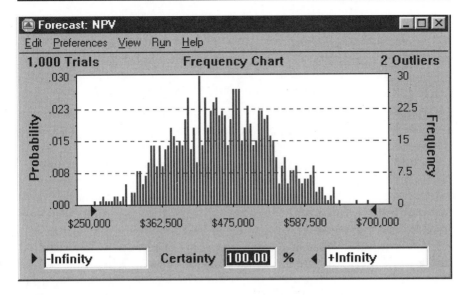

**Exhibit 8.8a   NPV Results During a Second Group of 1000 Iterations—
Frequency Chart**
Source: © 1988–1998 Decisioneering, Inc. Reprinted with permission.

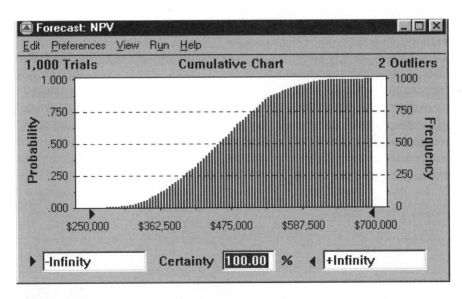

**Exhibit 8.8b   NPV Results During a Second Group of 1000 Iterations—
Cumulative Chart**
Source: © 1988–1998 Decisioneering, Inc. Reprinted with permission.

degree of probability one chooses. For example, from this chart it appears that there is approximately a 90 percent $(1 - 0.1)$ probability that the NPV will be greater than $360K.

Adjusting the Model Based Upon Critical Assumptions

Before making an interpretation of the NPV distributions, it is important to consider how the Monte Carlo Method can be used to highlight the important uncertainties. Although many different factors are unknown in every projection, the significance of these uncertainties is not equal. In every model there are usually one or two variables whose uncertainty determine substantially all the uncertainty in NPV. Identifying such critical variables can be very useful because reducing the uncertainty in these quantities greatly improves the quality of the prediction.

Shown in Exhibit 8.9 is a sensitivity chart produced by Crystal Ball for the 1000 iterations shown in Exhibit 8.8a and b. What is shown in Exhibit 8.9 is that the two most important sources of uncertainty in NPV are first, the uncertainty in COGS, and second, the uncertainty in SG&A plus R&D. This may be surprising given the natural inclination to place high importance on the assumptions behind the revenue line, namely the assumed number of units sold and the average selling price. However, the COGS and SG&A plus R&D numbers have a direct and important bearing on operating margin and, therefore, cash flow. For the assumptions made here, these effects are actually much more significant than the revenue model.

In a license valuation situation, one would then direct attention to the values assumed for COGS and SG&A plus R&D and, if additional precision in NPV is needed, make additional investments to develop more precise estimates of these numbers to the extent possible. In some cases, it may be practical to conduct additional proof of principle experiments to demonstrate, for example, that the cost of manufacture (COGS) is either lower than previously assumed (good for the seller's position) or known to a higher degree of certainty (better for both party's negotiations).

Interpretation and Valuation of NPV Distributions

As discussed in Chapter 7, there are two general perspectives on dividing NPV between seller and buyer: (1) the seller deserves 100 percent of the NPV because the RAHR (k-value) has the justified return built in for the buyer, or (2) the NPV should be split between the seller and buyer because the RAHR produces an NPV that only minimally accounts for the risk, making the buyer "whole" so that all the excess value (NPV using such k-value) is the true benefit of the opportunity. The normal perspective is the first perspective.

Often, buyers use k-values that provide the required internal return

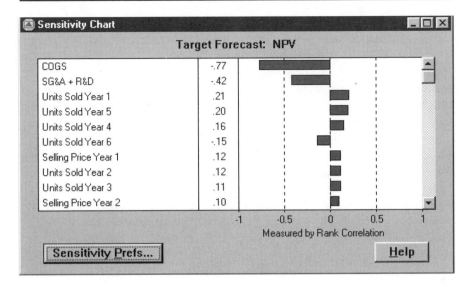

Exhibit 8.9   Sensitivity Chart for the 1000 Iterations in Exhibits 8.8a and 8.8b

Source: © 1988–1998 Decisioneering, Inc. Reprinted with permission.

given the riskiness of the project. For such a situation, all excess NPV justifiably belongs to the seller. Buyers will still want to have as much of the excess NPV as possible because business is all about paying $5 for $10, when possible.

Assuming such a perspective, how might a seller use the results of the Crystal Ball forecasts to support a negotiation position? With the buyer's assumed "right" to 100 percent of the NPV, what NPV does one choose? Clearly, if the seller settles on the maximum observed NPV ($662K) then there is less than one chance in a 1000 that the buyer will meet its targeted RAHR. At the other extreme, using the minimum observed NPV ($282K), there is less than one chance in a 1000 that the buyer won't achieve its RAHR and, on average, it will obtain a substantial additional return (in addition to its RAHR) of $176K ($458K less $282K) and could receive (one time in a 1000) as much as $380K ($662K less $282K) of additional value.

There is no simple way to decide such matters. If a single one-time payment is the remuneration approach favored by the parties, then it is a matter of dividing the uncertainty. If the parties "split it down the middle" then the result in this case is not much different than would have been obtained by using a straight DCF method without the Monte Carlo structure.[3] The argument for or against the seller receiving more than half of the NPV hinges on this: Where is it more likely to find surprises? If the surprises are more likely to be found in new markets and applications

(more than considered in the model) and/or in cost efficiencies of manufacture and/or synergies with other products or processes controlled by
the buyer, then the seller should get more than the 50 percentile NPV. On
the other hand, if the surprises are more likely to occur when bringing the
technology to commercial fruition or as a result of new and superior
products and technologies unexpectedly introduced by the competition,
then the seller should get less than 50 percentile NPV.

The results of a Monte Carlo analysis can provide the basis for other
payment structures that can more fairly reward the parties based on the
uncertainty. One example would be that the buyer pays the seller 33 percent on closing with a second 33 percent payable based upon well-defined outcomes of the key assumptions (such as the COGS value in the
previous example). Thus, the deal might be that the buyer pays $420K on
closing, approximately the thirty-third percentile, and the difference between the sixty-seventh percentile (approximately $485K) and the $420K
(i.e., $65K) would be payable in, say, three years if the COGS (carefully
defined) did not exceed 57 percent.

Other Issues Relating to the Monte Carlo Method

There are many theoretical issues that can be argued about the use of normal or bell distributions for a selling price. There is no mathematical or
scientific basis justifying such use. (Statistical purists have probably already discarded this book by now anyway.) However, the distribution
closely clusters values around the expected value and, given all the other
uncertainties, seems to offer reasonably useful results.

Likewise, one can argue about the interrelationship between price and
volume distributions, namely that one should account for higher pricing
causing lower volumes and vice versa, rather than permitting both of
these variables to act independently and be represented by different distributions to boot.[4] Again the answer is that, given all the uncertainties
one deals with in technology licensing, such arguments should not cause
immobilization. The physicist Diderot told of the man walking in the absolute darkness with a poor torch-lamp who encountered another man
who said "it is very dark here, turn out the light!" Diderot, a champion of
science and the Enlightenment, said of the second man: he was a theolo-
gian. The joke, weak as it may be, applies here: a poor light in the midst
of great darkness is better than no light at all.

RISK-ADJUSTED NPV METHOD

The rest of this chapter will consider two additional advanced[5] valuation
methods: Risk Adjusted NPV and Option Pricing. Both methods have

arisen to treat longer term/higher risk valuation which may not be well handled by other approaches.

The Risk Adjusted NPV Method builds on the DCF Method of Chapter 7.

Regarding DCF calculations (Chapter 7), when one value of RAHR (k) is used for long term projects, the equations compute very little value in later years because of the compounding effect of the value of k. For projects that end, by IPO or strategic acquisition, in five years or less, this compounding effect can be serious but not catastrophic. For pharmaceutical projects, where the first revenues may not occur for seven or even 10 years after a technology license, using high values of RAHR make it virtually impossible to justify any investment. Yet, everyone recognizes that with the technical, regulatory, and market hurdles, new drugs are high risk projects. What to do?

One approach is to "de-aggregate" the RAHR into its respective components: a component that represents the time value of money, a component for the opportunity cost value of money, a component for the technical risk, another for the regulatory risk, and so on. By this means, one can use lower values of RAHR as various hurdles are successfully passed and that particular risk is eliminated.

In a recent paper, Ashley Stevens has extensively described the use of such a stage-gating process on RAHR.[6] He also notes that Research Corporation Technologies applies a similar approach in deciding whether to invest in a university discovery. In this paper he contrasts such adjusted NPV, designated by raNPV (for risk adjusted NPV) with valuation models done by Larry Smith of Hambrecht & Quist[7] and Mary Tanner of Lehman Brothers.[8]

The examples he presents shows that such raNPV provides a higher estimated valuation of the opportunity, more in line with common sense. The reader is referred to the paper for the details of his approach and results.

OPTION PRICING METHODS

As discussed here and in Chapter 7, long-lived projects are not analyzed well by the use of single values of "k" to compute DCFs and NPV. When "n" (the number of years) is large, the discounting effect causes very small DCFs in the later years, even for projects with very significant cash flows. For example, $DCF = B/(1.3)^{10}$, for k = 30% and 10 years results in DCF = B/13.8. So even if the buyer has a cash flow of $100 million in the tenth year, the perceived value is only 100/13.8 or $7.25 million. For projects involving long development times, new pharmaceuticals would be a noteworthy but not unique example; this circumstance arises all the time.

Another problem with the DCF approach is that it assumes that all the investment money will be spent, regardless of intermediate outcomes. What actually happens is that a technology commercializer can terminate a project early if it looks like the risks are going to be higher than anticipated (or the profit less), thereby saving some or much of the investment that would have been committed and lost.

Option pricing techniques that can deal with such complexities have been developed. The preponderance of such work has been in creating investment hedges primarily for European and American call options, which requires extensive data to be able to characterize various traits of the investment, such as volatility. In some respects this creates the same distinction made in Chapter 1 between sales of businesses and licensing of technologies: businesses have track records. Similarly, option pricing methods have been developed and applied to investments, such as stocks, that have extensive track records. Although such highly mathematical methods are now widely used in analyzing investment vehicles, their use in technology licensing is restricted to more simplified approaches as will be discussed next.

STRATEGY AS A PORTFOLIO OF REAL OPTIONS

Timothy Luehrman has published a series of papers in the *Harvard Business Review* on decision-making strategy from the perspective of taking and exercising options. In his most recent paper, he defines an option space determined by two variables: one based upon NPV modified to incorporate the time value of the ability to defer investment, and the other a measurement of volatility illustrating how much circumstances can change prior to the commitment of a decision.[9]

The underlying goal is to recognize that having an option to an NPV in high-volatility situations is an opportunity to spend a little and learn a little, deferring decisions of major investments until there is much higher certainty. In this sense, the concept is similar to the raNPV approach.

Professor Luehrman also describes the use of a modified NPV—APV, or adjusted present value—in modeling the present value of future returns.[10] In another article, he shows how such options relate to the Black-Scholes Model.[11]

A useful, concrete example is provided in a related paper by Dixit and Pindyck.[12] The description here is adapted from their example and applied to a licensing context. For simplicity we will focus attention on the option aspects; no time-value of money calculations will be made. The situation is this. A buyer is given an opportunity to acquire a license for an initial payment of $5 million after which the buyer will have to expend $10 million in additional R&D. After careful analysis, the buyer has concluded that the ultimate additional cost to commercialize the technology (after the $5 million plus $10 million) will be (1) $40 million, (2) $80 million, or (3) $120 million, based upon certain assumptions. At the moment, all three outcomes are believed to be equally probable. The payoff from a successful implementation is predicted to be either (A) $50 million or (B) $130 million. Should the buyer license the technology?

Identifying the two payoffs as A and B, and the three costs as C1, C2, and C3, there are six equally likely possibilities. AC1, AC2, AC3, BC1, BC2, and BC3. The payoffs are as follows:

AC1 = $50 – $40 = +$10 million
AC2 = $50 – $80 = –$30 million
AC3 = $50 – $120 = –$70 million
BC1 = $130 – $40 = +$90 million
BC2 = $130 – $80 = +$50 million
BC3 = $130 – $120 = +$10 million.

However, in all cases, there is a $15 million investment required just to determine which outcome is expected to occur, so including this cost there are only two outcomes that are net positive, BC1 and BC2.

If one takes a decision tree approach and weighs the outcomes according to their relative probabilities, then one finds the following:

$$\text{Value of the opportunity} = 1/6(10-30-70+90+50+10)-15 = -\$5 \text{ million}$$

where the $15 million is always subtracted from the net payoff because in all cases, under these assumptions, it requires a $5 million license fee and $10 million of initial R&D to determine which of the six outcomes occurs. From such an NPV perspective, even if the seller cuts the license fee to zero, the opportunity does not yield a positive value to the buyer.

However, through option pricing, these authors illustrate that such NPV approaches portray a faulty thought process because by the $15 million investment, the buyer acquires an *option* to determine which of the three costs and two payoffs will occur. Once that is known, one does not incur the poor outcomes because if that is the perceived outcome, then one does not exercise the second option. To illustrate, if the outcome of the R&D is AC3 (payoff of $50 million and cost to commercialize of $120 million), no rational buyer will proceed any further because the buyer will lose an additional $70 million to the sunk cost of $15 million.

If the outcome is BC2 (payoff of $130 million and cost of $80 million), the buyer would then proceed with the project and net $50 million less the $15 million for the option, yielding $35 million net profit for having taken and implemented the option. Finally, if the outcome is C3, at a cost of $40 million, then the buyer should go forward in either payoff A or B (because the $15 million is an already sunk cost), yielding a net profit either –$5 million or +$75 million.

The six possible net profit outcomes are shown in Exhibit 8.10. At the left of each cell is the net of payoff (A or B) less costs (C1, C2, or C3). At the right of each cell is the net profit including the $15 million cost of obtaining the option.

The two unshaded cells show outcomes which are clearly positive even accounting for the $15 million option cost.

The two lightly shaded cells show a profit of $10 million by exercising the option, but when the option cost is considered show a net of –$5 million.

The two dark shaded cells show outcomes which would cause the buyer to terminate the project, incurring a net loss of the option cost ($15 million).

Since it was assumed that each of these six outcomes was equally probable, an option valuation shows the following:

$$\text{Value of the option} = 1/6(-5 - 15 - 15 + 75 + 35 - 5)$$
$$= 1/6(70)$$
$$= \$11.7 \text{ million}$$

Therefore, by viewing this opportunity from an option pricing perspective, it is worth a positive $11.7 million to the buyer instead of the negative result found by NPV analysis. The difference is a result of the actions taken for the two darker cells in Exhibit 8.10. In the NPV case, it is assumed that the buyer would commercialize these two possibilities just as is done in the other four cells and lose even more money than the sunk $15 million in option cost. Whereas in the option perspective it is recognized that the buyer will not ever lose more than $15 million net for any outcome.

Exhibit 8.10   Net Profit Table for the Option Pricing Example

		Commercializing Cost		
		C1 **$40 million**	**C2** **$80 million**	**C3** **$120 million**
Pay off	A $50 million	$10 –$5	–$30 –$15	–$70 –$15
	B $130 million	$90 $75	$50 $35	$10 –$5

Therefore, the license fee could actually be up to $11.7 million *higher* and still be net positive for the buyer.

CONCLUSION

Option pricing is the subject of active research. Monte Carlo techniques are being more widely applied. The challenge is in applying such insights to the technology valuation problem at hand and dealing with the scarcity of data available to be able to exploit these tools.

However, as shown in the Monte Carlo example, it is now quite easy to develop much deeper insights into risk and reward using software available for the PC and the Mac. Some study of the software manuals is required, but experience will be gained mostly through use. The software vendors offer helpful courses and seminars. Also, insights can be gained with some simple math by viewing technology investments as options.

Valuation tools will continue to be an area for active development in order to assist businesspeople trying to make important valuation decisions in conditions of high uncertainty.

NOTES

1. "Closed form solution" means that all the variables involved in the problem can be arranged in equations such that the value being solved for can be determined by simply substituting for all the variables. A simple form of such a solution is $z = ax + by$, where z is the thing sought, x and y are variables for which one has values (known or assumed) and a and b are known constants. For any x and y, one can always determine z in "closed form." Complex problems cannot be reduced to such simple forms.

2. Justified True Belief (JTB) deals with beliefs that are not only *true* (lots of people believe things that are false) but also *justifiable* (it is possible to hold a belief that is true but for false or unjustifiable reasons).

3. In general, the assumption cells are not uniformly centered about the most likely value as was shown here. For instance, one could build in a probability of total project failure (such as due to FDA non-approval). In such more general cases, the median NPC valve will be skewed lower (or higher) than the corresponding simple DCF Method calculation.

4. The Crystal Ball software provides a very easy means to correlate, either positively or negatively, any pair of assumption cells. A further refinement of this example could include the use of a negative correlation between selling price and units sold.

5. The use of the term "advanced" is meant to designate methods that involve more complex mathematical calculations than the DCF Method and which are not as widely used.

6. Ashley J. Stevens, "Risk-Adjusted Net Present Value—A New Approach to Valuing Early Stage Technologies," *Journal of Biotechnology in Healthcare*, Vol. 2, No. 4, January, 1996.

7. Larry D. Smith, "Valuation of Life Sciences Companies—An Empirical and Scientific Approach," *Hambrecht & Quist Monograph*, January 4, 1994.

8. Mary Tanner, "Financing Biotechnology Companies," presentation at Association of Biotechnology Companies, NYC, September 1991.

9. Timothy A. Luehrman, "Strategy as a Portfolio of Real Options," *Harvard Business Review*, Sept.-Oct. 1998, p. 89 ff.

10. Timothy A. Luehrman, "Using APV: A Better Tool for Valuing Operations," *Harvard Business Review*, May-June 1997, p. 145 ff.

11. Timothy A. Leuhrman, "Investment Opportunities as Real Options: Getting Started on the Numbers," *Harvard Business Review*, July-Aug. 1998, reprint 98404.

12. Avinash K. Dixit and Robert S. Pindyck, "The Options Approach to Capital Investment," *Harvard Business Review*," May-June 1995, p. 105 ff.

APPENDIX 8A

Crystal Ball Report

Crystal Ball Report
Simulation started on 3/10/99 at 17:18:06
Simulation stopped on 3/10/99 at 17:21:34

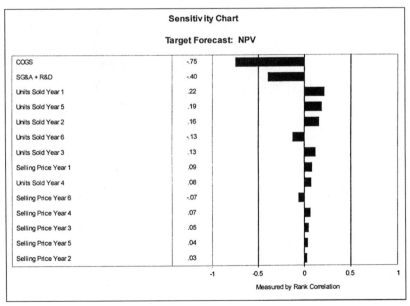

Forecast: NPV   **Cell: C18**

Summary:
   Display Range is from $250,000 to $650,000.
   Entire Range is from $282,179 to $661,632.
   After 1,000 Trials, the standard Error of the Mean is $2,257.

Statistics: *Value*
  Trials   1000
  Mean $457,773
  Median $458,247
  Mode   —
  Standard Deviation $71,362
  Variance $5,092,594,733
  Skewness   0.14
  Kurtosis   2.58
  Coeff. of Variability   0.16
  Range Minimum $282,179
  Range Maximum $661,632
  Range Width $379,452
  Mean Std. Error $2,256.68

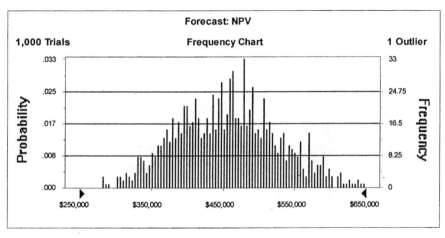

Percentiles:

Percentile	Value
0%	$282,179
10%	$366,192
20%	$393,817
30%	$414,635
40%	$438,070
50%	$458,247
60%	$477,084
70%	$493,614
80%	$517,890
90%	$555,341
100%	$661,632

End of Forecast

Assumptions

Assumption: Selling Price Year 1   Cell: C3

Triangular distribution with parameters:
    Minimum $9,000
    Likeliest $10,000
    Maximum $11,000

Selected range is from $9,000 to $11,000.
Mean value in simulation was $10,002.

Assumption: Selling Price Year 2   Cell: D3

Triangular distribution with parameters:
    Minimum $9,000
    Likeliest $10,000
    Maximum $11,000

Selected range is from $9,000 to $11,000.
Mean value in simulation was $9,990.

Assumption: Selling Price Year 3   Cell: E3

Triangular distribution with parameters:
    Minimum $8,550
    Likeliest $9,500
    Maximum $10,450

Selected range is from $8,550 to $10,450.
Mean value in simulation was $9,496.

Assumption: Selling Price Year 4   Cell: F3

Triangular distribution with parameters:
    Minimum $8,100
    Likeliest $9,000
    Maximum $9,900

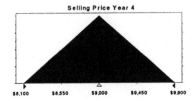

Selected range is from $8,100 to $9,900.
Mean value in simulation was $8,982.

Assumption: Selling Price Year 5   Cell: G3

Triangular distribution with parameters:
   Minimum $7,200
   Likeliest $8,000
   Maximum $8,800

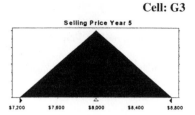

Selected range is from $7,200 to $8,800.
Mean value in simulation was $8,006.

Assumption: Selling Price Year 6   Cell: H3

Triangular distribution with parameters:
   Minimum $7,200
   Likeliest $8,000
   Maximum $8,800

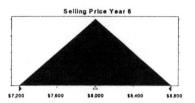

Selected range is from $7,200 to $8,800.
Mean value in simulation was $8,007.

Assumption: Units Sold Year 1   Cell: C2

Normal distribution with parameters:
   Mean   100.00
   Standard Deviation   10.00

Selected range is from –Infinity to +Infinity.
Mean value in simulation was 100.07.

Assumption: Units Sold Year 2   Cell: D2

Normal distribution with parameters:
   Mean   200.00
   Standard Deviation   20.00

Selected range is from –Infinity to +Infinity.
Mean value in simulation was 199.82.

Assumption: Units Sold Year 3   **Cell: E2**

Normal distribution with parameters:
   Mean   300.00
   Standard Deviation   30.00

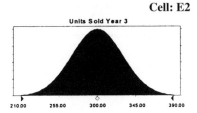

Selected range is from –Infinity to +Infinity.
Mean value in simulation was 301.56.

Assumption: Units Sold Year 4   **Cell: F2**

Normal distribution with parameters:
   Mean   350.00
   Standard Deviation   35.00

Selected range is from –Infinity to +Infinity.
Mean value in simulation was 348.79.

Assumption: Units Sold Year 5   **Cell: G2**

Normal distribution with parameters:
   Mean   400.00
   Standard Deviation   40.00

Selected range is from –Infinity to +Infinity.
Mean value in simulation was 400.98.

Assumption: Units Sold Year 6   **Cell: H2**

Normal distribution with parameters:
   Mean   400.00
   Standard Deviation   40.00

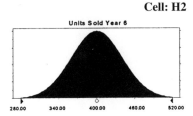

Selected range is from –Infinity to +Infinity.
Mean value in simulation was 399.06.

Assumption: COGS   Cell: B6

Uniform distribution with parameters:
Minimum   55%
Maximum   59%

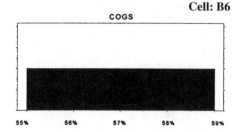

Mean value in simulation was 57%.

Assumption: SG&A + R&D   Cell: B7

Custom distribution with parameters: *Relative Prob.*
   Single point   34%   0.300000
   Single point   35%   0.500000
   Single point   36%   0.200000
Total Relative Probability   1.000000

Mean value in simulation was 35%.

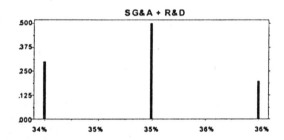

End of Assumptions

Source: Crystall Ball 4.0g, Decisioneering, Inc., Denver, CO. © 1988–1998 Decisioneering, Inc. Reprinted with permission.

9

Method Six: Auctions

INTRODUCTION

While the Monte Carlo Method and the various option pricing techniques discussed in this book are fairly recent, this chapter deals with the oldest form of valuation known: obtaining bids under an auction format.

Since antiquity, auctions have been used as a simple, powerful means of determining the value of goods offered for sale. Auctioning is similar to the Industry Standards Method of Chapter 4 in that both methods are based on direct market determinations. However, the Industry Standards Method used market information for *previous* transactions *similar* to the one in question; the Auction Method uses existing and pending offers for precisely the technology being valued.

In a certain sense, one can interpret typical negotiations as being "auctions." Even in mundane contexts such as bananas in a grocery store, the offering price is based upon the seller's perception of the price buyers are willing to pay, given the benefits and the alternatives. There really is nothing inherent in a banana that says it should sell for $X a pound. If for some reason buyers begin to want more bananas than are available, the sellers (all the sellers in the value chain) sense the demand and use it as a signal to deliver more bananas and to charge a higher price. Because bananas are perishable commodity items, the supply will eventually increase to the point where the abundance of bananas will cause sellers to reduce the price in order to clear out stock and a new market equilibrium price and demand will be established.

In offering technology for license, sellers typically call on multiple potential buyers to determine interest. The response from such inquiries can influence a seller's pricing decisions, even though no formal offer or bid has been made. Even if there are only discussions with one prospective buyer, imagine what a seller would think if that buyer said

189

something like, "This is the best opportunity I've ever seen,"; "We absolutely have to have this technology," and "Hey, look, money is no object here, how much do you want?" Would not such words, or equivalent body language, be interpreted by the seller as bidding language even without formal bids? This is why, in the author's experience, the seller instead hears: "It looks very risky," "It's going to take a lot of money to get this to the market and then I'm not sure anyone is going to buy it," and "Maybe, just maybe, if we can get it for no upfront license fee and for a very reasonable royalty, I might be able to persuade my boss to take a chance on this."

The Auction Method is a way for a seller to structure a series of parallel, very short-term discussions with multiple prospective buyers and reduce all positioning statements into a simple monetary bid in a winner-take-all framework.

WHEN AUCTIONS ARE FEASIBLE

Before going into the operational issues of the Auction Method, it needs to be noted that the use of the method presumes a certain bargaining power on the part of the seller. If such power does not exist, then auctioning does not work. Also, from the perspective of the buyer, it is hard to envision circumstances where the use of auctions as a valuation method should be encouraged.[1]

In all five previous methods, there is no inherent limitation on the seller in making use of the described tools and techniques. There is always the challenge of gathering data, developing models, and applying good judgment, but there is nothing about these previous methods that requires a particular circumstance for the methods to be applied by either the buyer or the seller. Also in all the previous methods, there is nothing inherently disadvantageous to either the buyer or seller in the method itself. In the case of auctions, the buyer is at a disadvantage, and it requires some special circumstances in order to induce prospective buyers to "play."

Buyers always hope to be in a position to buy below the market value. It is important to recognize that if a seller and buyer each independently value a particular opportunity and, miraculously, both conclude that it is worth $10 million on an NPV basis net of an identically-assumed royalty, that it is the nature of buyers to try to pay something much less than $10 million. It has been said that business is about paying $5 for things worth $10; that is certainly the buyer's perspective. So, from a "win-win" negotiating standpoint, one might expect this situation to result in a quick settlement on the $10 million NPV. More often, what seems to happen is that the buyer will work very hard to see if the opportunity can be acquired for less than $10 million. The last thing that a buyer wants is a competitive bid situation with other buyers because such a situation would, in this hypothetical example, inevitably lead to a bid of $10 million, thus extinguishing the buyer's hope of paying $5 for a $10 item (Lest buyers feel abandoned, a counter-measure buyers can use to avoid auctions will be briefly discussed in the last section of this chapter.)

The other special circumstance of an auction is that it presumes (1) an inherently strong bargaining position on the seller's part and (2) that the technology in question can be apprehended relatively quickly by prospective buyers. Considering first the issue of bargaining power, buyers will resist being herded into an auction. The only reason buyers will go along with this method is that the licensing opportunity is so compelling that passing it up is even worse than bidding. Unless the seller can attract at least two or three bidders, the auction method is unlikely to produce a desirable result, although a sole buyer who is unaware of the non-existence of significant (or any) competition could be induced to making a full-NPV bid. Three or more bidders are optimal because it is common to have "low-ball bidders" at auctions—buyers who have not conducted a serious valuation but who bid a number so low that they are confident they can make money regardless of what it is they are buying (which by the way, is not reliably true of technology opportunities). In some cases, low-ball bidders even construct their offer in such a way as to tie up the technology for little or no money for the purpose of conducting their due diligence in a non-competitive environment. (This approach will be included in the buyer's alternatives to auctions section.)

A variant of low-ball bids is "fire sale" bids. The term refers to the insurance industry's practice of offering for quick sale goods that have been damaged in a fire. The insured had already been paid the full value for the damaged goods; a fire sale was a way for the insurance company to recoup something on its loss. The fire sale also carried the notion that what was not sold immediately was literally trashed, so any offer above zero was considered a potential winning bid.[2] Sellers should, of course, do everything they can to avoid the fire sale perception, signaling buyers that the auction is a disposal situation. Savvy buyers, as part of their due diligence, investigate the selling circumstances for exactly this reason. In the previously-cited Arthur Miller play, *The Price*, the used furniture buyer does not quote a price until he is able to determine the circumstances of the sale, wherein he learns: (1) neither heir can or will take the furniture, (2) there are no other bidders or takers, (3) the lease is about to run out on the apartment in which the furniture is being stored, and (4) the buyer's family is in a "get it over with" frame of mind. Did this affect his price? Not for nothing did a 90-year old man spend the entire first act pumping the seller for information. (Did Arthur

Miller want us to think about our self-limiting natural inclinations, causing us to sell ourselves cheaply)? (Ah, back to work....)

If an auction fails, due to a lack of bids or only low-ball bids, then the seller is at a bargaining disadvantage in seeking out subsequent buyers (assuming such buyers knew of the auction) because they would know that there was little or no interest by other buyers. Therefore, one of the seller's big risks in auctioning is that it can fail, which then can make it difficult to sell at all. At the very least, the seller might have to propose terms even less attractive than would have otherwise occurred sans auction.

The second assumption behind conducting an auction is that a buyer can reasonably apprehend the opportunity without a significant level of due diligence. To use estate auctions as a colloquial example, typical formats provide a catalog description of all the items offered for sale and an inspection period during which all bidders can examine the merchandise. When the goods being auctioned are seen and valued in a few minutes' time, then it is possible to get a large number of bidders to make the small investment in their time for the prospect of making and winning a bid. Even if a buyer's perception is that the odds of winning a bid are low, the investment required to ascertain the potential value is also low. In the case of technology, such low apprehension cost situations are rare if not non-existent. All the risk issues discussed in Chapters 2 and 7 normally need to be evaluated through a serious investment of time and, sometimes, testing (laboratory, manufacturing, and/or market). In such circumstances, buyers tell sellers that they simply will not exert such due diligence without some reasonable chance of being able to acquire the license if the opportunity checks out and the terms are affordable. Serious buyers will often express such a position by counter-offering an option agreement (discussed in Chapter 11), together with a cash payment to maintain an exclusive right to bid for a prescribed period. To some extent, sellers can help reduce the buyer's investment requirement by creating extensive data packages and even disclosure "rooms" where prospective buyers can study comprehensively prepared background information. It is in the seller's interest to make the due diligence burdens as low as possible in order to induce as many bidders as possible.

From time to time a particular auction-related selling concept is tried, that of having a technology "fair." At such fairs, all technology sellers are in individual booths hawking their wares to prospective invitee-buyers, a technology flea market, so to speak. There are many problems with this concept. The principal underlying hypothesis is that it is possible, while standing in front of display tables with patents and prototypes, for a buyer to conduct sufficient due diligence to make a purchase decision and engage in negotiation. Such a process works well for baseball cards, collectible dolls, and shishkabob, but not for technology.

In summary, the more complex the opportunity, the more the seller must do to make it easier for buyers to conduct due diligence, and despite such efforts, the less likely it is that enough prospective buyers will take advantage of the opportunity. Likewise, the less compelling the opportunity, the more infeasible it becomes that a group of buyers will follow a seller's schedule in reviewing the opportunity and offering bids.

ROCKEFELLER "FAT GENE," AND OTHER EXAMPLES

One recent example of an auction that turned out very well for the seller has to do with a "fat gene" discovered by Rockefeller Institute.[3] Investigators at Rockefeller discovered a gene that appears to control obesity in mice and filed a patent application. The invention was described as "the hottest property to come out of biotech in years,"[4] a characterization not surprising given the ever-popular subject of weight loss. The inventor left Rockefeller and joined a startup company (Millennium) and sought to obtain rights to the patent. Rockefeller, reasonably concerned about obtaining fair value by an arm's length negotiation, invited the interest of about a dozen pharmaceutical firms including Amgen, Eli Lilly, BMS, and others. The interest turned out to be very high, and Rockefeller found itself being pursued with ever-increasing terms. To create order, Rockefeller formalized a review and bidding process in January and February of 1995. Then on February 28, 1995, Rockefeller announced that Amgen agreed to pay a $20 million "signing fee" for a license; royalties (to be determined) were estimated at an additional $70 to $80 million. According to the Rockefeller Vice President for Academic Affairs, "Amgen purchased a scientific concept."[5]

This example has received a lot of press and may have created unrealistic expectations in some sellers. Clearly the Rockefeller auction was a case where the two necessary factors for a successful auction were present: strong bargaining power on the part of the seller, and relative ease in conducting due diligence by potential buyers. As further evidence of the bargaining power, in 1998 Pfizer was reported to have paid Phytopharm PLC up to $32 million for exclusive rights to an experimental drug to treat obesity based upon extracts of plants native to South America.[6] Clearly, market demand for drugs to control obesity creates intense interest in identifying promising technologies.

Although the price obtained by Rockefeller may be unusual, the use of an auction process for technology is not uncommon. The following are briefly summarized examples of auctions used to value and sell technology. They are based upon a recent paper by Bob Bramson which was written using publicly available information:[7]

Exponential Technologies offered semiconductor patents alleged to cover Intel's Merced architecture. Rights were acquired by S3 for a price in the range of $10 to $12 million. Apple Computer has sued Exponential Technologies over the proceeds of the sale.

Wang offered 200 patents organized in 34 technology groups. Certain groups sold during a so-called "quiet period." Additional groups sold through the auction process.

AR Accessories Group, Inc. sold its patents at a bankruptcy auction.

Carl W. Cooke had a patent on a child-resistant closure for pharmaceuticals. Its bankruptcy plan appraised the value of the patent at $375 million. An auction was conducted supervised by the Internal Revenue Service, but no bids were received.

Cray Computer Corporation had patents on various technologies relating to supercomputing manufacturing packaging and processes. These patents and related intellectual property were acquired by Dasu L.L.C. for $100,000.

IL Med had patents relating to surgical laser scanners. Under an auction format these patents were acquired by Laser Industries.

Lamplighter Industries had patents relating to electroluminescent light technologies. The patents were offered at a bankruptcy auction and were acquired by CEL Technologies.

Orca Technology had patents relating to disc drives which it had bought three years previously from Priam for $500,000 as part of a technology package. At a bankruptcy auction, Orca received $3.65 million by a Samsung winning bid.

BioPolymers, Inc. had patents on medical adhesives which also were sold off also via a bankruptcy auction.

Thinking Machines Corporation's massively parallel process patents were on track to be offered at auction. It is unclear whether such an auction took place. Likewise, VideOcart Inc.'s patent of shopping cart video display terminals was planned to be auctioned but the results are unknown.

These examples and others show not only the feasibility of using auctions but also act as another category of "Industry Standard" data to assist both buyers and sellers in performing technology valuations.

TYPES OF AUCTIONS

At the heart of the Auction Method is establishing an unambiguous process that prospective buyers can rely upon as being fair. Integrity in the process is essential as prospective buyers must believe that the highest qualifying bid will in fact be the successful bid. From the standpoint of a buyer, the nightmare scenario is that the seller has a hidden understanding with one of the buyers enabling the favored buyer to make a final bid after learning of all the other bids. Not only is such behavior unfair, but it also runs against the seller's own interests because it saves the favored buyer from having to make an aggressive bid by enabling that company to make only a matching or a slightly higher bid (known in the industry as a winning "McBid").

A simple form of an auction is to establish a time and place for written, binding bids to be submitted and the arrangements and time period whereby due diligence can occur. The seller should do everything possible to maintain the confidentiality of the number and identity of the bidders, although on many occasions the bidders all learn who the other parties are. Nevertheless, in some cases the prospective buyer views its interest as highly sensitive information, and the seller needs to take all reasonable steps to protect it as such.

Some "buyers" are really just doing competitive intelligence by participating in the process. Such buyers know or believe that someone will acquire the technology and put it into the marketplace, and they want to understand what the competitive effect is likely to be. Although such parties do not directly harm the auction process, they do take time and resources away from assisting serious prospects. Sellers have the right to exclude parties who they believe are not serious buyers. Strong non-disclosure agreements can act to dissuade some "tire kickers" because of the fear of later legal exposure if they independently develop features or products that appear to be derived from what they learned in the due diligence process.

The process normally involves written offers rather than calling out numbers as in estate auctions, although oral bidding processes have been used. The seller should create a standard form for such bids to assure that bidders respond with answers to all terms relevant to the seller. Otherwise, it can be impossible to know what exactly a buyer has bid.[8]

The seller then reviews the bids, which may take some time because each bid could be structured in such different ways that it requires "moving money around in time" using the Discounted Cash Flow Method. Of course, as part of such money movement, a risk factor must be selected which could vary from bidder to bidder depending upon the assets they can deploy in support of commercialization. The Rating/Ranking Method can be useful in comparing the various bids and bidders. The Industry Standard Method can help the seller compare all the offers received with those received by others in other auctions. Finally, the seller can use the Monte Carlo Method to create multiple return scenarios with various bidders or with various options under each bid.

The seller is not precluded from proposing modifications in the winning bid. Of course, the buyer is not obligated to accept such variations. However, it is possible that some changes advantageous to both parties could be found, (or at least changes that are advantageous to one and neutral to the other).

It is important upon selection of the winning bid that the consummation of the sale take place quickly as the losing bidders are likely to lose interest and go on to other projects. If for some reason the winner bidder does not complete the transaction, the seller wants to be able to conclude a deal with the next best bid. This hurdle can be cleared by having a complete agreement already drafted, one that outlines many of the key terms and requires all bidders to accept such terms for their bid to be "qualified" and considered for award. The U.S. Government has conducted such auctions for various contracts and in some cases even requires all bidders to sign the contract with their bid. The Government then executes only the winning contract. (It takes a *lot* of bargaining power to be able to do this.) In most licensing situations, the bids are sufficiently different in structure and the transaction complex enough that such pre-signed licenses are not feasible.

Sellers can further protect themselves by requiring that a non-refundable license fee or partial licensing fee accompany a bid. If the seller accepts the bid and the buyer has a change in heart, the licensing fee is forfeited. Such a fee is sometimes known as a "break up" fee, although that term is also used for the exit price paid by the party that terminates the deal after it has been executed. The rationale of this lost fee in an auction context is that the seller has been harmed by the buyer's refusal or inability to consummate its successful bid.

Open bidding auctions such as those commonly used for paintings, antiques, and cars work best when there are many items to be sold and many bidders to be managed. For technology deals, such an approach is generally not feasible.

However, other variants of auctions could be useful. One such variant is the "short list" auction. The initial bidders are pared down to (usually) just two or three parties who make "the short list." Then more detailed negotiations (and possibly further due diligence) are held, and a last, "best and final" bid is made by the two or three parties. This approach is particularly useful if an ongoing relationship between the seller and buyer will be needed; the negotiating period will permit each party to discern what working with the other party will be like. Such discussions can also be helpful to a seller who is attempting to determine the likelihood of actually receiving future payments or royalties based upon a buyer's successful commercialization.

Appendix 9A, courtesy of Dale Hogue, provides a sample letter used to conduct an actual patent auction.

APPROACHES BUYERS CAN USE IN LIEU OF AN AUCTION

As discussed above, buyers generally find auctions to be to their disadvantage and, consequently, they seek ways of avoiding such situations. There are several techniques that buyers can use to prevent auctions.

The reason sellers seek auctions is to maximize the price and to have followed a process that can be argued to have done so. Buyers, then, can meet the desires of a seller by (1) offering a "preemptive," attractive bid, and (2) providing information that will persuade the seller that their offer is in fact fair and attractive. Further, the buyer can (when legitimate) create a reasonable sense of urgency. Focusing on concluding the negotiations as soon as possible will speed the subsequent commercialization of the technology.

At the beginning of this chapter there is the hypothetical example where the seller and buyers both have the same perception of value, that is, an NPV of $10 million. A buyer can use a business model to justify a bid of $10 million. Being greedy or attempting to get $10 for $1 may result only in getting forced into an auction process and a lost opportunity. This will certainly increase transaction cost and time spent. Instead, a buyer can sometimes induce a seller to accept somewhat less than the full $10 million for a quick deal. In the end, if the buyer believes that such NPV was calculated using an appropriate risk-adjusted hurdle rate (k), then the buyer should be prepared to pay the full $10 million.

CONCLUSION

In one sense, the Auction Method is the easiest valuation method because the seller does not have to calculate or develop a valuation model. However, it involves significant work of a different sort: the seller has to create and manage a valuation process that attracts a sufficient number of prospective buyers. Overall, it may not be simpler, or easier, or even faster. The greatest value of auctions is that when they succeed they provide concrete evidence of market value by virtue of the fact that multiple buyers are each making offers in their own reasonable self-interest. For those circumstances where it makes sense, the Auction Method can be very useful, but overall it is not the norm. Its frequent use in bankruptcy settings and other emergency liquidations is testament not to the desirability of the method but rather to the need for a rapid resolution of the sale, much like our earlier reference to fire sales.

NOTES

1. There is a least one case of buyer-encouraged auctions. If a prospective buyer believes that it has made a very high offer and, for reasons unique to the buyer, can afford to pay more for the technology than can other buyers, but the seller is still reluctant to sell because it believes that the technology is worth even more, then it could be in the buyer's best interest to encourage an auction, formal or informal, to dislodge the seller from its position.

2. In cases where there is a significant disposal (trashing) costs, even offers below zero, (i.e., the *seller* pays the buyer), can actually be advantageous to the seller. This situation is what buyers dream about in alpha-state sleep.

3. The source of the information provided about the Rockefeller Institute auction is based upon *Business Week* articles, March 13, 1995, p. 46; March 20, 1995, p. 100; and August 7, 1995, p. 29.

4. Ibid.

5. Ibid.

6. "Pfizer Gives Phytopharm a Boost; Pact Centers on Obesity Treatment," *Wall Street Journal*, August 25, 1998.

7. Special thanks to Bob Bramson of Bramson and Pressman for the examples cited, as given in his paper, "Patent Auctions, An Alternative Method of Generating Value from Patents," presented at the 1998 Annual Meeting of the Licensing Executives Society in Miami, October 28, 1998.

8. Some buyers create ambiguity on purpose. If a seller who does not fully understand such an ambiguous offer enters into negotiations with such a buyer, other buyers are likely to vanish and the seller could be left in a negotiating situation very different from what had been anticipated.

APPENDIX 9A

Bidder's Agreement

This agreement made between _____(hereinafter Bidder) and Hogue Management, LLC (Hereinafter Auctioneer) is for the purpose of allowing Bidder to participate as a bidder in a live auction of U.S. Patent No. 5,664,115, Interactive Computer System to Match Buyers and Sellers of Real Estate, Businesses and other Property Using the Internet, now owned by Richard Fraser.

If the Bidder is the highest bidder, he agrees to pay his bid amount payable to the transfer agent, Antonelli, Terry, Stout & Kraus, LLP, 1300 North Seventeenth Street, Suite 1800, Arlington, Virginia 22209, by 5 PM EDT, Friday, May 15, 1999 at the above address. Payment may be by cashiers check or a wire transfer of good funds. Payment made after this time period may be accepted at the sole discretion of Richard Fraser. If there is not timely payment or acceptance by Richard Fraser of a late tender, Richard Fraser may reject the bid and resell the patent at the cost of Bidder and may recover any negative difference between the ultimate sale price of said patent and the Bidder's highest offer.

Bidder agrees that he will clearly communicate his bid to the auctioneer. Once the auctioneer acknowledges the bid it is final and may not be withdrawn.

Bidder agrees to abide by the laws of the Commonwealth of Virginia pertaining to the sale of intangible property sold by auction.

The Bidder may bid anonymously. If he wishes to do so he must identify his nominee to the auctioneer in writing by June 11, 1999, no later then 5 PM EDT, addressed to the auctioneer at the address of the Antonelli, Terry et al. law firm above identified.

Bidder will be assigned a number for bidding purposes and will receive a numbered bidding card. Bidder agrees to bid by this assigned number and is responsible for retaining possession of said card and all bids made using that number. Auctioneer will not disclose the identity of any bidder.

The auctioneer will cause to be delivered an assignment of all right, title and interest in said U.S. Patent 5,664,115 upon payment in good funds of the successful bid price to the transfer agent. The assignment will include all rights, past and present. Richard Fraser will warrant that there are no claims to title or licenses granted under said patent, or claims as to validity or enforceability of said patent. No other warranties or representations will be made nor indemnifications given.

Accepted by: Accepted by:

_____   _____
Signature   Signature

_____   _____
Title   Principal Manager

_____   _____
Company Name and Address   Hogue Management, LLC
Tele. No.

_____   _____
Date   Date

Source: Dale Hogue, Hogue Management, LLC, Hilton Head, SC, dchoguesr@aol.com.

10

Equity Considerations

INTRODUCTION

As discussed in Chapter 2, there are many possible forms of payment (or consideration) of interest to buyers and sellers in licensing negotiations. In this chapter we will consider the special circumstances where the buyer offers equity (stock) in an entity already created or to be created in order to commercialize the subject technology. Although stock can be considered as partial or full compensation for a license by performing a fair market valuation (FMV) of the stock, and as such, could be treated by any and all of the previous valuation methods, frequently there are special aspects of such a transaction that warrant treatment in a separate chapter.

INHERENT ADVANTAGES OF
PERFORMANCE-BASED PAYMENTS

First, it is useful to distinguish among cash payments, royalties, and equity as forms of compensation in a license. Cash is the simplest rumuneration. Once the amount has been settled upon as a result of valuation, pricing, and negotiation, the cost to the buyer and the benefit to the seller is fixed, certain, and immediate.[1] If the licensed technology turns out to be more successful than the parties envisioned, then this fortuitous outcome benefits the buyer and the buyer only; likewise, if there is an unfortunate outcome, the direct financial consequences are felt by the buyer and the buyer only. In other words, "A deal is a deal." Once the parties have agreed on the worth of a technology, it is contrary to the nature of a cash license agreement for future events to cause the parties to change the valuation. It is precisely this certainty of valuation that makes it challenging to use only cash as the basis of a technology license. Sellers must make projections on the potential range of outcomes, high to zero, and settle on one number for which they are willing to part with the technology and live with that decision. Similarly, buyers need to reduce all the uncertainties to one number, and that number has to be equal to or higher than the seller's number or no deal will be possible.

In a sense, all cash license agreements can lead to a feeling by either the buyer or the seller that, in retrospect, the deal was unfair. This is because the NPV of what actually transpires will almost certainly be higher or lower than the license price. If, for example, it comes out higher, then the seller must face the fact that the deal is fair even though it did not receive the full value of the opportunity because it did not participate in the risk but instead opted for a certain sum. If the outcome is lower than originally agreed to, then the buyer has to remember that this is the price of agreeing to a fixed-cash license fee. The buyer took the risk of commerce and this particular time the outcome was unexpectedly low. A summary of these perspectives is shown in Exhibit 10.1.

Because of the difficulty in determining one single number as an equitable valuation, and the subsequent dissatisfaction that one or the other parties can be expected to feel, it is common for the parties to instead structure the valuation so that both the buyer and the seller share some of the risk and some of the reward associated with uncertain outcomes. Royalties are a very useful and simple means of doing this, which is in fact why they exist as an option—the marketplace created the royalty concept because of the need for dealing with vast future uncertainties. This "tying together" of like interests, (unlike the example shown in Exhibit 10.1) is one key advantage of a royalty structure. A second advantage is that it does not require the specification of one absolute dollar amount as the eq-

Exhibit 10.1   Perspectives of the Parties to Future Outcomes with Cash Licenses

	Seller's Perspective	Buyer's Perspective
NPV of the Outcome is Greater than Cash Payment for the License	I elected not to risk my payment and, so, did not deserve the unexpected upside.	By my risk-taking (and perhaps commercial skill), I have managed to do better than planned.
NPV of the Outcome is Less than Cash Payment for the License	At the time, I received what both parties believed it was worth; I did not have the right to any upside surprise and, so, I do not participate in a downside surprise either.	I took the risk that in the end I would receive more value than originally estimated, but with that risk was risk that I would not do as well as I'd planned.

uitable consideration for a license; so in this sense, it is easier to reach agreements between sellers and buyers, and it is easier for both the seller and the buyer to feel that what they are to receive is fair. This latter virtue is important because, in most cases, there are multiple individuals at both companies who must approve the deal in order for it to take place. A licensing negotiator can sometimes face more difficulty trying to negotiate a consensus in his or her own organization than with the other side. Royalties and equity make this easier than lump sum payments.

RATIONALE FOR EQUITY AS A PERFORMANCE-BASED PAYMENT

However (and there is always a "however") royalties do not completely mirror the profitability or cash flow that will result from putting a technology into commerce. Royalties, as the term is normally used, apply to a base of sales, the so-called "top line" of an income statement. Profitability, or cash flow, occurs at the "bottom line." In between are a lot of costs (and a lot of accounting). The buyer will feel success or failure, relative or absolute, by what happens principally at the bottom line.[2] Accordingly, it is possible that the seller could be quite happy with a royalty cash inflow based upon some percentage of sales, while the buyer is quite unhappy because after all the costs, including the royalty payment, the net on the bottom line is small, zero, or even negative. Because royalties are tied to sales, which occur only if there are customers, they are a step toward risk sharing between the seller and buyer, but a royalty structure does not equally balance the risks and interests between the parties.

From time to time, various buyers have proposed a modified royalty structure where the royalty base is in the bottom line, EBIT, or EAT (see Chapter 7), instead of being sales-based, arguing that such a net income basis is a truer reflection of the value of the license. However, because all the costs between the top line and the net income of the bottom line are largely controlled by the buyer, there are only rare and special cases where the parties agree to basing the royalty on any value below the top line and doing so is perilous to the seller.

There are various other lines below the top line (sales) and above the bottom line (EBIT or EAT) on which the royalty could be based. Gross Margin, defined as the sales less the cost of goods sold (the so-called direct costs), is one such possibility. In general, because of the auditing complexities in computing the royalty base anywhere below the top line, it is still rare that parties agree to such a provision.

There are certain other issues that arise with royalty agreements. Consider the following situation. The seller licenses patents and trade secrets (know how) to the buyer and, in so doing, launches the buyer in a new business. As the technology is developed and optimized, the buyer creates and then sells products that look generally like the licensed subject matter, but such products are outside the claims of the licensed patents and the scope of the licensed trade secrets. As a result, the buyer argues that it owes the seller nothing. The seller, in looking carefully at the terms of the license agreement, concludes that although the buyer is technically correct, an unjust outcome has occurred because despite having put the buyer in business, the seller will not receive any future compensation. The buyer's response is "a deal is a deal" and I have no obligation to pay for what I am not using (i.e., I am not benefiting from the scope of the licensed patent claims or trade secret information). Equity-based agreements can help prevent this situation.

With equity agreements, the seller receives a share in the company that receives the licensed technology. If the above scenario unfolds, it would not limit the seller's future prospects because it owns stock *in the company*, not a royalty right in specific kinds of *sales*. In this sense, the consideration received by the seller is somewhat like ownership of a mutual fund comprised of anything and everything the buyer can or will create in terms of value. Even if the buyer abandons the licensed technology and instead opens a hamburger stand, as long as the corporate entity remains, the seller will retain its equity share in a burgers and fries enterprise.

Equity deals can also create a downside outcome for the seller. Consider a buyer that has two products, one based on the licensed subject

Exhibit 10.2   Contrasting the Benefits and Limitations of Royalty and Equity-Based License Agreements

	Royalty Agreements	Equity Agreements
1. Base of payment	Sales of licensed subject matter	Value of the buyer-entity
2. Upside Potential	Increased sales of licensed subject matter	Increased value of the company
3. Downside Potential	Decreased or no sales of licensed subject matter	Failure of the company
4. Payments Made to Seller	Quarterly or annually on sales	Conversion (sale) of stock
5. Payment Stream to Seller	Each quarter for the life of the agreement (could extend to 10 years or more)	No payments until an equity conversion (realization) is possible and exercised
6. Importance of Patents and other forms of IP	Crucial to the seller receiving payments under the terms of the license	Relevant to the general competitive position of the buyer, but irrelevant to the rights of the seller

matter and one developed independently. In this scenario, the licensed subject matter is wildly successful in both a top line and bottom line sense. However, the second product turns out to be a disaster and causes the loss of all the profits of the firm. Had the seller a royalty-only interest, it would have received payment unaffected by the misfortune occurring elsewhere in the buyer's company, providing the buyer continued to make sales of the licensed technology. But with an equity interest, the "mutual fund" right the seller acquired could result in the destruction of all value of the company. Other concerns of sellers, which are outside the scope of this book, have to do with liability. Exhibit 10.2 summarizes the principal distinctions between a traditional royalty interest and an equity interest.

THE EXTREME UPSIDE POTENTIAL OF EQUITY-BASED AGREEMENTS

There is one additional, and extremely important, factor that explains the keen and increasing interest in equity-based agreements: the upside potential to the seller. Consider the following situation. In Case A, there is a straight royalty agreement of 5 percent of sales and such sales are $100 million per year for 10 years. Ignoring DCF considerations for simplicity, the math for the seller looks like this:

Annual Royalty=5% *$100 Million=$5 Million * 10 years=$50 Million.

In Case B, assuming somehow there is a parallel universe where the exact same technology is put into practice under an equity-based agreement where, instead of a 5 percent royalty, the seller received 10 percent of the pre-public stock, the math for the seller could look like this:

Annual Royalty = $0. Value of the company, as determined by the market at an initial public offering (IPO) turns out to be 10 times the company's revenues (which are solely from the licensed technology), then the value of the seller's stock = $100 million * 10 * 10% = $100 million (ignoring, for the moment, dilution), at the date of the IPO which is in (say) three years hence.

So for Case A, the seller received a total of $50 million in equal $5 million payments over 10 years, whereas in Case B, the seller received $100 million in one payment three years after the license was signed. Most sellers would prefer Case B to Case A; if the perceived risks were the same, no rational seller would prefer Case A. The key driver for value in Case B is the market's perception of company value scaled on the company's sales at the time of the IPO. In this example, 10 times sales was used; had the valuation been two times sales, then the seller would have received:

$$\$100 \text{ million} * 2 * 10 \text{ percent} = \$20 \text{ million}.$$

For most sellers, this would look less attractive than the Case A outcome. The general recipe for comparison is as follows:

$$\text{Case A/Case B} = \text{Royalty} * \text{Sales/Share} * M * \text{Sales} = \text{Royalty/Share} * M, \text{ where royalty is the royalty rate as a percentage of sales,}$$

share is the percentage of the company owned by the seller at the time of IPO, and M is the market's valuation of the company as a multiple of sales at the time of the IPO.

Historically, companies were valued at approximately one to three times sales. Using two times sales, the formula becomes:

$$\text{Case A/Case B} = \text{Royalty/2} * \text{Share}.$$

This equation shows that without consideration of risk or the time value of money (and the attendant timing of an IPO), Case A would be preferred by the seller if the royalty percentage was more than twice the share ownership at the time of IPO. If the share ownership is greater than half the royalty (again expressed as a percentage), then Case B would be more attractive to the seller. Using 5 percent royalty as an example, and again neglecting the issues of risk and time value of money and taxes, the seller should prefer an equity deal (Case B) for any circumstance where the share interest exceeds 2.5 percent at the time of an IPO, and should prefer a royalty deal (Case A) when the shares offered were less (or projected to become less) than 2.5 percent at the time of an IPO. All these values are derived from the assumption that the market value is twice the annual revenues.

If the market valuation (M) is 10 times revenues, then the crossover value for preferring equity over royalty is one-tenth the royalty rate, namely, the seller is better off in an equity model, rather than a royalty payment, when the shares offered make up greater than 0.5 percent of the company at the time of an IPO. Exhibit 10.3 shows how this works for various values of M.

The historical basis for valuations in the range of one to three times revenues is this: If a company produces after-tax profits (EAT) of 10 percent of revenues, then $100 of annual sales creates a stream of profits of $10 per year. What would an owner pay for a stream of payments of $10 per year? Using the Discounted Cash Flow equation (Chapter 7), the present value of each $10 payment is equal to $\$10/(1 + k)^n$ where k

Exhibit 10.3   The Relationship Between Royalty Rate and Market Valuation Multiple that Makes an Equity Realization More Attractive to a Seller

Royalty rate for a royalty-based agreement (the Case A alternative)	Market Valuation Multiple, M (Value at IPO/Annual Revenues)	Share ownership that would create a more attractive return to a seller than a royalty interest
5%	2	2.5%
5%	10	0.5%
5%	20	0.25%
1%	2	0.5%
1%	10	0.1%
1%	20	0.05%

is the risk-adjusted hurdle rate and n is the year in which such payment occurs. What is the sum of an infinite stream of such payments made year by year? It turns out that the equation is very simple: Present Value of an infinite stream of annual payments = B/k, where B is the magnitude of such annual payments. So for a k-value of 7 percent (0.07), PV = 14.3 $*$ B. In other words, an investor believing that the future benefit of owning an asset will be "B" dollars per year, and perceiving the overall risk and time value of money as being 7 percent, would be willing to pay up to 14.3 times the value of B. Further, if the buyer believed that "B" would increase with time, perhaps as a result of expanding markets, then a value higher than 14.3 would be warranted. What this represents is the the price/earnings ratio (P/E ratio): the earnings are "B," and the buyer is willing to pay 14.3 (or more) to own such future earnings. Historically, common stock has traded (been sold) at P/E ratios of 15 to 20.

Putting this together, the value of a company expressed as a percentage of its annual sales would be as follows:

Value of a company = (P/E) $*$ (B/Sales) $*$ Sales. For a P/E of 20, and B/Sales (i.e., earnings after tax, or EAT) of 10 percent, the resulting valuation is two times sales. The general result is shown in Exhibit 10.4.

The values shown in Exhibit 10.4 presume constant sales and profitability. Because the IPO market has recently valued many start-ups at very high multiples of revenues—the so called "dot com" effect—sellers have become increasingly interested in participating in equity realizations. When multiples on revenues at an IPO reach 10 or more, then even very small ownership percentages can create tremendous valuations.

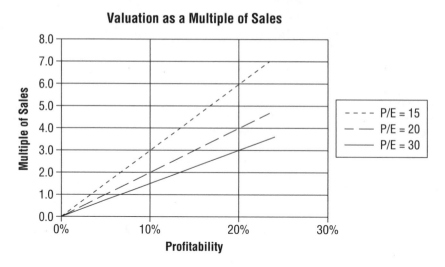

Exhibit 10.4   Valuation as a Multiple of Sales for Various Values of P/E Ratio and Projected Profitability

SHARE STRUCTURES AND VALUE

When a company is publicly traded, such as on the NASDAQ exchange, the share price is known daily, even hourly, with great precision. The reason for such precision is that there is a continuous auction underway with numerous buyers and sellers, and imbalances in supply and demand cause the price of a share to go up and down. Such market determination is not present in a technology license to a start-up, because there is no public market.[3]

There are two licensing situations to be considered here: (1) the buying company pre-exists the license negotiation with previous investment and valuation, and (2) the buyer exists as individuals who will start a company, raise funds and hire additional management to commercialize the licensed technology. In the former case, there is some basis of valuation for the existing company because previous investors had to have determined how much each share was worth in order to rationalize their investment. In the latter case, the initial valuation of the company will be determined at the time of the license. We will deal with the latter case first because it's a more common situation.

The easiest way to perform a valuation is to assume a number of shares outstanding. For convenience we shall use 10 million shares, a commonly used number in technology start-ups. What is needed to create a company to commercialize a licensed technology is equity investors, parties who may not have any day-to-day management involvement but who invest money in the start-up with the expectation that at some future time (1) there will be a way to get their money out of the company (a liquidity event), and (2) there is a reasonable prospect that a return on the investment will occur that is commensurate with the risk. Equity investment is critical because start-up companies often find it impossible to obtain debt investment (loans), because the start-up will require money to complete the technology, hire all the employees, perform market development, and manufacture and sell products, all before there are substantial or even any revenues, and because lenders want security for such loans: Creating a business of unknown value is not what such lenders consider ideal collateral. Usually the finance model assumes only equity investment until the company's profitability can support its operations and growth needs for capital; at such time, debt as a form of financing normally becomes available.

In order to determine the magnitude of such equity investment, a business plan that projects all the investments and future revenues and costs is needed. Equity investors typically like to release their funding in phases, known as "rounds." A round is typically defined as a time period of 12 to 24 months, at the end of which additional funding will be needed in a subsequent round. A common business model shows the need for three or four rounds before a start-up becomes publicly traded through an IPO (Initial Public Offering) or becomes acquired by another company seeking a foothold in the business.

A START-UP CAPITALIZATION EXAMPLE

For simplicity, let us assume the business plan shows the need for $5 million for one year, then $10 million for the second year, and $20 million for the third year, at the end of which the start-up will have demonstrated sufficient sales and perhaps profits to enable it attract an underwriter and a public market. Such a plan would ask its founding investors, those capitalizing the start-up in Round 1, for $5 million with the understanding that the plan calls for additional capital infusions totaling $30 million before the company can stand on its own. Now the question becomes, how much of the company at founding does $5 million buy? Put another way, what is the price per share of the 10 million initial shares?

Apportioning the Value to Start-up Contributors

Generally this question is answered by looking at three primary contributions to the start-up: technology, management, and money, but not necessarily in that order. For simplicity, let us consider a case where the management is not a source of any money, so their stake in the company is determined solely by their commitment to the fortunes of the company. Further, for simplicity, let us also assume that the management is not the source of the technology. In such cases, investors tend to provide 10 to 20 percent or more of the founding stock as the management share, awarded (and vested) over time, based upon meeting certain milestones. In this example, we shall assume 20 percent, or 2 million shares are so allocated. Now, of the remaining 8 million shares, how shall they be divided between the money (investors) and the technology (the seller)?

This is a negotiation between the seller (the technology owner) and the buyer (the start-up investors) just like the ones considered previously in this book. What is different here is that these investors will develop a model for the future valuation of the company based on various scenarios, with a built-in expectation for a rate of return (k-value) from which a calculation can be made of how much of the company they should have (in their mind) given the risk they are taking. Likewise, sellers can perform the same business model assessment to determine a future cash value that can then be brought back to the present time using the DCF method (with a k-value appropriate to the risk). The seller then compares such DCF (or NPV) value to that obtainable from other licensing approaches, such as a royalty-bearing license, to an existing company using any of the methods and tools of the preceding chapters, and decides upon the minimum number of shares that would make this equity deal attractive. If the expectations of the seller and buyer overlap, then a deal will be possible. If they do not and cannot be made to overlap by further discussion and negotiation, then no grounds for an agreement will be reached on an equity model[4].

The Use of "Step-Ups" to Characterize Round by Round Valuations

The challenge both the seller and buyer (investors) face is that the business model is based not only on a product that does not yet exist but also on a company that does not exist with customers who also do not yet exist. Accordingly, the uncertainty in the financial model tends to be very high. One tool commonly used to develop a valuation is the use of "step-ups." Let us suppose that in this example, the seller and the buyer agree to split the remaining 8 million shares 50:50 so that the founding capital structure is as follows: 2 million shares for management (albeit earned over time), 4 million for the technology (the sellers), and 4 million for the money (the investor-buyers). Thus, $5 million invested purchases 4 million shares. This ratio fixes the initial share price at $1.25/share ($5 million divided by 4 million shares). Thus, the management allowance of 2 million shares has an initial paper value of $2.5 million, and the technology has a value of $5 million, although because there is no market for the company's stock, none of the stock is sellable (there are also legal and contractual reasons why such shares cannot be sold, but these are outside the scope of this book).

A year hence, an additional $10 million will need to be raised. To do so, the company will issue and price additional stock, which leads to the infamous "dilution" problem for the seller and for management. Here's how the dilution problem is usually stated. If the future stock is priced at $1.25/share, then to raise $10 million, it will be necessary to issue 8 million new shares, creating a total pool of 18 million shares. Now management's 2 million shares, which had been 20 percent of the company, have become 11 percent of the company, and the seller of the founding technology has seen its 40 percent initial share become "diluted" to 22 percent because it still owns 4 million of the now 18 million shares. However, the value of the company has gone up as a result of the second round of funding. There are now 18 million shares with a value of $1.25/share or total value, known as the market capitalization (or market cap), of $22.5 million. When the management and technology sellers multiply their respective company shares against the $22.5 million they discover that their dollar value has not changed since the founding round, but their "say so" in company operations at the board level has been reduced by the addition of other seats for the new investors.[5]

This example of a second round of funding being priced the same as the founding round is known as "flat round" or a "step-up of 1.0." A step-up is defined as the ratio of the share price of the later round to the preceding round. Step-ups greater than 1.0 mean that the stock has become more valuable from one round to the next, and step-ups less than 1.0 mean that it has become less valuable.

Founding investors expect that the value of the shares at the time of the second round will be higher than at the founding round because the overall risk of the project should be less, and the time to liquidity should most certainly be less than faced by the founding investors. However, if there are significant problems in developing the technology or the market or building the management of the company, Round 2 investors could well conclude, based upon their projections of future rewards, that the risk is as high and the time to liquidity is as long as the first round investors perceived it to be. In business terms, either nothing was accomplished during the first year, or founding investors paid too much for the technology, or the market attractiveness has deteriorated.

Founding investors normally expect a very nice step-up to occur in the course of a year because the product should be defined and perhaps even prototyped, prospective customers should have been identified, and all the key management posts filled. Continuing with this example, let us assume that the results of the first year warrant a step-up of 2.0; that is, it is possible to find Round 2 investors who are willing to pay $2.50/share, or twice what founding investors paid. In this case, the number of new shares required to raise the needed $10 million is 4 million shares. Thus, there would now be 14 million shares, all valued at $2.50/share. The new "market" price is based on what cash investors at the one-year juncture are willing to pay, making the total value of the company (the market cap) equal to $35 million. The technology seller's ownership of the company has declined from 40 percent to 29 percent (4 million shares divided by the new total of 14 million shares) but its valuation has *increased* from $5 million (4 million shares at $1.25/share) to $10 million (4 million shares at $2.50/share). Likewise the management allowance has been "diluted" but become more valuable.

Let us assume that during the second year significant progress is made in that a product has been completed and demonstrated and customers have placed orders necessitating another $20 million for Round 3 in order to complete manufacturing and begin running the factory. As a result, let us assume that a step-up of 4.0 is attainable, making the price $10/share. Thus, only 2 million new shares must be printed (making a total of 16 million shares) for the Round 3 investors who are putting in $20 million, making the total value of the company $160 million. Accordingly, the seller of the technology has been diluted to 25 percent of the company (4 million shares divided by 16 million shares, the new total) but the value of each share is now $10/share (4 times the $2.50/share at Round 2) so that the total value of such shares is now $40 million.

Summary of All Capitalizations and Returns through IPO in an Example

Finally, let us assume that the company goes public at the end of the third year for $25/share, or a step-up of 2.5 over Round 3, which raises $100 million. This would require issuing 4 million additional shares, bringing the total to 20 million shares. The seller would now own 20 percent of the company, which is exactly half of the starting ownership percentage, but with a publicly traded (and liquid) value of $100 million! How is it that the seller can be diluted by a factor of two and yet the value is incresed by a factor of 20? The answer is that the share price has been stepped up three times by factors of 2, 4, and 2.5. Multiplying these three factors together yields exactly 20, which is why the seller's value has gone up by this factor.

The step-up example is further illustrated in Exhibit 10.5. Following the row and column headings, we see in Row 3 the investment raised in each of the four rounds, including the IPO as the fourth and final round. A total equity capitalization of $135 million is shown. The seven shaded cells contain the key assumptions on which this example hinges: the initial share distribution among the investors, the technology sellers, and management; the initial share price of $1.25 which determines how much

Exhibit 10.5 Sample Start-up Company Valuation as a Function of Step-ups

		C	D	E	F	G
1	Year	1/1/00	1/1/01	1/1/02	1/1/03	
2	Round	Founding	2	3	IPO	
3	Round Investment	$5,000,000	$10,000,000	$20,000,000	$100,000,000	
4						
5	Post Round Shares	10,000,000	14,000,000	16,000,000	20,000,000	
6	Step-up in Share Value	-	2.0	4.0	2.5	
7	Post-Round Value: $/Share	$ 1.25	$ 2.50	$ 10.00	$ 25.00	
8	Post-Round Market Cap	$12,500,000	$35,000,000	$160,000,000	$500,000,000	
9						
10	Founding Investors' Shares	4,000,000	4,000,000	4,000,000	4,000,000	
11	Ownership	40%	29%	25%	20%	
12	Valuation	$5,000,000	$10,000,000	$40,000,000	$100,000,000	
13						
14	Technology Seller's Shares	4,000,000	4,000,000	4,000,000	4,000,000	
15	Ownership	40%	29%	25%	20%	
16	Valuation	$5,000,000	$10,000,000	$40,000,000	$100,000,000	
17						

(Continued)

Exhibit 10.5 *(Continued)*

A	B	C	D	E	F	G
18	**Management Shares**	2,000,000	2,000,000	2,000,000	2,000,000	
19	Ownership	20%	14%	13%	10%	
20	Valuation	$2,500,000	$5,000,000	$ 20,000,000	$50,000,000	
21						
22	**Round 2 Investors' Shares**		4,000,000	4,000,000	4,000,000	
23	Ownership		29%	25%	20%	
24	Valuation		$10,000,000	$ 40,000,000	$100,000,000	
25						
26	**Round 3 Investors' Shares**			2,000,000	2,000,000	
27	Ownership			13%	10%	
28	Valuation			$ 20,000,000	$ 50,000,000	
29						
30	**IPO Round Investors' Shares**				4,000,000	
31	Ownership				20%	
32	Valuation				$100,000,000	

214

of the company the investors receive for their $5 million, and the three succeeding step-ups at Rounds 2, 3, and 4. With these assumptions, all the other values of this exhibit can be calculated. Focusing on Column C, the ownership percentages are determined by calculating the ratio of the shares owned by the total of 10 million shares outstanding (an arbitrary number). The post-round market capitalization of the company is determined by multiplying the share price ($1.25) by the number of total shares (10 million).

In Column D, the second round requires $10 million in new investment. The assumed step-up of 2.0 determines that the share price for the new money is $2.50 (2 times the $1.25 at the end of Round 1). Thus the investors providing the $10 million will receive 4 million shares ($10 million divided by $2.50/share), creating a total of 14 million outstanding shares. The number of shares owned by the founding parties (shown within the lightly shaded outline) does not change. However what does change is the value of such shares: $2.50 instead of $1.25. Accordingly, the paper valuation of the founding investors, the technology sellers, and management has doubled to the values shown in Cells D12, D16, and D20. Their respective ownership as a percentage has declined as shown.

In Column E, the Round 3 investors provide $20 million. At the assumed step-up of 4.0, the share price corresponding to such new money is now $10, so only 2 million new shares need to be issued, raising the total to 16 million shares outstanding. The rest of the calculations follows what was done for Column D.

Finally, in Column F, it is assumed that the IPO investors will pay $25/share, the so-called IPO price.[6] At this juncture, with these assumptions, the value of the company is $500 million, and the shares belonging to the technology seller are worth $100 million. At this time, and subject to lockout restrictions (a specified period as an IPO where insiders cannot sell their shares), the seller can convert such shares to cash.

Now, in order to perform the initial valuation of share price, which determines how many shares the investors providing $5 million receive and how many shares are left for the technology sellers, this model has to be analyzed to provide a basis for all the aforementioned assumptions.

The first and most important assumption is the underlying business plan, which is not shown. At founding, the company had to create a "pro forma," a projection (based upon certain assumptions and models) of its future sales and profitability. In Exhibit 10.4, we considered how valuation depends upon profitability and P/E ratio. In order to obtain the IPO valuation of $500 million, for a sales multiple of 5, sales of $100 million annually would need to have been demonstrated, at the end of the third year. If the sales multiple were 10 times, then the sales needed would be $50 million to support the $500 million IPO valuation. Remarkably, there are examples of companies with lesser annualized sales supporting a more than $1 billion market cap at the initial public offering.

The determination of such multiples are figured, generally speaking, using the Industry Standards Method. Fortunately, because of the public nature of IPOs, there exist in any given year more than 100 examples of market valuations. By analyzing such recently-public companies (sales, growth, profitability, industry trends, etc.), investors and technology sellers can develop a range of expectations for future value based upon assumed performance. Likewise, there is a surprising amount of data available to determine step-ups. Although the companies receiving pre-IPO funding are not public, and thereby are not obligated to disclose their funding sources and valuation, normally such information is obtainable through a little digging. Sophisticated and experienced venture capitalists are much better able than technology sellers to create such models and estimates because of their experience and contacts in the industry.

Another tool for checking the overall sanity of the step-up assumptions is to use the DCF method of Chapter 7. Working backwards from the IPO, the question can be asked, what would lead the Round 3 investors to pay $10/share? And, again, would a Round 2 investor see $2.50/share as reasonable? Finally, would the founding round investor accept $1.25/share? Exhibit 10.6 analyzes all the investments from Exhibit 10.5 to determine what the corresponding "k" value is to each round's investors.

Looking at Row 14 of Exhibit 10.6, we see the k-value, or return on investment (ROI), on a round to round basis. What this means is: If after raising Round 2 funding as shown for 1/1/2001, and perceiving a paper value of the 4 million shares as $10 million, what would the founding investor have experienced as a ROI? Referring back to the DCF equation where $B/A = (1 + k)^n$, or solving for $k = (B/A)^{1/n} - 1$, and substituting $B/A = 2$ and $n = 1$, results in $k = 1.0$ or 100 percent. Likewise, considering the effect of Round 3 funding and valuation, the ROI from the time of the second round is 300 percent; and the year-over-year return to the IPO round is 150 percent. Overall, from the founding of the company until the IPO event, the founding investor perceives an ROI of 171 percent, which corresponds to a 20 "bagger" (multiple) in just three years. Would a 171 percent ROI make a founding investor happy? Yes and no. If it were guaranteed, and the value of other comparable guaranteed returns was 7 percent, then of course the answer is "yes." But because it is not guaranteed, such an investor would review all the assumptions in the business plan and determine how speculative or realistic they are. If they were reasonable, then the answer should still be "yes," but investors would not be shy about trying to get an even better deal, especially if there are even better opportunities available to them elsewhere. In recent years, the overall range of ROI for the more successful venture capital investors has

Exhibit 10.6 Return on Investment to the Various Round Funders of Exhibit 10.5

	C	D	E	F
Year	1/1/00	1/1/01	1/1/02	1/1/03
Round	Founding	2	3	IPO
Round Investment	$5,000,000	$10,000,000	$20,000,000	$100,000,000
Step-up in Share Value	-	2.0	4.0	2.5
Post-Round Value: $/Share	$ 1.25	$ 2.50	$ 10.00	$ 25.00
Post-Round Market Cap	$12,500,000	$35,000,000	$160,000,000	500,000,000
Founding Investors' Shares	4,000,000	4,000,000	4,000,000	4,000,000
Valuation	$5,000,000	$10,000,000	$40,000,000	$100,000,000
Round-to-Round ROI (k)	-	100%	300%	150%
Cumulative	-	100%	183%	171%
Round 2 Investors' Shares		4,000,000	4,000,000	4,000,000
Valuation		$10,000,000	$40,000,000	$100,000,000
Round-to-Round ROI (k)		-	300%	150%
Cumulative		-	300%	216%
Round 3 Investors' Shares			2,000,000	2,000,000
Valuation			$ 20,000,000	$50,000,000
Round-to-Round ROI (k)		-	-	150%

217

been over 40 percent, a number obtained by a mixture of outcomes, some at 171 percent and some total losses.

Looking at Exhibit 10.6 for the Round 2 investors, their 216 percent overall return is even higher than the founding investors', because their capital was tied up for only two years. Finally, the Round 3 investor experiences a 150 percent return.

In order to refine the assumptions, one would need to look carefully into the business plan and ascertain what risks will occur at what point in time and with how much money invested. The plan should be that the ROI of the founding investors should be higher than any of the later investors because joining the party at start-up entailed the highest risk. Statistically speaking some start-ups will never have a Round 2 and will fail out of the starting gate, losing all the founding capital, which is why investors who join only in the later rounds should receive a lower rate of return.

By adjusting the ROI projected for each round's investors in the context of the expected risk at that point, this model can be refined to provide a more rational prediction. Then, by comparing the return to the founding investor, compared to their alternatives, and to the technology seller, compared to their alternatives, the relative balance between their initial contributions can be analyzed. If the technology is genuinely the substance of the start-up company, then it is not unusual for the technology seller to receive founding shares equal to the investment, or even higher. On the other hand, if the investment yet required to commercialize is large and progress is likely to be slow, then founding investors will not fund a deal that allocates so much of the stock to the technology. To do so would not leave room for later investors to infuse additional needed money at attractive rates of return.

DILUTION ISSUES

Earlier we considered the effect of dilution, and we now need to return to the subject to consider what happens when things go more poorly than expected. If the step-ups are greater than 1.0, then the value of founding shares increase with each round. As shown in Exhibit 10.5, even as the percentage of the company owned goes down, the value of shares held goes up. That is the magic of step-ups.

For flat rounds, where the step-ups are exactly 1.0, the technology seller's ownership is diluted as a percentage, but the value of the shares held are unchanged. This is because there are more shares issued but the value of the shares remains what it was in the preceding round, and the start-up company has more money infused to support its operations and further development.

If a technology seller wanted a deal where its ownership percentage is unchanged even with the infusion of later investors, the founding investor would receive very poor returns on its investment because the dilution that occurs would come out of the founding investors' shares. Unless the percentage awarded to the technology seller was extremely low, then no investor is likely to want to fund the start-up company.

There is one other means that a technology seller, or founding investor, can use to avoid dilution: continue to invest in the company in all later rounds to maintain a larger share of ownership. Such a provision is common in start-up deals. The difficulty that arises is that technology sellers are not always in a position to make such investments, whereas founding investors exist for the purpose of making such investments. Ordinarily, founding investors are also second and third round investors. Perhaps they maintain their share, perhaps they are diluted a little as other investors are admitted to the club, but technology sellers, who have the right to match investments, often may not have the means or will.

Assuming that such funding is secured through legitimate means using fair market value negotiations at each of the subsequent rounds, then technology sellers are not innately harmed by their inability to maintain their share. However, if the start-up is a success they will regret not having found the funds somehow and somewhere.

There is another phenomenon, however, that should be of great concern to a technology seller. In all the previous examples, the step-ups have been 1.0 or greater. What happens if progress during the year has been poor, or the market looks more distant, or competitors have emerged that were unexpected or stronger than expected? It is entirely possible for legitimate business reasons that the value in a later round is less than at the founding round. If this happens, then a true dilution will occur to a holder of previous round stock who does not invest to maintain his or her share: not only will the share of the company as a percentage decline but the aggregate value of their share holdings will also decline.

In such a situation, frustration arises when the adverse round is a result of management blunders over which the seller had no control. It should be recognized that technology sellers are not normally going to have a controlling interest or right to manage the company. In many cases, the reason for a start-up in the first place was that the technology seller wanted to put the technology is someone else's hands to develop and commercialize it. Otherwise, there would be no licensing situation. In essence, even though the technology seller may have one or more board seats and may express its opinion on various strategic matters, it is an opinion only. Decisions at the board level are made by the board majority. As a result of some bad decisions, the technology seller may, in retrospect, perceive that its dilution in value is unfair. However, the other owners also have incentive to increase the value of the shares (because they own shares too), so usually the board's decisions can be expected to have been made in good faith. The only defense in such circumstances is for the technology seller to invest in subsequent "down rounds."[7]

There is, unfortunately, another kind of down round known in the industry as a "cram down" round. One technique that founding investors can use to unjustly dilute technology sellers (and management) is to lead a second round of funding at a valuation substantially below the founding round valuation. For Exhibit 10.5, say that instead of the second round being priced at \$2.50/share, a step-up of 2.0, it was priced at 25 cents a share, step-"up" of 0.20. After the infusion of second round capital, primarily from the founding investors perpetrating this plan, the original allocation of stock among the founders has been significantly altered to the detriment of those founders who are not able to make the second round cash investment.

There are numerous such issues present in equity deals, more so than in licensing situations. Although there are various protective techniques that can be negotiated by technology sellers, they are outside the scope of this book. The general lesson here is to know with whom you are dealing. The same holds true for the management. This segment will receive a significant share of the founding stock, and the success or failure of the company will depend in large part on their skill, their industry, and their ethics. So, "Who am I dealing with?"—ever present in any licensing negotiation—is an even more significant question in an equity transaction.

EQUITY WHEN LICENSING TO
AN EXISTING, PRE-PUBLIC COMPANY

The governing assumption in the previous discussion is that the start-up company is being created at the time of the license for the purpose of commercializing the licensed technology. At the beginning of this chapter, licensing to a public company was briefly discussed. What remains is to consider the intermediate situation: licensing to an already existing, pre-public company in exchange for stock.

If, in this circumstance, the start-up company is effectively restarting its operations (perhaps abandoning its previous technology for the subject license), then this reverts to the case considered in Exhibits 10.5 and 10.6. The founding valuation needs to be considered by all the parties as though it were a fresh start. The fact that significant sums were expended in a fruitless endeavor should not penalize the technology seller. Sunk costs are irrelevant. The re-started up company can argue that it has now established a management team and some market awareness that deserves recognition. That may be so. On the other hand, it is possible that the management team assembled is not particularly suited to the new direction of the company, or that the management has demonstrated only a lack of business acumen in its previous efforts. In any case, the seller should consider all these arguments just as though it were a true start-up, and value each party's contributions independently.

Another possibility is that a pre-public company seeks the seller's license to create a second product or to enhance its first product. Instead of paying a cash license fee or royalties, the buyer instead may propose issuance of stock. In this circumstance, the seller should consider that it is, in effect, a second or third round "funder" by infusing the company with technology and rights. The approach that should be used follows the structure of Exhibits 10.5 and 10.6. The seller should assess all the valuations that have gone into the company to date, the business plan and the actuals at the negotiation date, and determine what is the highest stock price, or fewest number of shares, it needs to get a fair return at the time of an IPO or strategic acquisition.

Such analysis is difficult for the seller because it necessarily involves performing due diligence on a company, its management and technology, and its business plan, without the advantage of having been part of the company's formation. Further, the seller may not have sufficient knowledge about the existing technology in the pre-public company to enable a fair assessment of its worth. The seller in these circumstances is really playing the role of a later-round venture capitalist without the experience and tools that come with doing this for a living. For these reasons, this form of valuation is more difficult than either getting stock in a true start-up or stock in a public company. In the former case, the founding technology is the seller's, and should be known; in the latter case, the value of the shares is determined by a public market and so it is known. This intermediate situation may have both little-known technology and hard-to-know share price.

The uncertainties might possibly be narrowed by performing due diligence, perhaps with support from an outside consultant. If the uncertainty remains large, then this can be reflected by a high "k" value in a DCF calculation. If the buyer's offer can meet the seller's requirements through an appropriately high discount rate, the seller then needs to decide whether it wants to take a high-risk opportunity. Such decisions are always best made when alternatives exist.

CONCLUSION

Equity as partial or sole recompense for the seller's technology is becoming an increasingly common and important event. There are certain innate advantages to equity participation that suggest its use when the opportunity is sufficiently valuable to warrant the attendant increase in deal costs because of the complexity of such arrangements.

In start-up situations, the nature of the technology, money, and management are so different that it is a challenge to put them all on the same scale. There is a widespread perspective by technology sellers that, as a rule, they do not fare well in the monetization of their contribution. The thought is nicely captured in the Dilbert cartoon shown in Figure 10.1; note the enthusiastic tongue of the inventor, sardonically portrayed in panel 2.

Management's perspective is that in many start-up situations they make the difference in achieving commercial success (though the reciprocal is not true of failures!). There are numerous examples of start-up companies creating value by evolving away from the founding technology to reach more attractive market opportunites. Finally, there is the argument on behalf of the people investing the money. It is a special kind of high-risk adventure. Unlike other investments, there is a serious probability that every dime will be lost without any return—nada, zip, nothing. Also, overseeing the company as a board member is another kind of adventure and investment. People investing such risk capital are normally bringing much more than money to the venture.

It should be noted that all six valuation methods discussed in this book can be applied to determine equity valuations, just as they can be used to determine a royalty or any other form of compensation. However, the non-liquidity of stock and the complexity of ownership bring with them a whole array of other business issues; those most-directly related to valuation were considered in this chapter.

In Chapter 11 we will consider other issues of structuring licensing agreements and payments.

Figure 10.1
DILBERT © distributed by United Feature Syndicate. Reprinted with permission.

NOTES

1. It is possible for cash payments to have some indeterminancy and/or to be paid for a period of time. Such matters will be considered in Chapter 11.

2. There are some exceptions to this broad statement that are outside the scope of this book.

3. Of course, publicly-traded stock could be part or all of a payment for a license. However, in such a case, the stock represents its cash equivalent because the seller receiving stock from the buyer could immediately convert the stock into cash (at the current trading price) or, conversely, if the seller wanted stock in the company it could take a cash license payment from the buyer and covert such cash into stock. The scope of this chapter deals with a more complex situation: when the stock of the buyer is not publicly traded and thereby not available and, generally speaking, is not valued in a well-defined way.

4. Investors in start-up companies are often not interested in a royalty relationship. They realize that the company will be a cash burner for many years and want to structure the company to limit such cash outflows. Royalty is simply another cash outflow. Accordingly, investors will attempt to defer royalties until the company is profitable, or encourage reducing or eliminating the royalty in lieu of stock.

5. In many cases the "new" investors are the old investors putting in additional money.

6. Once the initial selling price is determined, the company receives such proceeds one at a time, less expenses to the underwriters, and thereafter the ups and downs of the market even on the opening day does not generate any additional cash for the company. Of course, the company could elect later to print and sell additional stock.

7. There are, in addition, various down round protections known as "ratchet" provisions. Such provisions act to revalue, in whole or in part, previous round investments. Ordinarily only the founding investor expects to be the beneficiary of such provisions. A thorough discussion of such matters is outside the scope of this book.

11

Structure of Licensing Payments

INTRODUCTION

In the preceding chapters we have discussed methods of valuation and expressed the results in terms of royalty rates, DCF or NPV, and equity shares. This chapter discusses many different forms and structures of payment that can be used individually or in combination to establish the total value contained within a license agreement.

Although there are an infinite number of ways that payments can be structured, especially when considering non-monetary forms, this chapter reviews the principal forms and attempts to provide a framework for connecting the six valuation methods considered in Chapters 4 through 9 and the equity case reviewed in Chapter 10. Chapter 10 also provided a brief review of the advantages and some of the issues surrounding cash-only licenses versus royalty licenses versus equity licenses. This information is a useful backdrop for this chapter.

LUMP SUM LICENSES

Lump sum licenses are known by a variety of terms: cash licenses, up-front licenses, "paid-ups" (as in paid-up licenses). What is meant by such an agreement is that the parties will agree on a fixed amount to be paid by the buyer to the seller.

The most straightforward means of determining such an amount is by use of the Discounted Cash Flow method of Chapter 7. Recall that this approach uses "k" values, known as risk-adjusted hurdle rate (RAHR) or discount rate, to convert each future royalty payment to a discounted present-cash equivalent. Adding all the DCF values for all the years of the agreement yields the Net Present Value (NPV) of the agreement. For a single, lump sum cash agreement paid at closing, the amount simply equals the NPV of all the cash flows. The buyer usually performs a wire transfer to the seller's bank account on the day of the closing, immediately following the signing of the license agreement. In some cases, with trusted buyers, the license agreement stipulates that such payment be made within a short time, such as ten days.

In Chapter 10, some of the limitations of using this form of agreement were discussed. The primary difficulty arises because all future predictions of value have to be reduced to one single number. A related difficulty is that, years later, either the buyer or the seller is likely to believe that they were at a disadvantage because it is unlikely that the commercial outcome will be identical to the terms of the agreement.

However, there are some advantages to lump sum agreements. Buyers often have a preference, if affordable, to conclude the relationship with the seller and avoid the accounting issues associated with making annual, semi-annual, or quarterly royalty payments. Normally, license agreements provide for auditing rights on behalf of the seller. Although there are limitations on the frequency of audits, and the seller must give fair notice before an audit, audits are still a burden on both parties. Further, the results of an audit can lead to a dispute. Furthermore, the disclosure of sales information is very sensitive business information and even though the seller is normally under confidentiality provisions, buyers do not like having to make such detailed disclosures to anyone.

From the seller's point of view there are also some advantages to paid-up licenses. The most obvious advantage is that the seller gets its money; there is no uncertainty of payment. Also, the payment is made now, so the seller can use such funds to invest in its other businesses. The seller also avoids the cost of administering the license on its end. Although royalties should be "checks in the mail," there are administrative costs involved, including reminding buyers to remit payments. In some cases this requires more extensive (and expensive) actions such as auditing the payments received, collecting and reporting the numbers, and making forecasts to management as to expected future royalties.

In the case of field of use licenses to multiple buyers, problems between different buyers can arise that will require the seller's intervention. For example, Buyer A could be exclusive in Europe, and Buyer B exclusive in the U.S.; however, Buyer B discovers (or thinks it discovers) that sales from Buyer A are being imported and wants the seller to put a stop to it and even negotiate reparations. If these parties have a competitive history, finding an amicable solution can be harrowing.

Other issues can relate to the minimum royalties. Buyers are not shy about coming back to sellers and arguing for a reduction in the minimums previously negotiated The seller can simply say "no," but if the buyer ends up terminating the license due to economic necessity, the seller may be left with a technology it cannot easily license a second time.

Buyers have also been known to argue (even years later) for a reduction in royalties, not just minimum royalties. New management at the buyer's company can seek to change the deal because some of the projections have not borne out or simply because they believe that previous representatives agreed to pay too much. Future arguments about licensing terms will be further discussed later in this chapter.

When licensed patents are retained in the name of the seller, there can be disputes over filing or maintaining the patent in a particular country, or dealing with oppositions (as in Europe, where such oppositions are permitted).

Infringement (real or apparent) can arise. Buyers logically do not want to compete with companies who are not paying royalties to the seller, even in the case of a nonexclusive license. Buyers are even more concerned when they have paid a premium to obtain an exclusive right and other manufacturers turn up in the marketplace. How these issues can be handled in a license agreement are outside the scope of this book, but the point here is that because of an ongoing relationship between the buyer and seller, such infringement concerns can lead to complex issues requiring further negotiation.

Issues may arise surrounding future inventions made by the seller. Even though a license agreement might clearly state that the seller is not obligated to provide such future improvements to the seller, or to offer other technologies it may invent that could be used for similar products, the buyer may believe it is entitled to such rights because it is paying royalties year-by-year and it views the relationship as an informal partnership. Likewise, a seller can feel restricted in its options, not because of a legal requirement, but because it does not want to alienate a company paying annual royalties into its coffers. Sellers may likewise develop expectations that it should be entitled to invention rights to developments made by the buyer in the same technology area as the license.

In general, because royalty-bearing licenses can last 10 years or more, it can be expected that the particular individuals participating in the negotiation will have gone on to other jobs during the life of the agreement. Then the interpretation of the agreement will fall to individuals who were not privy to the original negotiation and who may not feel the same commitment or enthusiasm for the deal as the originators did.

All these issues have to be weighed against the difficulty of reaching an agreement on a lump sum payment to determine whether this form of an agreement makes the most sense. One factor not mentioned above is a subjective human one. In some negotiations the two parties were or are adversaries and do not want to work with each other because of a lack of trust or other issues. This situation would favor a lump sum agreement so that the parties can bring the negotiating relationship to a quick close. At the other extreme are cases where the parties have a longstanding strategic relationship that is much broader than the specific license and it is in each party's interest to stay involved with the other; this view would favor some form of royalty or even equity relationship.

Assuming the parties have agreed on a lump sum, how should it be determined and structured? If the valuation has been done by agreeing on a royalty rate and base, the creation of a sales projection is needed. This is done using a DCF method to bring all future payments back to the time of the negotiation, as described in Chapter 7. If a 25 Percent Rule of Thumb has been used to split profitability, then a profitability projection also must be made and discounted to create an NPV. If a DCF approach has been used, then the number has already been obtained. Monte Carlo techniques as described in Chapter 8 can be used with any of these projections to develop a "best guess" for the range of uncertainties.

One standard of payment that comes up regularly is a lump sum tied to the costs of the seller in getting the technology to its present stage. One could argue that a cost basis is yet a seventh method. As discussed in Chapter 3, there are rare circumstances where a cost basis would be a useful proxy for determining value. One way that it does come up is when the seller is closing down an R&D activity that created something of value but not something perceived to be significant in value. In such a situation the seller may be willing to settle for a quick deal to simply get back what it put into developing the technology. If the buyer perceives that all the R&D activities would have been similarly costed in its own operation, then the buyer could view such a payment as reasonable. However, it is possible that the seller has spent an enormous sum and created a small opportunity, or a small sum and created an enormous opportunity. In the former case the buyer will never agree to pay such costs, and in the latter case the seller would be foolish to sell the opportunity solely for its costs.

One very practical situation that arises in such lump agreements has to do with budget issues within the respective organizations. For large sums, buyers may not wish or be able to make such a payment all at once. In some cases, sellers may prefer to receive payment in several years, also for budgetary reasons. One way to handle this is to create two or more lump sum payments instead of just one at closing. In such cases it needs to be made clear that future payments are not conditional on future outcomes and simply represent a payment schedule. Subsequent payments should be escalated to reflect a "k" value appropriate to inflation and lost opportunity to the seller, because presumably the earlier payment could have been invested elsewhere. The formula for performing such escalations was developed in Chapter 7: $B = A * (1 + k)^n$, where A is the payment which would have been made now but instead will be made "n" years later, and B is the magnitude of such future payment.

Normally such multiple lump sum payments are limited to two or three payments made over two or three years. If they stretch out longer than this, then the parties will normally prefer some form of a royalty payment.

PURE ROYALTY LICENSES

Royalties are a payment made by the buyer to the seller based upon sales made by the seller of the licensed technology. Sometimes they are called "earned royalties" or "running royalties" to distinguish them from minimum royalties or other forms of payment. They are usually expressed as a percentage of sales made by the buyer, but they can also be expressed in dollars per item, per pound, or per anything. When expressed in fixed dollar amounts, it is generally a good idea to provide some form of inflation factor so that 10 years later (particularly if inflation has been significant) the amount paid is still reflective of the value of the license. In certain technology areas buyers may require that a deflating factor be included because the selling price is expected to decline with time; computer chips are an example, but not the only example, of such a phenomenon. For these reasons it is usually a good idea to simply express the royalty as a percentage of selling price.

Pure royalty licenses are licenses for which there are no lump sum payments. The buyer pays the seller a royalty based on sales and pays only once sales begin. Such agreements are rare, because ordinarily the seller expects to receive some form of down payment and, possibly, progressive payments before such earned royalties begin. Later in this chapter the more common case, a combination of upfront and running royalties, will be considered.

The advantages of royalties were discussed in Chapter 10. To review, they provide an opportunity for the seller to receive more than the parties would have or could have expected because the outcome of the license has been greater than expected. Likewise, they can be an advantage to the buyer if the market turns out to be much smaller than expected. With royalty structure, it is more likely that both parties will feel that they got a fair deal years later. However, there are the complexity issues of a long term relationship which were discussed earlier. The more uncertain the future, especially with large upside uncertainties, the more likely it is that a royalty form of payment will work best.

If the Industry Standard Method has been used, then a royalty is normally the direct result. If a 25 Percent Rule approach has been used, then a calculation must be made to infer what royalty rate will produce the agreed profit split. This can be done using the same spreadsheet income statement projections presented for the Discounted Cash Flow Method. Using DCF, the royalty rate should be adjusted by iteration, or using the "solve" spreadsheet function so as to create an NPV value of zero (or any arbitrary value). Again, the Monte Carlo Method can be used in combination with other methods to examine the sensitivity of various factors, such as growth in sales and costs of goods sold, upon profitability as a function of various royalty rates.

Often overlooked is the importance of the royalty basis. What is important to both the buyer and the seller is the magnitude of the check, not the royalty percentage itself. The magnitude of the check is determined by the royalty rate multiplied by the royalty base. Although it may appear that the royalty base is obvious, it should be recognized that the license agreement will last ten years or more, and the way products get built and sold is likely to change dramatically during that term. The license agreement must carefully define both the licensed subject matter and which sales values are subject to the agreed upon royalty. If different products with different margins or with different mixes of licensed and unlicensed subject matter are envisioned, then some means of determining a fair split must be devised.

One example of such a situation is as follows. The buyer presently envisions making product A, which is covered by the definition of licensed subject matter, and then selling it to a customer who incorporates A into product B. However, in the future, the buyer decides to go into the business of making product B. Now, how shall the royalty base be calculated? If the buyer is still selling A, then that price can be used as an inferred selling price (known as a transfer price) to the part of its operations that makes product B and a royalty paid on both sales made externally and internally. If the buyer no longer sells A, then there needs to be some other means of determining a royalty base. Various methods have been used in such situations. One approach is to use a market-based price for A based upon sales made by third parties. Another is to calculate a selling price by some formula such as multiplying cost of goods sold by some factor. Yet another way is to create a recipe that determines the value-percentage of B that contains A. The use of different, lower royalty rates on sales of B is yet another way. All of these approaches can be made to work, although there are complexities involved that are beyond the scope of this book.

To the extent possible, the parties should consider all the possible manifestations of the licensed technology so that an agreement can be reached on all matters at the time of the license. If not so done, or if unforeseen circumstances arise, then the parties will have to conduct a future negotiation to determine the appropriate base.

As discussed in Chapter 10, basing the royalty on numbers below the sales line on an income statement creates other problems. Costs on a product income statement can be quite arbitrary, based upon allocations determined within the company among its various divisions and product lines. Such accounting could be adjusted to the disadvantage of a seller.

LICENSE (DOWN PAYMENT) FEES AND PROGRESS PAYMENT FEES

When creating a royalty form agreement, the seller typically expects a down payment on the license. This is particularly true when the license involves some form of exclusivity because the seller is then precluded from selling to others.

The framework for this thinking is similar to leasing a car or buying a house: There is a payment schedule in both cases which parallels a royalty, but there is also a down payment. One of the purposes of the down payment is to ensure that the buyer fulfills the commitment by risking the forfeit of the down payment. In licenses, particularly ones involving exclusivity, the seller wants to be assured that the buyer is not just "tying up" the technology without a serious intent to commercialize it.

How much should the down payment be? From the buyer's point of view, in many cases the view is that it should be as small as possible. The buyer makes the case that it will have to make significant investments in commercializing the technology, so it "cannot afford" to pay a license fee. This argument is strongly made by small start-up companies that are strapped for cash. On the other hand, the seller can say to the buyer: "Where were you when the page was blank?"[1] The seller logically believes that it has been investing in the technology for a long time and is entitled to payback in recognition for getting it to this state. Further, the seller can point out to the buyer that if the buyer's own R&D organization had created the technology, it would have already spent a significant sum before it could begin its design for manufacturing process.

One common basis for determining a down payment is to perform an NPV analysis and take some percentage as the down payment. A number in the range of 5 to 10 percent is common, but there is no hard and fast rule. Another approach is to take one year's royalties (at maturity) as a down payment; that is, if the royalty climbs from initial sales starting in year three to near maturity in, say, year seven and is then paying $1 million per year in royalties, parties have been known to use such a figure as the basis for the down payment. Yet another technique is to use some cost basis for the down payment; one example would be for the seller to recover their project costs in the down payment, assuming that the total value of the deal significantly exceeds such project costs. A key factor in determining a down payment is the importance of instant cash to the seller. In cases where the seller is meeting or exceeding the current year's budget, there actually may be a desire to defer upfront payments to a second or third year, or to have those payments made solely as royalties; in other cases where there is pressure to meet current year goals, a seller can be highly motivated, even too motivated, to take as large a portion of future gains in a present payment as possible.

If one assumes the formal DCF model for determining royalties, then a down payment is really a pre-payment on royalties due. In the DCF model, the royalty should be iterated to provide the total NPV owed to the seller. Then, for any given down payment, the royalty should be iterated so as to provide an NPV to the seller exactly equal to this down payment. Some money owed in yearly payments is being moved to form such down payments.

When determining a royalty rate using an Industry Standards Method, sometimes the parties agree to an arbitrary upfront payment that is not scaled on a DCF model because one has not been created yet. For instance, the seller and the buyer could agree that the subject license closely follows a certain comparable agreement that had a 5 percent royalty and, in addition, $100K as an upfront payment. Again, subject to negotiations between a willing buyer and a willing seller, the parties could agree to such terms without formally considering the $100K as a royalty pre-payment.

Another variation that occurs is that the buyer wants such a down payment to offset royalties. Following the example in the preceding paragraph, the buyer could insist that it pay no royalties until it receives "back" (gets full credit for) the $100K it paid as a down payment. From a seller's perspective, it is usually not a good idea not to receive any royalties once such a structure is agreed upon. Therefore, it may agree to credit some (or all) of the down payment but at a credit rate such that the buyer can credit up to half the royalties due (as an example). This approach at least enables the seller to receive diminished royalties, beginning with the initial sales.

Another form of down payment is known as "progress payment" or a "license maintenance fee." When the delay from the time of the license until initial sales are made is long, sellers often expect to receive some additional lump sum payments after the down payment but before the initial royalty. The rationale is similar to that invoked for the down payment: it assures continued commitment by the buyer, and it provides some cash flow to the earliest investor (the seller). From the buyer's perspective these payments are additional prepayments against the royalties and, as such they resemble a lump sum agreement with a "kicker" (discussed later). Again, whatever is reasonable to both parties is subject to negotiation. Using the DCF model makes it straightforward to establish lump sum payments to the seller in any given year and then iterate on the royalty such that the NPV of the opportunity is unchanged. In principle, if this is done correctly and providing the sums are not large with respect to the total opportunity, both the buyer and seller should be indifferent to how money is moved around.

ROYALTY WITH FIXED SUM LICENSES

The most common form of royalty license involves one or more fixed sum payments, either down payments paid over multiple years, or down payments in conjunction with progressive payments.

As discussed in the last section, such fixed sum payments are normally viewed as prepayment of royalties. However, they need not be, especially if the amounts are small compared to the perceived opportunity.

The DCF Method is the primary tool for computing such licenses. As discussed, the royalty rate can be iterated to provide any pre-determined NPV, taking into account upfront and progress payment lump sums paid by the buyer. Normally, the "k" value used to perform DCF calculations on lump sums after the down payment is smaller than the "k" value used for the royalty rates, because the lump sum amounts are guaranteed by the contract.

A negotiation issue that arises is: What happens in the event of an early termination by the buyer? Such a situation presumes that the buyer is not going to make, use, or sell the licensed subject matter so no future royalty obligations exist. If all the lump sum payments have been made, then the remaining question is: Is there a termination fee? If all the lump sum payments have not been made, then there is the additional question: Are such payments still due upon termination? The answer to the latter question is usually yes and should be so worded in the contract. However, the matter is negotiable and the parties could agree that no further lump sums are due upon termination. Likewise, any termination fee is subject to negotiation, although because it deals with an event not expected to occur, it is not typically modeled as in a DCF approach.

ROYALTY "KICKER" LICENSES

One interesting variation on royalty agreements involves a bonus factor commonly known as a "kicker." The situation arises as follows. The parties agree on a reasonably certain financial projection of sales, costs, royalties, and profitability, say sales of $100 million per year at maturity and a royalty of 5 percent. However, the seller believes there are other markets that could be reached by the commercialized technology that are much larger and more profitable. The buyer counters that if such additional sales occur then there will be additional royalties at the rate of 5 percent. However, the seller argues that the 5 percent figure was agreed upon by considering certain fixed investment costs and other operating costs (overhead) that do not scale up linearly with volume. Put another way, if this is a $500 million per year sales opportunity, it will be much more profitable than the $100 million scenario, and the seller would be entitled to a higher royalty rate.

One way to handle such a circumstance is by means of a "kicker" that adds a payment to the seller after certain sales thresholds have been reached. Continuing with this example, the parties could agree that if the sales in any given year are more than $300 million, there will be an incremental royalty of 1 percent of sales over $300 million, and a second "kicker" of another 1 percent for sales over $500 million. The resulting payoff table would look like this:

Sales = $100 million   Royalty = 5% = $5 million
Sales = $300 million   Royalty = $5% = $15 million
Sales = $400 million   Royalty = 5%, + 1% of $100 million = $21 million
Sales = $600 million   5%, + 1% of $300 million + 1% of $100 million
                       = $34 million

In the third case above, the "kicker" provided an incremental $1 million over what would have otherwise been paid. In the fourth case, the "kicker" provided an additional $4 million.

Such kickers could be applied to a series of lump sum payments. As another example, the parties could agree that the deal will be a license fee of $6 million, paid in three equal $2 million lump sums—one at closing, one at the first anniversary, and one at the second anniversary. In addition, a kicker of an additional $2 million will be paid if sales in year five exceed $200 million. This provides some of the advantages of a royalty structure but with less complexity.

As in our discussions on royalty bases, using as the trigger or scale of a kicker some value below the sales line on an income statement is perilous. Buyers, especially large buyers, have enormous discretion in creating bottom line numbers at the product, product line, or division level. Also, buyers are subject to reorganizations that could cause the application of bottom line provisions to be incomprehensible. Buyers should likewise be concerned about tying kickers to "product profits" because it opens up the possibility of a costly dispute and an interpretation beyond the limits of the original negotiation.

ROYALTY SCALING ON SALES

A common issue that arises when implementing royalties is the use of what is known as "wedding cake" rates. They work like this. If the parties agree to a 5 percent royalty, the buyer typically proposes that this rate should be scaled down with increasing sales as is commonly done in purchase agreements, perhaps proposing something like this: 5 percent for the first $1 million in sales (i.e., resulting in a payment of $50,000), and 3 percent for the next $1 million in sales (an additional payment of $30,000), and 1 percent for all sales beyond $2 million ($10,000 per each additional million in sales).

There are many problems with this approach. First the underlying premise of volume discounts is sharing the benefit caused by a larger orders by the buyer. If the buyer places an order for paper clips, it expects to pay less per clip for a box car full of them than it does for a single box full. Why? Because there is a built-in economy of manufacture and delivery for the paper clip vendor. Because of the buyer's large-volume purchase, a volume value opportunity is credited that can be apportioned between vendor and buyer. This is a widely recognized concept—even at the grocery store: 50 pound bags of dog food are priced less on a per pound basis than 5 pound bags.

But does this make sense in licensing? No. There are no manufacturing and delivery costs or economies of scale to be shared in technology licensing.

What about declining profitability with increased sales? This can be possible but, in the absence of data, the more likely case is *increasing* profitability with sales because the buyer is enjoying a volume value opportunity. It is the seller who should, on this basis, make the argument that the royalty rate should go up with increasing sales because of the increased value (profit) to the buyer.

Sometimes buyers propose a variant of the wedding cake structure on cumulative sales. Using the 5/3/1 royalty rate example given earlier, this might be expressed as follows: 5 percent on the first $50 million in cumulative sales under the license, 3 percent on the next $50 million, and 1 percent on everything over $100 million. This approach could be based on a rational examination of margins because it could happen that with time (expressible in terms of cumulative sales) that competitive pressures will erode margins and so should erode royalty rates.

The seller is cautioned to not casually adopt such structures without thinking through their potential implications, especially in the context of the total valuation determined beforehand. This is another example where the DCF Method can be very useful because all such wedding cake proposals can be evaluated and compared.

An extreme form of a wedding cake structure is a royalty cap, which works something like this. The seller says to the buyer, "After I've paid you royalties on $10 million in sales that year, or on $100 million in cumulative sales for that form of structure, all subsequent sales should be royalty free." This is the of "enough is enough" argument and you, the seller, should not want more than the cap.

The seller's response to this should be to explore ways that both the buyer and seller can jointly contribute their profits to some charitable purpose, rather than just restricting such opportunity to the seller. The cap of the seller's profit should be similarly shared by the buyer. This usually puts an end to this line of negotiation.

Sellers can and do propose "inverse wedding cakes," royalty rates that increase with sales because, as argument goes, the margins increase with volume. Conceptually there can be a solid argument for such an approach, but this would normally require some fairly detailed modeling to convince both parties of its legitimacy.

AGREEMENTS TO NEGOTIATE ROYALTIES

Because technology licenses deal with so much uncertainty, parties have agreed to defer negotiations until the products and margins are better known. This can be done in a variety of ways. One is simply to agree to negotiate in good faith and, if negotiations are not successful, to submit the matter of royalty rates to some designated third party to act as an arbitrator. At this stage, both parties would submit their basis for their rates and the arbitrator would evaluate the arguments and set the rate.

This approach has been widely used, but the actual need for bringing in the arbitrator is rare because neither party wants to deal with the uncertainty of a third-party decision.

A variant of this approach is to provide a cap of the royalty *rate* with the rate to be negotiated subject to such cap. To be fair to the seller, at the same time there should be a floor, so the range is bookended.[2] When possible, the parties can also agree on principles or even a recipe for how the royalty rate will be determined within the prescribed range.

There are great advantages to deferring a royalty calculation to a time when commercial utility can be better predicted. Although this can appear advantageous to the seller because the buyer is advancing the technology without knowing the royalty rate that will ultimately be used, there are also advantages to the buyer. Later in the negotiations, the buyer will have a much better understanding of the value and use than the seller. Also, the buyer has the power of termination or selected use. Also, if the parties have an ongoing relationship and expect to do other deals, there should be a mutual confidence that both parties will act reasonably in the process.

AGREEMENTS TO RENEGOTIATE ROYALTIES

A variant of the deferred negotiation strategy is the renegotiation provision. This usually works as follows: The seller proposes that the rates agreed to will exist for a prescribed period, say five years, at which time the parties will renegotiate the license.

Buyers are understandably not keen on this idea because they fear that after all the investment in manufacturing, creating the market, and developing sales relationships, excessive claims will be made by the seller.

The seller can argue that the rate can also go down, benefiting the buyer, so the provision is not one-sided. The key issue hinges on what happens if the parties do not agree. If the seller can effectively terminate the license by demanding an increase in royalties from 7 percent to 70 percent, then the buyer will see this as one-sided because it does not have a comparable club to wield.

Two provisions can help equalize this situation. One is the use of a third party arbiter in the event negotiations break down. The other, and better, approach would be to "pre-agree" on the criteria by which any new royalty rate would be established. For example, suppose a polymer will be introduced that initially will go into the general industrial market at low margins and a low royalty (say 3 percent). However, there is a possibility that it could have medical device applications, but this will not be known for years. Although the parties could pre-agree on the royalty rate for such medical applications, there is good reason to agree to renegotiate the license in 5 years to take into account the markets being served and the margins enjoyed.

ROYALTY BUYOUT AGREEMENTS

In some circumstances, the parties (especially the buyer) may seek to have a buyout provision. Such a provision is basically an option, exercisable by the buyer, to pay off the remaining financial obligations of the license by making a previously agreed upon lump sum payment.

The way it would normally work is that there is some formula for the buyout option that varies with time. If the buyout is exercised early in the license, then the lump sum payment is large because the foregone royalties were expected to be large due to the number of years remaining. The lump sum would decline with time as the number of years bought out declines. One way this can be done is to multiply the current year royalty by some ratio of the remaining number of years. For example, the parties might agree that the buyer can buy out the license by making a lump sum payment equal to the current year's royalties in dollars multiplied by half the remaining years of the license. In other words, the buyout takes place for 50 cents on the dollar, assuming the royalties were to stay flat for the remaining life of the agreement.

The financial basis is the Discounted Cash Flow Method. For each year of the license, the model calculates the NPV of all subsequent royalty payments using an appropriate "k" value. Based upon the perceived risk and estimated sales, a guideline can be developed.

Generally, such a provision is advantageous to the buyer, because the buyer has an option only it can exercise and that presumably, will only be exercised if it results in a better deal for the buyer. Sellers may find such risk acceptable if the formula used to calculate a prepayment provides a reasonable return. Care must be given to variabilities in royalties paid year by year. For example, it could happen that there would be a "down" year in royalties because of some problems with supplies, or a factory fire, or a one-year blip in the market; the seller would not want to enable the buyer to use a low royalty year as the basis of calculating a prepayment of the remaining royalties.

EQUITY LICENSES

In Chapter 10, equity licenses were considered in some detail. The subject is raised again here because equity can be used in combination with lump sum payments and royalties (and kickers, for that matter). For example, a license agreement with a start-up company could involve a nominal upfront lump sum payment, a low royalty, and some stock. The combined consideration would then reflect fair value for the transaction. In this case the seller receives a certain, immediate (though usually small) payment; the assurance of some payment based on sales, regardless of what happens to the stock; and finally, some share of the equity realization in the event the company has a big IPO gain. This could be attractive to the buyer because it minimizes the stock it must give up, yet it carries lower royalty payments than would otherwise be made, an important consideration when cash is tight. In some circumstances, buyers actually favor having the seller be a stock holder because they want the seller to be involved and supportive of the buyer's company. It can also add to the buyer's credibility to have the seller so involved.

Combining royalty and equity returns creates a lot of deal and management complexity. This must be balanced against the benefits of the multiple forms of compensation. Further complications (and creative solutions) are possible. There can be provisions to convert a royalty interest into additional stock, or vice versa. The primary concern of the seller would be that the buyer who controls the start-up might not decide to create a liquidity event such as an IPO. Under such circumstances, the seller would own a minority share of stock in a company that could remain small and private indefinitely. The seller would like to have some way to cash in on the value of the stock held; having a conversion right to increase the royalties would be one way of doing this.

MINIMUM ROYALTIES

Minimum royalties are fixed annual payments that the buyer pays the seller unless the earned royalties exceed the stated minimum. In other words, the buyer owes the seller the larger of the earned royalties or the minimum royalties.

Clearly buyers want to have low minimum royalties (or none), and they want payments to start far in the future. Sellers, on the other hand, want significant minimum royalties, approaching in magnitude the expected earned royalties according to a pro forma income statement. They want payments to begin at a time when such earned royalties are reasonably expected.

Like everything else in a license agreement, the minimums are negotiated through back and forth bargaining. If the pro forma has been conservative, i.e. assuming most circumstances do not turn out favorably, then the parties may agree that the royalties projected should be the minimum royalties. If the pro forma has been optimistic, then a fraction should be counted as minimum royalties. Parties seem to negotiate in the range of 25 to 75 percent of the most likely royalties, with sellers pressing for values of 50 percent or higher and buyers arguing for 25 percent.

One of the realities of licenses is that if the minimum royalties exceed the earned royalties for a number of years, the buyer can be expected to come back to the seller and ask (or demand) some relief. If the low return comes despite vigorous investment and development by the buyer, then the seller could be faced with a terminated license if it doesn't go along with a reasonable proposal. Also, a seller who gets back a technology years later as a result of a termination is often unable to license it to a third party because the market window may be gone, the key inventors may be gone, and the start-up investment to a third party simply may be too large to find an interested buyer. A third party would also (quite reasonably) question what it was that made the original licensee abandon the technology and its investment.

In the case of nonexclusive licenses, buyers often argue that minimum royalties should not exist because the seller can license the technology to as many buyers as it wishes. From the seller's perspective, each license, though nonexclusive, represents a commitment made and loss of opportunity to do something else. For example, a seller could end up with just two buyers, each with nonexclusive all-fields and all-territories licenses,

If one of these buyers is not practicing the technology, and without a minimum has no incentive to terminate its license, then the seller cannot take advantage of creating an exclusive license with its other buyer; such a circumstance could arise because the non-practicing buyer simply wants to preserve its options to enter the market but doesn't really intend to do so. Accordingly, there is no innate reason not to have a minimum royalty even for nonexclusive licenses.

OTHER FORMS OF CONSIDERATION

In all the previous discussions, the form of compensation considered has been money, in the form of initial payments, royalties, minimums, kickers, and so forth. There are many other possible forms of compensation.

One example is a supply contract. A seller could license technology to a buyer and receive as compensation the right to purchase the buyer's licensed products at a discounted price (compared to fair market value) in lieu of any royalty or other payment. Alternatively, the deal could be structured so that the buyer pays a royalty to the seller for sales to third parties and must supply a certain minimum quantity of the product to the seller.

Another example is a purchase contract. In this case, the buyer is obligated to buy raw materials from the seller as part of the license agreement. (Note: In both of these examples there are some potentially significant legal issues that need to be carefully reviewed by legal counsel.)

Another common form of compensation in technology licenses is the payment for additional R&D by the seller. In many cases the reason a technology license arises is because there is an R&D capability within the seller that is not or can not be used directly for commercial purposes. In these and other cases, the seller can be highly motivated to receive funding to support the people and labs doing such work. This can also be important to a buyer because it can speed the commercialization process and/or lead to enhanced features in a second generation embodiment.

The following question arises; Should payment by the buyer for such R&D services come out of the NPV of the deal? Using the $10 million NPV example, suppose that the seller proposes an upfront cash payment of $500,000, the balance of the $9.5 million in royalties, and that the buyer commits to funding $1 million in additional R&D at the seller's lab. From the buyer's perspective, this now looks like an $11 million deal.

What happens here depends on the nature of the R&D and the rights flowing from such work. If the $1 million in R&D was to be precisely the work that the buyer was going to have to do anyway, and the buyer obtains, for no additional consideration, all rights to the fruit of such R&D, then it should not be considered as coming out of the $10 million (assuming that is the agreed upon figure) to which the seller is entitled. Taking the other extreme, if the R&D is not going to aid the buyer's commercialization, and the buyer receives no rights to the results, then the buyer will naturally take the position that the seller may spend its money however it likes but that it should come out of the $10 million (or elsewhere from the seller's budget), not as an additional buyer's payment.

The typical situation is somewhere between these two extremes. The proposed work is related "but not exactly" the same. The seller is willing to include an option to obtain rights to the new results but under terms to be negotiated when the time comes. In this case, the seller is really offering the buyer an option to a second grocery cart of technology rights as an add-on to the deal for the $10 million opportunity. The use of options will be discussed in the next section. However, the short answer here is that the parties should separately value the benefit of the option to the buyer and the funding to the seller to determine a valuation in addition to the $10 million. In order words, the seller is now offering more than the original deal (an option to additional rights), and the buyer is paying more (the R&D funding that will create such additional rights). This circumstance should be treated as a separate valuation, although there may be some economy of scale to consummate this additional agreement at the same time as the base agreement.

OPTION AGREEMENTS

An option is the right to make a future decision. Normally it presumes an exclusive right: If a buyer seeks an option on a license, it normally expects to receive the exclusive right to acquire such license. However, there are cases where the buyer is only seeking assurance that he can acquire a freedom to practice at some future point. In such cases an option to a non-exclusive license is sufficient.

Option agreements can be very useful in technology licensing because they allow a buyer a period of time to conduct due diligence, including possible test marketing. During this period the buyer has the assurance that the deal will not be sold "out from under him" (the phrase refers to the retailer who repossesses a bed while the occupant is still in it). For seller's options there is good news and bad news. The good news is that a serious buyer exists, and there has been some payment for the option. However, the bad news is that during the due diligence period the seller normally (for exclusive options) is prohibited from further marketing the opportunity (the so-call "no shop" provision) and other interested buyers must be turned away. Thus, it is possible that a more motivated buyer could offer more than the buyer holding the option but would have to be turned down. Finally, if the buyer-optionee elects not to exercise the option, other prospective buyers are likely to find out; this casts a pall over subsequent marketing efforts. Some options require a termination fee to compensate sellers for the "pall effect." Although not common, some options provide for "march in" provisions similar to conditional offers in real estate: If a third party shows up with a bona fide offer, then the optionee has a shortened period of time to exercise the option or lose it.

Another issue to be considered in option agreements is what happens if the buyer says yes. If the buyer wants to know all the financial and other key terms prior to exercising the option, then essentially that means the entire agreement will have to be negotiated upfront, a costly exercise in both time and money. Without such agreement, what would a "yes" entitle a buyer? Generally the answer is, only a good faith effort to negotiate within a prescribed period.

The key elements of an option agreement are (1) the scope of the option (defining the TR, or technology rights), (2) the duration of the option, (3) restrictions and obligations on the seller, (4) rights of the buyer (access to information, consultation, etc.), (5) what happens if the buyer says "yes," and (6) payment(s) by the buyer to secure the option.

Like upfront fees, option fees can be considered to be down payments on the opportunity. Consider a case where the parties agree that the NPV of the opportunity is $10 million, subject to confirmation by due diligence. They might agree to the following approach: an option fee of $250,000 upfront and non-refundable (or creditable), an option termination fee of $250,000 in the event the option is not exercised, an upfront fee for the license of $500,000, and the balance of the value expressed in royalties. Normally the option fee does not subtract from the NPV of the deal because the buyer got more than the deal itself: It received the option to the deal, which has value of its own, and then the opportunity to acquire the deal.

Options can be very useful when two parties anticipate doing deals regularly. In that case, an almost form-like agreement can be negotiated once and used quickly many times. Such an approach also allows the option to have unspecified execution value, subject to negotiation, because parties expecting a long term relationship have confidence that both parties have a stake in being reasonable.

CONCLUSION

In this chapter we considered many of the ways that the economic value of a technology can be structured. The wonderful flexibility of technology licenses enables parties to customize the terms of payment to meet their respective goals. In many instances, the issues addressed in this chapter are a delight to work out because it becomes a mutual discovery process for how to meet the needs of all stakeholders.

In the final chapter we will deal with some of the negotiation principles that are part of converting valuations to prices.

NOTES

1. Reportedly said by Truman Capote to a film director who was changing the story line of the screenplay of a Capote book.

2. An example "bookend" structure would be as follows. At the time of the licenses the parties reach agreement on the most (reasonably) pessimistic and optimistic projections for the use of the technology, and these correspond to a royalty rate of 1% and 5% respectively. The agreement could then provide for a royalty rate to be negotiated at the time of commercial introduction that would be bound by these values. The parties could further provide a formula, or basis, by which future events or findings could be used to determine the neighborhood or even exact value in this range.

12

Pricing, Negotiation Readiness, and Conclusion

INTRODUCTION

In this chapter we return to some of the "soft" issues originally introduced in Chapters 1 and 2, issues of risk perception and personalities. By means of the six valuation methods developed in Chapters 4 through 9, it is possible to make a judgment as to what a specific licensing opportunity is worth. Normally such an estimation contains inherent uncertainties due to computing a value based on future events. Through the use of a royalty or equity structure, and perhaps sweetened with "kickers" or renegotiation provisions, some of the effects of such uncertainty can be mitigated. Finally, through negotiation the seller and the buyer, can come to a price agreement or, in terms of the *TR R A DE™* acronym, *"DE" (Deal Economics)*.

For a valuation to be realized, it is necessary that a negotiation take place between a willing buyer and willing seller in which, at the end, both parties agree on the same number with the associated terms. Because each party tends to look at matters in an egocentric way, even if the buyer and seller make use of the same method, it should be expected that their initial positions will not agree or overlap. One reason has to do with conservatism. Sellers know that they will never get more than they ask for, and that once an agreement is struck it will not normally be possible to reconstruct it for more money. Accordingly, the safe tack is to produce a valuation on the high side so that if a buyer accepts the proposed figure, the seller can be at ease with the outcome. However, the buyer is inclined to look at things pessimistically, at least initially, so that the odds of meeting or beating the market-value assumptions are very high. In most cases, the initial perspectives developed by the parties do not overlap, that is, the desired valuation by the seller is higher than that of the buyer.

Although negotiation as a discipline is an extensive subject, not covered here, there are some basic points that are essential to implementing the work of previous chapters. Addressing these basic points and wrapping up some of the "soft side" issues is the goal of this chapter.

REVIEW OF THE SIX VALUATION METHODS

The six valuation methods are displayed visually in Exhibit 12.1. Shown at the top are the two most commonly used methods: Industry Standards (Chapter 4), and Rules of Thumb, such as the "25 percent Rule" (Chapter 6). The Industry Standards Method requires the identification of an appropriate comparable agreement. In many cases, no single agreement exists that closely matches the subject valuation. Therefore, a common practice is to create a comparable scenario from existing agreements. This can be envisioned as an interpretation exercise that interpolates and extrapolates from existing data to predict how the market would have valued the subject opportunity had it been given a chance to do so.

There is a useful metaphor for this process. Airplanes reference their positions from fixed ground stations that emit a special signal. These signals, known as VORs, are coded in such a way that an onboard instrument can determine the heading, or direction, of the airplane moment-by-moment relative to the ground station. Originally, such VOR stations were used as byways whereby pilots would "hop" their way across the country flying from one VOR to the next until they got close enough to their destination that they could use visual observation or other forms of navigation. Then a very bright guy came up with a simple but powerful idea: Instead of flying from VOR station to VOR station, why not use the VOR signals and create virtual stations anywhere, ideally in direct lines toward the destination? This was the birth of what is now known as R-NAV. The process of using Industry Standards is a lot like R-NAV. If one can find a comparable agreement, or better yet, a family of them that happen to be located exactly where one wants to go, it's like having a VOR station conveniently located at one's destination (a rare event). It is more common to find useful points of reference from previous agreements (similar to the scattered VOR stations). Analyzing the agreements through analysis such as Rating/Ranking, possibly coupled with Rules of Thumb and Discounted Cash Flow, one can create an R-NAV site directly where one needs to go. (The Rating/Ranking Method is particularly useful in this endeavor.)

The Rule of Thumb Method is commonly employed for three valuation purposes. First, it is a starting point for deriving a royalty rate, based upon an analysis of the benefit to the buyer, to create a price. Second, it is

Exhibit 12.1 The Six Key Valuation Methods

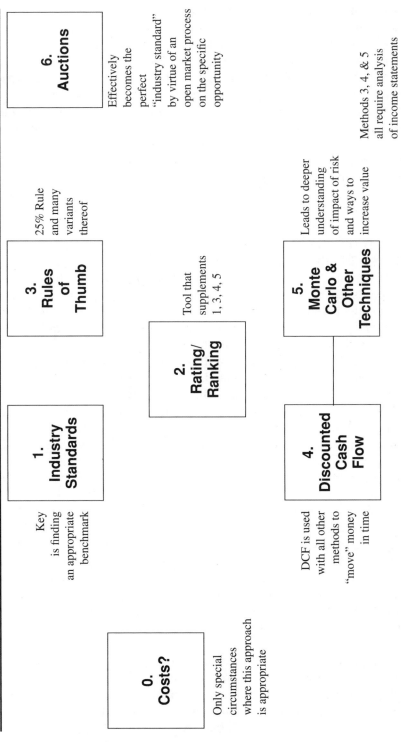

6. Auctions

Effectively becomes the perfect "industry standard" by virtue of an open market process on the specific opportunity

3. Rules of Thumb

25% Rule and many variants thereof

2. Rating/ Ranking

Tool that supplements 1, 3, 4, 5

5. Monte Carlo & Other Techniques

Leads to deeper understanding of impact of risk and ways to increase value

Methods 3, 4, & 5 all require analysis of income statements

1. Industry Standards

Key is finding an appropriate benchmark

4. Discounted Cash Flow

DCF is used with all other methods to "move" money in time

0. Costs?

Only special circumstances where this approach is appropriate a sanity check on a number created in some other way. For instance, the seller's use of the Industry Standard Method coupled with Discounted Cash Flow can create a valuation that does not take into considerion what proportion of the expected financial benefit to the buyer is being allocated in royalties and equity. The Rule of Thumb Method can check the reasonableness of other methods. Finally, Rules of Thumb can be used as an early basis of agreement between a seller and buyer to frame subsequent detailed financial analysis. For instance, if the parties can agree at the earliest stage of due diligence and negotiation that they will apply the 25 Percent Rule with the value "25," then this process agreement can create confidence that a deal can ultimately be struck and a fair final number calculated. Conversely, if a prospective buyer discerns early in the process that the seller aspires to 50 percent or 75 percent of the profits, and such a high range is clearly incompatible with the nature of the opportunity, the buyer can focus on realigning the seller's perspective or else cut off further investment in due diligence.

The Discounted Cash Flow Method (Chapter 7) and other advanced methods such as Monte Carlo (Chapter 8), are based on creating pro forma spreadsheets of estimated income and cash flow statements. Such approaches are the most formal, and complex, methods of valuation. They calculate a financial benefit that the buyer will accrue by virtue of the license. By applying Rules of Thumb to the projected profitability, a Net Present Value can be calculated, or a royalty such that the NPV is apportioned appropriately between seller and buyer.

In addition, these two methods serve other purposes. The DCF Method and its related equations enable money to be moved in time so that even if one performs a valuation solely based on the Industry Standard Method, it is possible to make rational judgments as to the appropriate upfront payments, or progress payments, or buyout value. Also, the DCF Method creates a way to think about and evaluate risk that is expressed in a concrete dollars and cents form.

Likewise, the Monte Carlo Method can be used to assess the effect of specific elements of risk or uncertainty and to understand its effect on the overall uncertainty of the project's profitability. Such analysis can suggest actions that sellers can take to reduce the business risk of a project and, thereby, attract more buyers and better terms. Also, such methods can help buyers construct agreements that provide conditional payments (such as kickers) to sellers based upon ultimate outcomes of highly variable risk factors.

Finally, the Auction Method (Chapter 6) is a way of creating an incontrovertible comparable, or as in the metaphor used earlier, creating a VOR site at the perfect location, by having the market bid for the specific opportunity. With perfect information, and multiple bidders, this process should yield a fair value to both the buyer and the seller.

What About Cost?

Reinforcing a key point made in Chapter 3 about cost, it must be remembered that costs are, with special exceptions, irrelevant.

It is easily conceivable that a seller has already made enormous investments in getting the technology to its present state, and these costs would not have to be laid out by the buyer. One reason this must arise is simply poor project and investment management on the part of the seller. Another reason is that the seller's timing was poor; the cost of creating a new technology is heavily dependent on when one starts. In starting too late, one misses the window. If one starts too early and is the so-called pioneer, one has to invent everything and endure a long gestation period before the market is ready. Numerous other reasons can exist. The seller may have locked into a needlessly complex and expensive way of creating the technology because of the mindset of the inventors or corporate policy.

On the other hand, a low cost project might "get lucky" in that it creates something of significant value quickly and for a very modest investment. This is normally not a fortuitous accident: key capabilities that already exist were previously paid for at the seller's labs.

In both of these extremes, the cost basis of the project will have no bearing on a valuation. In the former case, no rational buyer will pay more than an opportunity is worth, looking only forward in time; the buyer perceives itself as striking a deal to benefit itself, not to undo the misfortunes of the seller. In the latter case of the "fortuitous" project, no rational seller will sell it for less than it is presently worth just because its costs were low. Sellers recognize that, just as in each life a little rain must fall, so does a little extra sunshine from time to time. Realizing fair value for sunny days helps compensate for the rainy times.

Yet there are certain circumstances where a cost analysis is worth performing. Often within the seller's organization there are stakeholders who approve or influence the approval of a deal. These stakeholders may be cognizant of the project's costs and they will want to know why the seller is receiving less than it spent and why it is getting a smaller ROI than expected. There can be circumstances where in-process R&D has been booked as a balance sheet asset; upon disposition, there could be an adverse balance sheet effect. Such circumstances would indicate the need for a cost-analysis.

Performing the cost analysis will help stakeholders in the selling company to come to one mind on the valuation. Such a process may require reconciliation with earlier (and not-to-be-realized) ROI expectations. Even if R&D expenses do not show up on the seller's official balance sheet, they can show up in key people's bonuses and so affect behavior. As will be discussed further, license negotiations include negotiations within one's own organization. For the seller, such negotiations involve reconciliation of already sunk project costs with proposed selling prices or terms offered by the buyer.

Another reason to analyze cost is to determine how a buyer might value an opportunity. What are the buyer's alternatives to a negotiated agreement with the seller? One simple alternative for the buyer is to do nothing, which is equivalent to investing its funds in buying down its debt or buying back its stock. Another option is to invest in a completely different project unrelated to the one offered by the seller. A third option, and a crucial issue with regard perceiving the value of the seller's technology, is to create the same or similar business opportunity as might result from a deal with the seller but to do so independently of the seller. This can be done by following a different technology path, or by following the same path but working around the seller's patents and/or independently recreating the seller's trade secrets.

The seller's project costs could be a useful starting point for estimating what it might cost a buyer to recreate the technology. If it will cost the buyer X to recreate the seller's technology, then the buyer will not pay much more than X unless there is a significant time-to-market advantage in doing so. Other reasons to consider technology licensing would be if there is significant risk that the buyer's recreation might not work, or there is significant risk that the scope of the seller's patent claims might not be avoided, or the buyer wants to maintain good will between the parties because of broader business objectives, or for some other reason.

Accordingly, it is good practice to answer two cost questions: (1) What did it cost the seller to this point? (2) What would it cost the buyer to recreate the seller's technology? However, it is rare that either of such figures will be the basis of a final agreement.

Deciding on an Appropriate Level of Analysis

Using any of the described methods, it is possible to engage in an endless analytical exercise, leading to paralysis by analysis. This quote from Ross Perot captures well the frustration that can exist with excessive analysis:

> I come from an environment where, if you see a snake, you kill it. At GM, if you see a snake, the first thing you do is go hire a consultant on snakes. Then you get a committee on snakes, and then you discuss it for a couple of years. The most likely course of action is—nothing. You figure the snake hasn't bitten anybody yet, so you just let him crawl around on the factory floor.[1]

An appropriate question is to ask is: How much of my resources are justifiably spent on analysis? Or, put another way, what is an appropriate

cap on transaction costs, of which valuation analysis and other prepared-
ness activities are the initial component?

Let us consider a simple example. Suppose there is a technology that
a seller expects could result in a royalty of probably more than $100,000
per year, but probably less than $1 million per year; this is colloquially
termed a "six-figure deal." Further, it is believed that such royalties
might be paid over a period of five to ten years starting three to five
years hence. Using such approximate numbers, a seller might estimate
that it should be able to receive an upfront licensing fee of at least
$100,000, so in current-year terms the deal should be worth at least that
much money. Over the life of such a license, the NPV could be roughly
estimated as, say, seven times the DCF of a $300,000 royalty payment
(on the conservative side of midway between $100,000 and $999,999),
occurring seven years hence (about mid-term of the royalty payment after four years of further development). Using "7" as the multiple on the
DCF is a somewhat conservative estimate of the number of years that a
royalty would be paid. Overall, the risk level of the royalty stream (as an
example) may be estimated to be 30 percent. Thus, the NPV may be calculated as follows:

$$NPV = 7 * \$300,000/(1 + 0.3)^7 = \$330,000.$$

Such an estimate of potential impact can be done quickly, especially
with experience, and used to gauge priority and significance. It can be argued that the range in the assumed values is so vast that the calculated result is meaningless. It can also be argued that the entire process has
become circular because the calculation assumes the value which is to be
determined to decide whether or not it is worth the effort to determine the
value. However, making judgments about the importance of things without genuinely knowing the importance of things is something we all do
every day. When you get a telephone call soliciting the "opportunity of a
lifetime" do you invest time in figuring it out or not?[2] Sometimes it is impossible to invest all the due diligence time needed. Early, best-guess
judgments and selections must be made.

Following up on this example, if it is reasonable to assume, as a ballpark estimate, a current-year value of $100,000 (assumed to be conser-
vative) and a lifetime NPV value of $330,000 (modestly conservative),
what is the appropriate level of investment to make a deal? Like many
things, there is no hard and fast rule. One way to look at this from the
seller's perspective is, what is the opportunity worth without a license
agreement? If it is zero, then if there is even a 50 percent chance of
reaching an agreement with a buyer under the previous terms, it is
worth spending up to 50 percent of those figures. For sellers that think
appropriately in NPV terms, that would put a cap of $165,000 on the

transaction costs; for sellers who think in terms of current-year expenses and revenues, the cap would be $50,000. More accurately, the seller should view investment in creating a deal like any other investment made and, so, should be reasonably justified on an ROI basis. This might place the operational caps at 80 percent of these figures ($40,000 and $134,000).

Of course the goal of any seller is to determine rational behavior to maximize benefit, not to compute the worst tolerable performance. A way of valuing the benefit of perfect information is needed. Let us consider what might be meant by perfect seller information in a licensing valuation context. A good working definition of that number would be the most that any one buyer would be willing to pay after completing due diligence and hearing the seller's persuasive argument and that the transaction took place in a reasonable amount of time with reasonable selling costs. In many cases, such perfect valuation information would cause three to five buyers to take a serious look at the opportunity. Three might make serious counter-offers, all within a three-month period, and all with terms and conditions generally acceptable to the seller.

How would such perfect information differ from, say, the example proposed earlier? Because in that example the probable annual royalties varied by a factor of ten ($100,000 to just under $1 million); this would correspond to a royalty rate variation of 0.2 to 2 percent or 0.5 to 5 percent, a huge range. For the seller to be reasonably safe in quoting a figure, it would have to select a number at or close to the top end of the range. Such a figure may be so high as to dissuade any bidder. Alternatively, considering the range of 0.5 to 5 percent, what should the seller do if an early prospective buyer offers 1.5 percent "firm and final?" Most sellers, under these circumstances would view the investment of several tens of thousands of dollars as a prudent investment.

Sellers often find themselves at an information disadvantage with respect to the buyer. By definition, the buyer is planning to put the technology into commerce, so it should know many of the key issues of manufacturing and sales and marketing. If the opportunity is really significant, the buyer is not likely to tell the seller that it is valuing the opportunity too modestly.

Therefore, it is good practice for the seller to perform some preliminary analysis of potential significance to make a general determination of the value at stake. This can be done semi-quantitatively as shown in the previous example, or even more qualitatively by creating and using "high," "medium," and "low" categories. Then a seller can adopt deal investment levels and methodologies appropriate to the categories. For example, for a "high" opportunity (say, a potential of seven figures or more, i.e. $10 million or more), an extensive valuation will be performed using multiple cross checking methods and using outside experts to provide additional resources and confirmation. For a "medium" category (a six-figure deal), the seller could use one method, perhaps with external support and validation.

For "low" categories (a five-figure deal), judgment could be based upon an afternoon of thinking and consulting the records of previous deals (including networking with colleagues and friends). Also, for each of these categories a budget for selling and transaction costs should be established. Clearly for a five-figure deal one could spend more than the value of the deal in internal staff costs, especially for legal costs. If a seller has numerous opportunities in the "low" category, then it would be wise to create a very standard valuation approach with form licenses that are not subject to negotiation or customization to avoid consuming value in transaction costs. Also, there are some situations in which the opportunity is literally not worth the cost of creating the agreement to transfer the rights.

VALUATION VERSUS PRICING

As discussed in Chapter 1, we have used the term "valuation" to mean the worth of an opportunity and "pricing" as a communicated offer. When buying from street merchants in some countries, especially areas frequented by tourists, a seller's initial price can easily be ten times the product's value. In such circumstances, the number of potential buyers is practically endless. Sellers in such circumstances have little to lose by quoting enormus prices because there is literally always another buyer around the corner (or perhaps on the next cruise ship). Further, if the buyer is not responding favorably, the price can be dropped quickly often, without losing the transaction. Such backpedaling by a seller normally causes a buyer to distrust the seller's representations. In the case of street goods, this is generally not a significant loss because the trust was probably not high in the first place, but, more importantly, the buyer can conduct rapid due diligence without the "assistance" of an untrusted seller.

Consequently, it should be no surprise that street sellers the world over have learned to deploy strategies of high price multiples. How would such a strategy work in licensing a technology? Not well. First, the number of potential buyers is normally not large and certainly not endless. Therefore, it is generally not a good idea to risk losing any buyer's interest by quoting unreasonably high numbers.

In addition, technology licensing requires significant levels of due diligence by buyers. Buyers are not inclined to make such investments if they have reason to believe that the seller is just looking for naïve or desperate buyers. Further, trust is an important element in most licensing transactions. A buyer will tend to devalue an opportunity if it concludes that the seller is hiding or misrepresenting information. There are serious adverse results to being too aggressive in pricing.

So, although a seller can count on not being offered more than it asks, it does not serve its own interests to ask for much more than it is perceived to be worth. A very reasonable approach to finding the middle ground is for the seller to value an opportunity several times under varying levels of optimism, the so-called scenario analysis. A common approach is a low scenario, a high scenario, and a most likely scenario. The low and high scenarios are usually labeled according to the assumptions made about them. For example, the low scenario could be "niche market, U.S." and the high scenario "mass market, worldwide." For a seller to select a price valuation at the high end is reasonable, providing that there is some basis for making such an assumption. During the course of discussions with prospective buyers, the feasibility (or not) of the optimistic assumptions can be tested.

Obviously, buyers may disagree with seller's assumptions, particularly for the more optimistic scenarios. However, buyers generally will respect a reasoned approach. Further, if the seller's assumptions are communicated to a buyer, then the buyer can move forward by developing its own most likely scenario and present those findings to the seller. If the seller says, "I want 100" and the buyer says, "I'll give you 10," convergence will be difficult if not impossible. If instead the seller says, "You will be able to sell licensed products for three major applications in all the industrialized countries of Europe, Asia, and America, and so it is worth 100," then the buyer can reply, "If I believed I could, I would agree with your number, but here is where I can see applying it. . . ." And so on.

Although the pricing discussion has been primarily focused on a seller's position, pricing is also an activity performed by the buyer. "Low ball" offers by a buyer often poison the relationship with the seller and can, in particular, offend inventors whose technology is being sold. Even if the buyer later makes a more reasonable offer, offended inventors (and others) can sometimes sabotage negotiations. Although some buyers might relish the prospect of getting something for almost nothing, most sellers are not naïve and, furthermore, they have long memories.

MARKETING AND SELLING STRATEGIES: SELLER'S VIEW

Although "marketing" as a term seems to carry a more professional image, what a seller really is doing is "selling." Marketing has more to do with creating future products and services that the target segments will want. Selling is getting a buyer to take what exists on the shipping dock. Theodore Leavitt has put this succinctly: "Selling is getting rid of what you have; marketing is making sure you have what you can get rid of."

Selling as an activity focuses on the specific "product" in the sales bag and how it will benefit specific customers. This process leads a seller to consider how the intrinsic features of the technology translate to the benefit of the buyer and the buyer's customer. It is helpful to consider the buyer as a value-added reseller (VAR) as the term is used in the information technology industry. The key attribute of VAR-thinking is that the buyer is an intermediary to the ultimate customer and, as an intermediary, has to contribute to and benefit from the value delivered to such customer. It is generally a very good idea for the seller to be able to express in income statement terms (such as used in the DCF Method) how the buyer will make money with the technology. This is the basic concept behind the phrase, "Sell the benefits not the features."

Another key aspect of selling is market segmentation. Not all categories of buyers will view the same opportunity as equally valuable. An astute seller will focus on the category of buyers that is most likely to be interested in becoming a licensee and that will put the highest value on the opportunity because they can extract the greatest benefit. Next we will consider four distinct buyer segments.

One poor buyer category that is frequently but unwisely considered is the ultimate customer. To make this concrete, let us consider a technology for making a special-purpose laser. Sellers can often more easily identify potential customers of such lasers than potential licensees who would want to build and sell such lasers. The identity and enthusiasm of potential customers can be helpful in attracting licensees, but rarely will such customers find the opportunity so compelling that they will seek to become laser manufacturers.

A better buyer for this category is a company that presently uses similar technologies but for other markets and applications. Again using the laser example, let us suppose that the laser is particularly suited to medical applications, both diagnostic and treatment. If a prospective buyer exists that already makes lasers, but only for the *industrial* laser market, then it can be a significant stretch for that buyer to enter the medical market. This is because there are many aspects of the medical market that would be unknown to the company, such FDA approval processes, the buying needs and patterns of hospitals and doctor's offices, the economics of the industry, especially the important involvement of third party payers, and so forth. Also, having trade name value and company recognition definitely plays a role. Finally, one needs an experienced sales force to call on the ultimate customer. Thus, although it is a positive that the prospective buyer understands lasers, its lack of experience in the niche market is usually a significant barrier.

An even better buyer segment would be a company making high-tech devices for the medical industry. Even if it does not presently make lasers, it inherently possesses an in-depth understanding of the market environment and customer requirements, and it is the perspective that is generally more important and difficult to obtain. If needed, the buyer could have some or all of the laser manufacturing contracted out to one of its vendors. Obviously, the best buyer segment would be a company already making lasers for the medical industry because it would have both the technology and the market understanding, but finding such a buyer is not always possible.

Using such perspectives, a seller needs to develop a sales strategy. Because it will be necessary to induce a buyer to make a significant due diligence investment, it is helpful to be able to show the prospective buyer how and why the opportunity is beneficial. To do this intelligently requires some effort on the seller's part and limits the number of prospective buyers that could be cost-effectively analyzed. Usually a seller should consider more than just three or four buyers; depending upon the potential significance of the deal, a reasonable upper limit might be in the range of six to ten. If a seller were to choose six in the laser example, the distribution should favor the last two buyer segments. A reasonable distribution would be as follows: two or three companies that make lasers for the medical market, one or two companies that make other high-tech equipment for the medical industry, and possibly one company that is experienced in making and selling lasers for many markets, but not the medical market. This approach benefits the seller by providing different perspectives from different segments; however, most of the selling energy goes into the most-likely-to-succeed category.

Another selling question that arises is determining what size companies are most likely to be serious buyers. In other words, should a seller approach the existing market leader, a strong "number 2," or a market laggard? There are two generalizations that can be useful to answering this question. First, the size of the opportunity should be scaled to the prospective buyer. For instance, if the seller's expected price is going to be seven figures, it is generally not fruitful to consider buyers whose annual revenues are just seven figures. Big opportunities, particularly ones that will require large R&D and developmental investments, will need the resources and grand visions of big companies. Likewise, profitable but small opportunities seem to be more attractive to smaller prospective buyers; bigger companies are generally not interested in licensing opportunities that, even if successful, will be almost undetectable on their income statements.

The second generalization deals with the attitude of market leaders. It appears to be both a human and corporate trait that large size and success lead to hubris and the belief that one knows more than anyone else. Compounding this, market leaders normally have a vested interest in maintaining the status quo. Although there can certainly be exceptions, it is not surprising when market leaders turn down an opportunity, and later that decision proves to be a short-sighted judgment. At the other end of the market share spectrum, the smallest companies are often so limited in their resources that they are unable to effectively implement opportunities. Generally, the companies ranging number two through number four in terms of market size frequently are better targets than the market leader or the smallest players.

OPPORTUNITY PRIORITIZATION AND DUE DILIGENCE: BUYER'S VIEW

The high cost of conducting due diligence, coupled with the high mortality of even the most promising projects, makes a strong argument for a strategic approach for a buyer. If every prospective opportunity has to be analyzed from first principles, then the cost of analysis will be high and the likelihood of failure will be equally high. On the other hand, if licensing opportunities can be investigated from a pre-established framework of company priorities and strongest assets, success becomes more likely.

By being proactive, a buyer can increase its odds for being the first in line to negotiate. By having a checklist of key functions, features, and benefits sought, together with an understanding of the customer needs it seeks to meet, the buyer is also better able to quickly recognize significant opportunities.

An ability to understand the value of a license early in the process enables the buyer to do a reality assessment. In some cases such an assessment may actually precede the seller's own valuation activities (which from a seller's perspective, is not a preferred method). By being early, the buyer can create momentum for a quick and early deal that can induce the seller to accept a lower price than it might have otherwise. This is particularly so in a royalty-based agreement where the buyer can make the case that in its hands the technology will be exploited more fully and immediately because of the strategic fit and the proactivity of the buyer.

NEGOTIATION READINESS

Prior to a negotiation, there are certain basic preparations that are part of "negotiation readiness." The first two are obvious but often are not carefully thought through: (1) what do I have to offer?, and (2) What do I want in return? As discussed in Chapter 2, there are many things that can be offered and sought. Even if one considers only money, it can come in many forms. It can be tied to company value (equity), to sales (royalty), to profitability (a kicker), to fields of use and territories granted. Money can be fixed payments or conditional, and weighted to occur early (or not).

The nature of the buyer's commitment is another important element of a deal. Often this shows up as the diligence requirement of the license. This means that if the buyer/licensee does not fulfill the specified requirement, the license can be terminated, or made nonexclusive, or some penalty payment is made, depending upon what is negotiated. This is an example of an important "want" of the seller and "offer" of the buyer.

Another kind of commitment is future assistance by the seller, either in the form of tech transfer, troubleshooting, and/or improvement inventions. The ability of the seller to provide such assistance may be critical to the buyer's decision to enter the license agreement at all, no matter what the price.

A good practice is for both the buyer and seller to create a simple table of "offer" and "want" elements around which to frame a deal. A common way to communicate such elements is in what is called a term sheet offer, which can be made by either the seller or buyer. Usually a term sheet is one to three pages in length and deals with the principal elements that are being offered and what is proposed in return. It normally defers dealing with the details of a license agreement until it appears that there is consent to the basic terms.

In addition to offers and wants, there are two other elements that should be thought through prior to negotiations. The first is often known as a decision tree. In any negotiation, it normally happens that the offers and wants of each party do not exactly mirror the other. This leads to the need for compromise. In order to compromise effectively, it is necessary to formulate a decision tree by which comparisons can be made of the economic significance of each concession made or sought. In complex cases, there could be multiple rounds of such considerations and therefore multiple decision trees. By preparing alternatives of various decision trees in advance of negotiations, the parties can more readily propose compromises that preserve the value sought while still accommodating certain needs of the other side.

The alternative analysis, sometimes called a "Plan B Analysis," should always be: What happens if there is no deal? What are our alternatives, and the likely value of such alternatives, if we cannot reach an agreement with this party? For sellers who negotiate with only one prospective buyer and who believe that there are no other alternatives possible, this process reveals the vulnerability of not having a tenable Plan B. Accordingly, sellers should always sell and negotiate with a legitimate Plan B, even if it is significantly less desirable than Plan A.

Without a Plan B, the seller can be convinced to accept a very low valuation because "something is better than nothing," (if their Plan B is truly nothing). In many situations, buyers inherently have a Plan B. That Plan B can be to invest its money in some completely unrelated but profitable project.

In licensing negotiation, as in many other areas of life, the old saying holds true: proper preparation prevents poor performance.

BUYER-SELLER CONVERGENCE

At the beginning of this chapter it was noted that the seller's and buyer's positions commonly do not overlap when negotiations begin. If both parties have performed valuations based upon some rational methodology, and both have identified underlying assumptions, then there is hope that with an open exchange of information convergence can take place. It can be the buyer's valuation increasing to meet the seller's, or it can be the reverse. In other cases it might be movement by both parties, not just in the spirit of compromise, but due to a better understanding of the opportunities and risks.

Convergence is illustrated in Exhibit 12.2, which is based upon a similar figure in a book by Smith and Parr.[3] Early in this book, we intro-

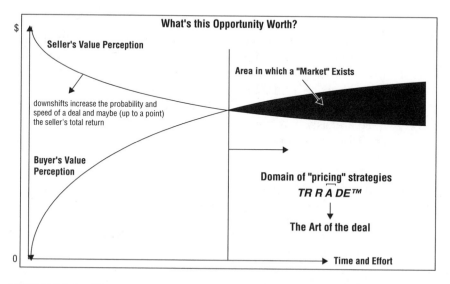

Exhibit 12.2 Illustration of the Conditions for which a Negotiation Opportunity Exists

Based on Figure 5.1 in Smith and Parr, *Valuation of Intellectual Property and Intangible Assets,* John Wiley & Sons, Inc., 1999.

Figure 12.1
DILBERT © distributed by United Feature Syndicate. Reprinted with permission.

duced the acronym *TR R A DE*™, where *TR* stood for *Technology Rights*, *DE* for *Deal Economics* (or Equity), and *R* for the risk characterized by the risk-adjusted hurdle rate (k). The final element in the acronym is the *A*: *A* stands for the *Art* of the deal.

Once the buyer's and seller's valuations overlap, a deal should be possible. The art of the process is discovering ways that make the deal as valuable as possible to both parties and to do so quickly.

CONCLUSION

Three other closing points remain. The first has to do with predicting the future. Technology, by definition, is unproven commercially. In some cases it carries with it bold promises of revolutionizing the way things are done. It is wise to have a little humility about such bold forecasts. At the World's Fair of 1893, a group of 74 social commentators, an expert panel, was convened and asked to reach consensus on key features of the world in 100 years. Here were some of their predictions:

> Many people will live to be 150.
> Prisons will decline and divorce will be considered unnecessary.
> The Nicaraguan canal is as sure to be built as the tides are to ebb and flow and the seasons are to change.[4]
> The government will have grown more simple, as true greatness tends always toward simplicity.

Secondly, it should be remembered that all of licensing is about creating value for end users. There is a Dilbert cartoon that has as its punchline: "Whoa! Are you saying we need *revenue* to make a profit?" Nothing good happens unless the buyer can sell something.

Finally, you bought this big, expensive book and were looking for a *number?* Based on having been asked this question many times, this author has developed an answer: 3.14. It's the best I can do without additional information.

NOTES

1. Ross Perot, "The GM System Is Like a Blanket of Fog," *Fortune*, 15, February 1988, pp. 48-49.

2. The author once received a collect long distance call from a man living in a homeless shelter in Florida who convincingly described the general outline of the "invention of the century." The deal was that he would offer negotiating rights in exchange for a Western Union transfer of $500, but that the deal had to be done now because the shelter lunch line was closing in two minutes. How does one decide such things?

3. Based on Fig. 5.1 in Smith & Parr, *Valuation of IP & Intangible Assets*, Wiley 1989 (p. 129).

4. This one is a personal favorite. The canal that got built just 15 years later under the leadership of President Theodore Roosevelt was the *Panama* Canal. The metaphor to express certainty is especially touching.

APPENDIX A

Technology Access Key Resource List

Here are important contacts for technology transfer professionals. Each listing is a window on hundreds or thousands of expert, helpful people and resources you can use to increase your returns from technology transfer. For more contacts, subscribers to Technology Access Report may call the Technology Access Hotline (see Technology Access Report entry below for contact information).

American Association for the Advancement of Science
Open membership organization of 200,000 includes subscription to Science, runs large annual meeting in February with a growing tech transfer track, and maintains an excellent update on S & T legislative action.
ACCESS: 1200 New York Ave., NW Washington, D.C. 200005, 202/326-6400, fax 203/371-9526.

American Entrepreneurs for Economic Growth
Founded (and wholly funded) by the National Venture Capital Association in 1989, this no-fee group now numbers over 4,000 emerging growth companies. Surveys, legislative alerts, directory and annual meeting.
ACCESS: 1655 N. Fort Myer Dr., Ste. 700, Arlington, VA 22209, 703/351-5269, fax 703/351-5268.

American Intellectual Property Law Association
7500 attorneys covering patents, copyrights and trademarks. Three meetings per year.
ACCESS: 2001 Jefferson Davis Hwy., Site. 203, Arlington, VA, 703/415-0780, fax 703/415-0786.

Association for Technology Implementation
Official consortium of Europe's national (governmental) tech transfer agencies. Chair rotates to different countries.
ACCESS: Mr. Gag Kavlie, Norges Forskningsraad, Sognsveien 720801 Oslo 8, Norway, 9(47-2)237-685, fax (47-2)181-139.

Asssociation of Federal Technology Transfer Executives
New in 1992, open to all, focuses on the details of administration of technology transfer in federal agencies.

ACCESS: Reid Adler, Director, Office of Technology Transfer, National Institutes of Health, 6003 Executive Blvd., Bethesda, MD 20892, 301/496-0750, fax 301/402-0220.

Association of University Technology Managers

1,000+ university and medical center licensing officers (and company scouts). Membership and meetings open to all; fall business-oriented licensing course.
ACCESS: Bayfield Resources, (management company), 71 East Rd., Norwalk CT 06851, 203/852-7168, fax 203/838-5714.

Best-North America

Database of university research faculty profiles.
ACCESS: Ken Blaisdell, President, Best-North America, 1615 Thames St., Ste., 301, Baltimore, MD 21231, 301/563-2378, fax 301/563-5389.

BioScan

Leading database of close to 1,500 biotech company profiles and 6,000 executives; includes R&D and licensing agreements, new products, etc.
ACCESS: American Health Consultants, www.ahcpub.com/ahc_root_html/products/newsletters/bsch.html

Center for Economic Conversion

Consults with communities and individual companies on positive actions to create economic benefits from base closings and cut-backs.
ACCESS: Michael Closson, 222 View St., Ste. C, Mtn. View, CA 94041-1344, 415/968-8798, fax 415/968-1126.

Commerce Business Daily

Notices of government contracts, RFPs, cooperative research opportunities.
ACCESS: Superintendent of Documents, Government Printing Office, Washington DC 20402, 202/512-1800.

Commercial Development Association

Merger of two chemical industry professional societies, with roots in marketing and commercial development, both sides dipping into technology licensing. Two annual meetings, foundation for training and scholarships in CD.
ACCESS: 1255 Twenty-third Street, NW, Washington, DC 20037-1174, 202/452-1620, fax 202/833-3636.

Community of Science

Commercial database collator, part-owned by Johns Hopkins University, with 46,000 U.S. and Canadian university research faculty profiles from some 125 U.S. and Canadian research institutions "Expertise", as well as funding opportunities, patents, Commerce Business Daily and the Federal Register, etc., searchable (for a fee), by entire organization domains.
ACCESS: Community of Science, 1629 Thames Street, Suite 200, Baltimore, MD 21231, 410/563-2378, fax 410/563-5389. Email: info@cos.com, www.cos.com

Corporate Technology Information Services (CorpTech)

Directory of 50,000 high technology companies public and private and 180,000 senior staff, including licensing contacts, in almost every conceivable format including paper, online, mailing labels, diskettes and in editions by state or region. Useful for targeted marketing of inventions by industry. Classifications are more up-to-date than old SIC codes.
ACCESS: 12 Alfred Street, Suite 200, Woburn, MA 01801-1915, 800/454-3647 (617/932-3939), fax 617/932-6335, www.corptech.com

Department of Commerce

The home of the Office of Technology Policy, "the only office in the federal government with the explicit mission of developing and advocating national policies that use technology to build America's economic strength."

ACCESS: Office of Technology Policy, Room 4418, 14th and Constitution Avenue, NW, Washington, DC 20230, 202/482-6102, fax 202/219-8667.

Disclosure, Inc.
Private service that maintains Securities and Exchange Commission filings by 11,000 companies on microfiche, including many documents detailing licensing and joint venture agreements.
ACCESS: 5161 River Rd., Bethedsda, MD 20816, 800/754-9690 (outside U.S., 44 171 278-8277).

Energy-Related Inventions Program/Innovative Concepts Program
Grant program "too small to cut" during Reagan-Bush years, has built enviable track record of successfully commercialized inventions, usually from independent inventors, by careful technical screening by NIST, and equally careful business training and supervision of grantees by ERIP staff.
ACCESS: Department of Energy, 1000 Independence Ave., CE521, 5E052, Washington, DC 20585, 202/586-1478, fax 202/586-8134.

European Association for the Transfer of Technologies, Innovation and Industrial Information (TII)
Private association of 300+ governmental private agencies and companies involved in various aspects of technology commercialization. Publishes cross-indexed directory.
ACCESS: TII asbl, 3 rue des Capuchins, L-1313, Luxembourg, (352)46.30.35, fax (352)46.21.85.

Federal Laboratory Consortium for Technology Transfer
Technology transfer officers for the 700+ federal laboratories, from every agency and department that perform research. Activities: a small demonstration grant program, a free newsletter, annual meetings, open to all. Fall meeting focuses on members' professional development; spring meeting includes displays of technologies available for license.
ACCESS: www.federallabs.org.

Federal Register
Proposed revised and enacted regulations, laws, including grant and procurement.
ACCESS: Superintendent of Documents, Government Printing Office, Washington DC 20402, 202/512-1800, fax 202/512-2250.

Find/SVP
Catalog of out-sourced product, market and technology reports.
ACCESS: 625 Ave. of the Americas, New York, NY 10011, 212/645-4500, fax 212/645-7681.

IBM Intellectual Property Network
The world leader in issued and new patents and patent licensing income had to create its own searchable database of all U.S. patents for internal purposes, then opened it to the public. It is slowly becoming a commercial venture, offering instant translation, document delivery, powerful patent analysis and graphing tools, both home-grown and by arrangement with outside vendors, and "pink dots," visible links from patents available for license to the owners' own websites.
ACCESS: www.patents.ibm.com

IC² Institute
Headed by George Kozmetzky, a founder of Teledyne Corp., then dean of the Graduate School of Business at UTA, and now widely heralded as the godfather of technology development in Austin and Texas, this research, publishing conference center focuses on Innovation, Creativity and Capital.
ACCESS: IC² Institute, 2815 San Gabriel, Austin, TX 78705, 512/475-8900 or 800/215-6782.

Industrial Research Institute

260 members, limited to for-profit companies conducting research in the U.S., across all industries; committees reach out to federal labs and universities. Company representatives are highest level managers of R&D. Publishes bimonthly journal *Research and Technology Management*, holds seminars and semi-annual meetings, conducts research on research.
ACCESS: Charles Larson, Executive Director, IRI, 1550 M St., NW, Washington, DC 20005, 202/872-6350.

Industry, Science and Technology Canada

Canada's government clearinghouse for information, online license opportunities and resources.
ACCESS: Ron Doherty, Market Intelligence & Technology Opportunity, ISTC, 235 Queen St., 1st Flr. E., Ottawa, Ontario K1A OH5, fax 613/954-5463.

Intellectual Property Owners Association

100 large with some small companies, universities, inventors and patent attorneys, advocating strong IP rights to government agencies. Publishes brief bulletins, awards inventor of the Year, and holds annual meeting.
ACCESS: 1255 23rd St., NW, Ste, 850, Washington, DC 20037, 202/466-2396, fax 202/833-3636.

Inventor-Assistance Program News

Free, limited circulation newsletter is the main information transfer mechanism of an Energy Department funded program to encourage inventor and inventor-assistance organizations. Short articles describe general business, entrepreneurship and technical information and assistance resources for inventors and the organizations that assist them. Also publishes Inventor Assistance Source Directory.
ACCESS: Robin Conger, Program Manager, Inventor-Assistance Program, Pacific Northwest Laboratory, P.O. Box 999, K8-11, Richland, WA 99352, 509/372-4328, fax 509/372-4369.

Japan Information Access Project

Non-profit, non-partisan, membership organization dedicated to training U.S. public and private decision makers to access, evaluate, and use Japanese scientific, technical and business information. Study groups and conferences organized by industry sectors.
ACCESS: Mindy Kotler, Exec. Director, 2000 P Street, NW, Ste. 620, Washington, DC 20036, 202/822-6040, fax 202/822-6044.

Japan Patent Information Centre

"Information offer forms," (for patent applications), retroactive, on-line searches, patent abstracts, status inquiries, "watching service" and statistics. (Non-resident applicants must file through Japan-resident patent attorney or administrator.)
ACCESS: 1-5-16, Toranomon, Minato-ku, Tokyo 105, Japan, (03) 503-6181, fax (03) 50l-3866.
ACCESS:Japan Institute of Invention and Innovation, 9-14, Toranomon 2-chome, Minato-ku, Tokyo 105, Japan, (03) 502-0511.

Knowledge Express

Online database package, with easy-to-use graphical, Al-enabled interface. Includes proprietary database of university inventions and data-bases of federal lab technologies, SBIR winners, federal research grants, etc.
ACCESS: 3000 Valley Forge Circle, Ste. 3800, King of Prussia, PA 19406, 800/529-5337.

Licensing Executives Society, U.S. & Canada

3000 corporate technology managers and scouts, inhouse and independent patent attorneys and consultants, increasing number of university and federal lab members. (Worldwide LES membership: 7,500.) Prospective members must be nominated by two

members. Meetings, quarterly journal and annual spring intellectual property law-oriented licensing seminar, open to all.
ACCESS: 1800 Diagonal Road, Ste. 280, Alexandria, VA 22314-2840, 703/836-3106, fax 703/836-3107.

Licensing, Innovation and Technology Consultants' Association
Promotes exchange of experience and information among members. Publishes annual catalog of technologies and services offered and sought, and bimonthly newsletter, annual convention in Hanover.
ACCESS: Dr. Paolo Cattapan, c/o Teknomedia Intl., Viale Restelli 3, 1-20124 Milan, Italy, 2 66801272.

Modernization Forum
Alliance of non-profit technology extension service providers to small and medium manufacturers, sponsored by the National Institute of Standards and Technology and its five Manufacturing Technology Centers.
ACCESS: 20501 Ford Road, Dearborn, MI 48121,313/271-2790, fax 313/271-2791.

MIT Enterprise Forum
30,000 members in 17 local chapters, open to all; chapters feature public critiques of selected entrepreneurs' business plans. National headquarters sponsors Venture Capital Network and meetings, including Entrepreneurial Tech Transfer.
ACCESS: MIT Enterprise Forum®, Inc., 28 Carlton St., Bldg. E32-336, Cambridge, MA 02139, 617/253-0015, fax 617/258-0532.

National Academy of Sciences
(Also: National Academy of Engineering, Institute of Medicine, National Research Council) Chartered by Congress but independent, non-profit, limited, honorific membership societies, which undertake studies of leading-edge developments and issues in science and technology. Advises government, holds conferences, publishes reports.
ACCESS: 2101 Constitution Ave., NW, Washington, DC 20418, 202/334-2138.

National Business Incubation Association
Maintains detailed statistics on incubators and their tenants; hosts practical annual meeting covering financing, best practices, economic development, international comparisons, etc.
ACCESS: 20 E. Circle Drive, Ste. 190, Athens, OH 45701, 614/593-4331, fax 614/593-1996.

National Commission for Economic Conversion and Disarmament
Focuses on legislation and other national plans.
ACCESS: Dr. Greg Bischak, Executive Director, 1801 18th St., Ste. 9, Washington DC NW, 20009, 202/462-0091, fax 232-7087.

National Council for the Advancement of Research
Founded in 1945 with a slightly different title (but same acronym), this loose association of some 250 high-level people from across industry, government and academe, holds annual meetings.
ACCESS: c/o Lt. Gen. Austin W. Betts, US Army, Ret., NCAR Executive Secretary, Consultant to the President, Southwest Research Institute, P.O. Drawer 78228-0510, 512/522-2202, fax 512/520-5505.

National Institutes of Health
The leading funder and creator of biomedical advances in the world, with funding growing faster. Lead licensor among federal research agencies, too.
ACCESS: Office of Technology Transfer, NIH, 6011 Executive Blvd., Suite 325, Rockville, MD 20852-3804, 301/496-7057, fax 301/402-0220, www.nih.gov/of/ott.

National Science Foundation
Independent federal agency, funds $3 billion in mostly basic research and education for o non-medical, non-military science, mathematics and (more recently) engineering, via competitive grants to non-profit institutions and individual investigators, and SBIR grants.
ACCESS: 4201 Wilson Blvd., Arlington, VA 22230, 703/306-1234.

National Technical Information Service
Part of the Department of Commerce, collects and publishes most government technology resources, reports, databases, facility descriptions, and many inventions.
ACCESS: NTIS, 5285 Port Royal Rd., Springfield, VA 22161, 703/487-4600, fax 703/321-8547.

National Technological University
Consortium of major engineering schools delivers credit courses and non-credit short courses on specific technologies and the innovation process, via satellite.
ACCESS: Lionel Baldwin, President, NTU, 700 Centre Ave., Fort Collins, CO 80526, 303/484-6050, fax 303/484-0668.

National Technology Transfer Center
Mission: to assist all other federal tech transfer efforts by building outreach and training, and answering initial inquiries of companies seeking technical expertise or specific inventions from federal labs. Funded by NASA.
ACCESS: c/o Wheeling Jesuit College, 316 Washington Ave., Wheeling, WV 26003, 800/678-NTTC(6882) or 304/243-2513, fax 304/243-2463.

National Venture Capital Association
Invitation-only (200 members), includes firms, corporate funds and individuals.
ACCESS: 1655 North Fort Myer Dr., Ste. 700, Arlington, VA 22209, 703/351-5269, fax 703/351-5268.

NERAC
Annual fee entitles companies to use non-profit center's technical and business problem-solving and tech transfer services, including access to its own technical team, automatic customized Tech Track® updates, Expert Match, fax document delivery, etc.
ACCESS: One Technology Dr., Tolland, CT 06084-9919, 203/872-7000, 203/875-1749.

North Carolina Biotechnology Center
In addition to assisting state-based biotechnology industry and academia, the center prepares national databases and directories of faculty, research centers, resources and companies.
ACCESS: Biotechnology Information Program, P.O. Box 13547, Research Triangle Park, NC 27709-3547, 919/541-9366, fax 919/549-9710.

Office of Science and Technology Policy
Staff of Science Advisor to the President, home of future Critical Technologies Institute.
ACCESS: John Gibbons, Director, OSTP, White House, Washington DC 20500, 202/395-6142.

Office of Technology Assessment
Analytical arm of Congress; produces and publishes thoughtful reports with options for action.
ACCESS: Director, OTA, U.S. Congress, Washington DC, 20510-8025, 202/224-9241.

Patent & Trademark Office
The world's largest and most compact collection of technological information. Essential for trend analysis and targeted searches. Accessible via commercial databases. CD-ROM, the central Public Search Room, and locally through 70+ Patent and Trademark Depository Libraries.

ACCESS: Room CM2-304, Washington DC 20231, General information, 703/308-HELP, Office of Information Product Develoment (electronic information only) 703/308-0322; PTDL Program: 703/308-3924.

Product Development & Management Association
Business and academic membership open to all; annual meeting, chapters, publishes *Journal of Product Innovation Management.*
ACCESS: www.pdma.org.

Regional Technology Transfer Centers
New in 1992, funded competitively by NASA (separately from NTTC) to assist businesses through fee for services programs: information retrieval, technical assessments, and technology and funding brokering.
ACCESS: Northeast: Westborough, MA, 508/8870-0042; Mid-Atlantic: Pittsburgh, PA, 412/648-7000; Southeast: Alahua, FL, 904/462-3913; Mid-Continent; College Station, 409/847-9217; Mid-West; Columbus, OH, 216/734-0094; Far-West; Los Angeles, 213/743-6132.

Science and Technology Council of the States
Designated representatives from every state and territory, supported by the Natl. Governors Assn.
ACCESS: Marianne Clark, NGA, 44 N. Capitol St. NW, Washington, DC 20001, 202/624-5300.

Small Business Administration
Loan programs, publications, central referral source for Small Business Innovation Research award programs (actual applications through each agency).
ACCESS: 409 Third St. SW, Washington, DC 20416, 800/827-5722.

Small Busines Innovation Research (SBIR)
Competitive, phased grants for proof of concept and prototyping set aside by each federal agency for businesses with fewer than 500 employees.
ACCESS: SBIR Programs, Office of Innovation Research & Technology, 1441 L St. NW, Mail Code 6470, Washington DC 20416, 202/653-7875.

Technology Access Report
Simply the best: concise, independent, highly *practical* monthly newsletter of analysis and opportunities in technology transfer, technology policy, defense conversion, economic development, and technology management. Includes comprehensive calendar of tech transfer events, technologies available for license, profiles of successful programs, and 400 to 500 contacts yearly, in every technology and industry. Editors in Washington, DC, Paris and San Francisco.
ACCESS: Technology Access, 8 Digital Drive, Ste. 250, Novato, CA 94949-5759, 800/733-1516; fax 415/883-6421.

Technology Exchange Ltd.
Annual forum for one-on-one appointments for buyers and sellers of technology; attendees receive book of 5-10,000 inventions prior to meeting.
ACCESS: Dr. David Lefever, Wrest Park, Silsoe, Bedfordshire, MK45 4HS UK, 44/1525-860333, fax 44/1525-860664.

Technology Targeting, Inc.
Database of 2000+ specific individuals in companies looking for inventions in technology areas they identified through detailed questionnaire.
ACCESS: Norman Brown, President, Technology Targeting, Inc., 2940 Warr Rd., Salt Lake City, UT 84109, 801/4887-9800, fax 801/486-0826.

Technology Transfer Conferences, Inc.
Bimonthly regional meetings present technologies from two dozen universities to audience of corporate scouts, with time for one-on-one sessions.
ACCESS: Lucy Malone, Executive Director, 325 Plus Park Blvd., Ste. 108, Nashville, TN 37217, 615/366-0680, fax 615/366-0695.

Technology Transfer Society
Individual open membership; publishes journal and newsletter; annual and chapter meetings.
ACCESS: 611 N. Capitol Ave., Indianapolis, IN 46204, 317/262-5022, fax 317/262-5044.

Technology Utilization Foundation
Affiliated with NASA and *NASA TechBriefs* publisher Associated Business Publications, presents Technology 2003 (1993) etc., annual showcase of federal lab and contractor technologies.
ACCESS: Bill Schnirring, President, 41 E. 42nd St., New York, NY 10017-5391, 212/490-3999, fax 212/986-7864.

Teknekron Corporation
Pioneer and exemplar of "open corporation" model for nurturing and spinning off technology ventures.
ACCESS: George Tuirin, Vice President, Technology, 1080 Marsh Rd., Menlo Park, CA 94025, 415/322-6390

Teltech, Inc.
Technology consulting service using a computerized search interface to draw from thousands of technology professionals who have agreed to provide the first hour for a pre-set fee.
ACCESS: Joseph Shuster, President, 2850 Metro Dr., Minneapolis, MN 55425, 612/851-7500, fax 612/851-7599.

United States of America
ACCESS: President William J. Clinton, The White House, 1600 Pennsylvania Ave., NW, Washington DC 20500, 202/456-1414 (voice mail 202/456-2226; to record comments on legislation: 202/456-2226), fax 202/456-2461. E-mail system upgrade is planned; MCI-Mail: View White House BBS. Compuserve: Go Whitehouse.American Online: Clinton pz.
ACCESS: Vice President Albert Gore, Jr., 202/456-2326 or 7125
ACCESS:U.S. Senate, Washington DC 20510, 202/224-3121.
ACCESS: U.S. House of Representatives, Washington DC 20515, 202/224-3121.

Wal-Mart Innovation Network
Quickly (since 1990) one of the largest company-sponsored programs for screening inventions for both technical merit and market potential. Uses network of 400-500 organizations as funnel. Recent pilot project used DOE's ERIP program to help screen and LES members to explore potential alternative commercialization route.
ACCESS: c/o The College of Business Administration at Southwest Missouri State University, 901 South National Ave., Springfield, MO 65804-0089.

World Intellectual Property Organization (WIPO)
Searchable database of published PCT applications.
ACCESS: http://pctgazette.wipo.int/eng/index.html

Source: © TECHNOLOGY ACCESS REPORT, newsletter for technology transfer and intellectual asset management professionals, NOVATO, CA, 800-733-1516, www.techaccess.com. Reprinted with permission from Michael Odza, editor and publisher of *Technology Access Report* and *Digital Drive*.

APPENDIX B

An Alphabetical Listing of Useful Resources

This resource material has been created by Daniel M. McGavock. Daniel M. McGavock is a founding Principal of IPC Group, LLC, a Chicago-based consulting firm specializing in damages analysis in commercial litigation and the valuation of businesses and intangible assets. His primary consulting focus has been in the area of intellectual property valuation and infringement litigation. He has valued intellectual property in connection with licenses and joint ventures, company purchase price allocations, sale-license back transactions, corporate reorganization/bankruptcy proceedings, Hart-Scott-Rodino Act requirements, and cross-border intercompany licenses (under Internal Revenue Code Section 482). In the tax arena, he has represented both corporate taxpayers and the IRS in assessing the fair market value of intangible assets. On numerous occasions, he has testified as an expert on intellectual property damages and valuation issues. He also has served as an arbitrator for the American Arbitration Association regarding valuation issues.

Mr. McGavock is Co-Chairman of the LES Valuation and Taxation Committee and has been a member of the International Trademark Association's Task Force and Forums Committee, the Business Valuation Association, the American Arbitration Association, and the American Institute of Certified Public Accountants. He has spoken before numerous professional groups and has been a guest lecturer at Northwestern's J. L. Kellog School of Management on the topic of intellectual property valuation. Mr. McGavock is a Certified Public Accountant in the State of Illinois and received his B.S. Degree in Accounting from Indiana University.

Almanac of Business & Industrial Financial Ratios
Balance sheet and income statement data along with key financial ratios, broken down by four-digit SIC code. Each SIC code breakdown shows data for current year and previous two years. Current data are further categorized down by sales ranges.

Publisher: Pearson Education
(201) 236-7000
(201) 909-6200
www.prenhall.com

American Statistics Index
Index of economic, demographic and statistical information. This resource is updated monthly and bound in annual volumes.

Publisher: Congressional Information Service
(301) 654-1550
www.cispubs.com

Bloomberg Financial Database
The Bloomberg Financial Database is extremely useful for finding significant amounts of information on public companies, broad industry news stories, stock prices, bond prices, and much more.

Provider: Bloomberg
(212) 318-2200
www.bloomberg.com

Bureau of Labor Statistics
This publication includes information on inflation indices, occupational earnings data, etc.

Publisher: United States Department of Labor
(202) 606-5886
www.bls.gov

Business Conditions Digest
This publication provides charts and statistical data for leading economic indicators. Information includes cyclical indicators, composite indicators and their components.

Publisher: U.S. Bureau of Economic Analysis
(202) 606-9900
www.bea.doc.gov

Census Bureau Database
The Census Bureau provides on-line access to its reports and studies. Some of the most useful information is found in the *Current Industrial Report* section. This on-line publication provides unit shipment and sales revenue data for specific products produced by domestic manufacturers. These products are categorized by SIC code.

Help-Line: (301) 457-1242
www.census.gov

Census of Manufactures
This publication provides useful information on industry statistics and ratios. The publication is broken down by SIC code; however, in many cases the SIC code is extended to cover very detailed subjects.

Publisher: Available through the Superintendent of Documents
(202) 512-1800
www.access.gpo.gov/su_docs

Dialog
The Dialog on-line database has access to a significant number of industry or company publications, articles, journals that cover a wide variety of topics. This database may contain significant amounts of information helpful in understanding the marketplace in which a product or potential product may compete.

Publisher: Knight-Ridder Information
(800) 334-2564
www.dialog.com

Directory of Companies Required to File Reports with the Securities & Exchange Commission
This report lists, alphabetically and by industry group, all the firms required to file under the Securities Exchange Act of 1934.

Publisher: Superintendent of Documents
(202) 512-1800
www.access.gpo.gov/su_docs

Disclosure Services
The Washington office of this organization maintains copies of all the documents filed with the Securities and Exchange Commission ("SEC"). Useful information that can be obtained from Disclosure Services includes company financials and license agreements.

Publisher: Disclosure, Inc.
(800) 777-3272
www.disclosure.com

Dun & Bradstreet Reports
Dun & Bradstreet credit reports provide information on over 3 million companies. It is one of the best sources of information for private companies. These reports cover both U.S. and international companies.

Publisher: Dun & Bradstreet
(800) 234-3867
www.dnb.com

Dun & Bradstreet Industry Norms
This report summarizes key financial data for various industries. The report includes common-sized balance sheet and income statement information, as well as fourteen financial ratios. These financial ratios summarize the average profitability, efficiency, and solvency positions of companies participating in the industry.

Economic Indicators
This publication includes basic U.S. economic indicators such as GNP, spending, personal consumption, corporate profits, production activity and security market data. Information includes most recent six years.

Publisher: Council of Economic Advisors
(202) 512-1800
www.access.gpo.gov/su_docs

Economic Report of the President
Annual report to the U.S. Congress from the U.S. President (as prepared in consultation with the President's Council of Economic Advisors). Discusses projected economic policy of the administration, economic outlook and provides current economic statistical data.

Publisher: Superintendent of Documents
(202) 512-1800
www.access.gpo.gov/su_docs

Encyclopedia of Associations
This set covers most major national associations. It lists the address, phone number, number of members, publications, and functions of the association.

Publisher: Gale Research, Inc.
(800) 877-4253
www.galegroup.com

Encyclopedia of Business Information Sources
This publication provides a detailed listing of publications that cover certain industries. It lists the address, phone number, fax number and purpose of the publications it covers.

Publisher: Gale Research, Inc.
(800) 877-4253
www.galegroup.com

Federal Reserve Bulletin
This report is published by the Board of Governors of the Federal Reserve System. It contains a wide variety of financial, economic and business statistics primarily related to the formulation and implementation of monetary policy. The report is published monthly and is particularly useful in tracking interest rate and exchange rate movements.

Publisher: Publication Services
(202) 452-3244
www.bog.frb.fed.us

Handbook of Economic Statistics
Economic statistics for selected countries. Covers economic profile of the country, data on economic trends, energy, agriculture, minerals and metals, chemicals, manufactured goods and foreign trade.

Publisher: U.S. Department of Commerce
(703) 482-4883
www.doc.gov

Ibbotson Associates' Yearbooks
This book provides a history of capital market returns in the United States from 1926 to the present. This information is particularly useful in determinations of costs of capital.

Publisher: Ibbotson Associates
              (312) 616-1620
              www.ibbotson.com

Ibbotson Associates' Cost of Capital Quarterly
This book provides useful information such as profitability ratios, cost of equity, cost of debt, and cost of capital for many different industries. The publication is broken down by SIC code.

Publisher: Ibbotson Associates
              (312) 616-1620
              www.ibbotson.com

Info-Trak
This database contains information on thousands of articles from a comprehensive list of trade publications.

Location: Public Libraries

Instant Information
Listing of nearly 10,000 organizations, associations and government agencies. Includes the name, address, phone number and a brief description of each listing. Part one is an alphabetical listing by state (including Puerto Rico and Canada). Part two is an alphabetical listing by organization title. Part three is an alphabetical listing by subject.

Publisher: Pearson Education
              (201) 909-6200
              www.prenhall.com

Investment Analyst Reports
These reports, if available, are an excellent source of information pertaining to specific companies covered in the report as well as the industry in which the company competes. Significant information that may be obtained in an investment analyst report may include projected company market share, profitability, and competition.

Publisher: Call specific analyst or use Investext
              (800) 662-7878
              www.investext.com

Investext Database
The Investext Database is useful for finding both industry-wide and company-specific reports prepared by investment analysts. The search of this database can be structured by product, date, and company.

Provider: Investext
              (800) 662-7878
              www.investext.com

Licensing Economics Review (LER)

this publication covers many issues of interest to the licensing executive. The cover of each issue provides the reader with a synopsis of recent royalty transactions discussed in the issue as well as other highlights.

Publisher: AUS Consultants
(609) 234-1199
www.ausinc.com

LES Nouvelles

The *LES Nouvelles* is the journal of the Licensing Executives Society which discusses licensing issues. This resource is useful in identifying recent trends and issues as well as experts that follow licensing in various industries.

Publisher: Licensing Executive Society
(703) 836-3107
www.les.org

Licensing Law & Business Report

This publication contains significant information in many of their feature articles that discuss licensing and other IP transactions.

Publisher: West Group
(800) 328-4880
www.westgroup.com

Market Share Reporter

This report is an annual compilation of reported market share data on companies, products, brand names and services. It is an excellent resource for identifying major competitors and their relative strengths within certain markets.

Publisher: Gale Research, Inc.
(800) 877-4253
www.galegroup.com

Mergerstat Review

This is a statistical reference guide on all announced mergers and acquisitions in the past year. Also includes historical data on mergers, acquisitions, reorganizations, etc. for both U.S. and foreign-based companies.

Publisher: Houlihan Lokey Howard & Zukin
(800) 455-8871
www.mergerstat.com

Moody's Bank & Finance Manual

This manual provides five to seven years of balance sheet and income statement data, along with key financial ratios for companies in the insurance, finance, real estate and investment industries. Includes, for each company, a narrative of its business and a listing of all subsidiaries. Also includes analyses of the various firms' debt and equity structures.

Publisher: Moody's Investors Service, Inc.
(212) 553-1658
www.moodys.com

Moody's Industrial Manual

This manual provides five to seven years of balance sheet and income statement data, along with key financial ratios for companies listed on the NYSE, AMEX, and regional stock exchanges. Includes, for each company, a narrative of its business and a listing of all subsidiaries. Also includes analyses of the various firms' debt and equity structures.

Publisher: Moody's Investors Service, Inc.
(212) 553-1658
www.moodys.com

Moody's OTC Industrial Manual

This manual includes industrial companies listed on the over-the-counter stock market. Provides data such as historical background, mergers, subsidiaries, products, plants, officers and directors. Also includes financial information and analyses of the various firms'debt and equity structures.

Publisher: Moody's Investors Service, Inc.
(212) 553-1658
www.moodys.com

Moody's Public Utility Manual

This manual includes five to seven years of balance sheet and income statement data, along with key financial ratios for electric and gas utilities, gas transmission companies, and telephone and water companies. Includes, for each company, a narrative of its business and a listing of all subsidiaries. Also includes analyses of the various firms' debt and equity structures.

Publisher: Moody's Investors Service, Inc.
(202) 553-1658
www.moodys.com

Moody's Transportation Manual

This manual includes five to seven years of balance sheet and income statement data along with key financial ratios for railroads, airlines, shipping, bus and truck lines. Includes, for each company, a narrative of its business and a listing of all subsidiaries. Also includes analyses of the various firms' debt and equity structures.

Publisher: Moody's Investors Service, Inc.
(212) 553-1658
www.moodys.com

Robert Morris Associates Annual Statement Studies

These statement studies contain composite financial data on manufacturing, wholesaling, retailing, service, and contracting lines of business. The financial statements on each industry are shown in common size form and are accompanied by widely used financial ratios. The report is organized by SIC codes.

Publisher: Robert Morris Associates
(215) 446-4000
www.rmahq.org

Standard Industrial Classification Manual
The SIC code was developed for use in the classification of establishments by the type of activity in which they are engaged. The code consists of 20 major industry groups which cover the entire field of economic activity ranging from manufacturing to distribution and service. Each business establishment in the United States has been assigned an SIC code according to the nature of its business operations. As a result, these SIC codes are useful for collecting and tabulating economic data on business activity in the United States. Many of the information resources used in market research organize their materials and data according to these SIC codes.

Publisher: U.S. Office of Management and Budget
Superintendent of Documents
(202) 512-1800
www.access.gpo.gov/su_docs

Standard NYSE Stock Reports
Provides financial data such as sales, earnings, book value, dividends and stock trading range for individual companies. Also provides a narrative about the background of the company, recent events and the outlook for the future of the firm and its industry.

Publisher: Standard & Poor's Corporation
(877) 481-8724
www.standardpoor.com

Standard & Poor's Analyst's Handbook
This handbook provides statistical industry composite data, including sales, operating profits, dividends, earnings and depreciation. Data cover over 90 industries.

Publisher: Standard & Poor's Corporation
(877) 481-8724
www.standardpoor.com

Standard & Poor's Bond Guide
This guide covers over 6,100 domestic and Canadian corporate bonds as well as hundreds of convertible and international bonds. Includes corporate and government bond yields, comparative financial data for each corporate bond, S & P debt ratings, rating changes and more.

Publisher: Standard & Poor's Corporation
(877) 481-8724
www.standardpoor.com

Standard & Poor's Industry Surveys
These surveys provide basic financial data on 36 key industries. Each industry report includes a financial comparison of the leading companies in that industry.

Publisher: Standard & Poor's Corporation
(877) 481-8724
www.standardpoor.com

Standard & Poor's Register of Corporations, Directors, & Executives
Volume one: Alphabetical listing of over 37,000 companies with a description of each business, the address and telephone numbers, and corporate officers and directors.

Volume two: Alphabetical listing of individuals serving as officers, directors, trustees or partners. Volume three: Indexed by SIC number.

Publisher: Standard & Poor's Corporation
                (877) 481-8724
                www.standardpoor.com

Standard & Poor's Statistical Service
This service covers current basic statistics for broad industry groups, including security price index record by industry group.

Publisher: Standard & Poor's Corporation
                (877) 481-8724
                www.standardpoor.com

Standard & Poor's Stock Guide
This guide covers stocks listed on all major U.S. stock exchanges. Provides information on institutional ownership, recent stock performance data, highs and lows for the past year and over a period of the past 20 years, balance sheet data, debt structure and earnings.

Publisher: Standard & Poor's Corporation
                (877) 481-8724
                www.standardpoor.com

Statistical Abstract of the United States
Summary of statistics covering social, political and economic organizations in the United States.

Publisher: U.S. Bureau of Census
                Superintendent of Documents
                (202) 512-1800
                www.access.gpo.gov/su_docs

Survey of Current Business
This survey provides national income and product account data for past three years, real GNP trends and cycles, regional economic analysis, international economic indicator comparisons, and more.

Publisher: Superintendent of Documents
                U.S. Government Printing Office
                (202) 512-1800
                www.access.gpo.gov/su_docs

TELTECH
This is an on-line database that provides information on how to contact experts for various industries.

Provider: TELTECH Technical Knowledge Service
                (800) 367-8358
                www.teltech.com

U.S. Industrial Outlook
This publication provides statistical and narrative analyses of recent trends and forecasts
for over 200 industries. It includes analyses of industries' supply and demand,
developments in domestic and foreign markets, employment trends and capital
expenditure trends.

Publisher: U.S. Department of Commerce
             Industry & Trade Information
             (202) 512-1800
             www.access.gpo.gov/su_docs

Value Line
This publication provides information that is useful for calculating a company's cost of
capital. It summarizes individual company financial performance over the last decade by
providing up to 15 years of simplified financial statement and ratio analysis data. The
report specifically addresses the company's most recent results. Moreover, the report
provides historical stock price performance and projections for the company.

Publisher: Value Line, Inc.
             (800) 531-1425
             www.valueline.com

Index

Ford Motor Company, 2
Forecasting, from past, 40
Franklin, Benjamin, 74

Gain, 96–97, 98
Georgia Pacific factors, 78
GM v. Dailey, 59
Going concern perspective, 99–100
Golden rule perspective, 100
Goldscheider, Bob, 78
Goodwill, 6
Gross cash flows (GCF), 138–146
Gross margin, 104
  as royalty basis, 203

Haas, David, 50
Hambrecht & Quist, 177
Handbook of Economic Statistics, 274
Harvard Business Review, 178
Headley, Tim, 87
Headley/Arnold value factors,
  87–92
Heads of agreement documents, 17
"Heuristic", 95
Hogue, Dale, 196
Horton, Corwin, 50, 78
Houston, University of, 62, 68–69

*Ibbotson Associates' Cost of Capital
  Quarterly*, 274
Ibbotson Associates' Yearbooks,
  274
IBM, patent licensing and, 61
IL Med, 194
Income statement, 147–154
  25 percent rule and, 105–118
  pro forma, 116, 118, 135
Industry standards valuation method,
  34, 189, 216
  auctions and, 195
  concept/limitations of, 43–46, 64
  review of, 246

royalties and, 229–230, 232
sources of
  court cases/judgements, 58–60
  expert judgement tables, 55–58
  personal database, 63
  price lists, 60–62
  publications/databases/
    consultants, 63
  published license agreements,
    62–63
  survey information, 46–55
  voluntary surveys, 50, 52–53
Inflation, 229
  RAHR (Risk Adjusted Hurdle Rate)
    and, 124–125
Info-Trak, 274
Infringement, 227
Innovativeness scale, 52
Instant Information, 274
Intel, 194
Intellectual property (IP), 3–4
  protection of, 80, 82
Intrinsic quality, valuation factors,
  88
Investext Database, 275
Investment Analyst Reports, 275
Investment, rule of thumb and, 97
IPC Group, Inc., 63, 271
Isuzu automobile company, 27, 29,
  15

Japan, 47, 49–50
*Journal of the Association of
  University Technology
  Managers*, 63
Justified true belief (JTB), 162–163

"k", *see* Risk-Adjusted Hurdle Rate
  (RAHR)
Kahn, E., 56–57
Kendall Square, 37
"Kicker" licenses, 116, 232,
  233–234